START YOUR OWN STORE

Managing, Merchandising, and Evaluating

Sidney Packard

Business Analyst, Small Business Development Center
Adjunct Professor of Marketing
Florida Atlantic University, Boca Raton

Alan J. Carron

Small Store Consultant
Assistant Professor
Fashion Buying and Merchandising Department
Fashion Institute of Technology

Prentice-Hall, Inc. / Englewood Cliffs, New Jersey 07632

Library of Congress Cataloging in Publication Data

Packard, Sidney.
    Start your own store.

    Bibliography: p. 181
    Includes index.
        1. Stores, Retail—United States—Management.
    2. Self-employed—United States.   3. Success.
    I. Carron, Alan.   II. Title.
    HF5429.3.P33   658.8'701   81–5165
    ISBN 0–13–842948–0   AACR2

© 1982 by Prentice-Hall, Inc., Englewood Cliffs, New Jersey 07632

Printed in the United States of America

10 9 8 7 6 5 4 3 2 1

Prentice-Hall International, Inc., *London*
Prentice-Hall of Australia Pty. Limited, *Sydney*
Prentice-Hall of Canada, Ltd., *Toronto*
Prentice-Hall of India Private Limited, *New Delhi*
Prentice-Hall of Japan, Inc., *Tokyo*
Prentice-Hall of Southeast Asia Pte. Ltd., *Singapore*
Whitehall Books Limited, *Wellington, New Zealand*

Contents

PART II
OPERATING A STORE (MERCHANDISING), 89

CHAPTER 7
Setting Policies, 91

CHAPTER 8
Planning and Control of Merchandise, 96

CHAPTER 9
Merchandising Research, 114

Foreword

Independently owned stores are the most numerous type of business organization and add up to one of the most significant components of an economic structure.

Despite increased competition and relatively recent widely publicized retail failures, thousands of fashion shops are flourishing and enabling ambitious people to realize the American dream of being one's own boss.

To say that opening and operating a store is an easy means to achieve financial success is a misstatement. What experts would claim are the ingredients for small success, it is certain, will vary. The one certainty is that retailing demands hard work not confined to five days a week, 9 AM to 5 PM.

Successful independent merchants, it is true, have entered business with scant knowledge, not infrequently because they had no other alternative to make a living. However, what they had in common was a thirst for success, a willingness to work hard, and the acumen to seek and listen to good advice to become management sophisticated. Their rigidity was their ambition, their flexibility was their attitude.

Start Your Own Store addresses itself to the manifold situations, requirements, and principles of management and merchandising in a realistic and logical manner. A reader/participant has the opportunity to perform as an entrepreneur in the most economical and reasonable way to prove readiness and competency for small store ownership. The authors emphasize a most worthwhile truism: "To plan and be aware is to be forewarned and forearmed."

For the interested, retailing is a fulfilling business endeavor in an "arena" with plenty of opportunities for those who have an abiding interest, a willingness and capability to work hard, and a sense of adventure.

Sam Andrews

Andrew's Apparel
Tacoma, Washington

Introduction

Entrepreneurship is alive and well in the United States!

Retailing in this country is actually just an extension of a long-term historical need for entrepreneurs — for individuals who express their creativity by investing in and operating small businesses. Retailing is a time-honored profession that can be traced back to the ancient civilizations of Greece and Rome, even though its activities vary from one period to the next, due to the influences of changing economics, social and cultural values, technology, and politics.

What precisely is this persistent form of business activity? Essentially, retailing is a middleman activity in which the store owner buys from producers and sells to consumers. Retail merchants are channels of distribution that satisfy people's wants. Retailing is a business that is for and about people — one that is never dull or monotonous. It offers you the opportunities to:

* make money,
* express your creativity,
* be your own boss,
* achieve rewards consistent with your effort, and
* gain the satisfaction of self-achievement.

Today, even in a business environment characterized by conglomerates, giant chains, and other multi-store organizations, small retailers have at least as much chance for success as at any time in the past, and possibly more. Retailing is the major contributor to the United States' gross national product. Retail sales for 1981 are estimated to reach $1 trillion, a figure that is generated by approximately 1.8 million stores. And those are small stores:

Of those 1.8 million, 36 percent have no paid employees and only 7 percent employ more than seven people. As a matter of record, then President Jimmy Carter said in February of 1980:

> The small business community constitutes the single most important segment of our free enterprise system. It accounts for forty-eight percent of our gross national product, more than half of the American labor force, and continues to be the major source of inventions and new jobs. Small business is truly the backbone of the American economy.

Perhaps the persistence of retail "smallness" is due, at least partially, to the negative impressions sometimes conveyed by retail "bigness" — impersonal service (or none at all), overcrowding, long lines, and mass merchandising. Today, perhaps more than ever, small store owners — with their personalized service, individual efforts, and special productivity — may enjoy great success while constituting a keystone in our economy.

In recognition of the entrepreneur's role, the government embarked in 1978 on a campaign to stimulate small business initiative. State delegates met regularly for a year and a half to discuss a list of recommendations for submission to a scheduled White House Conference on Small Business. In February of 1980, that White House meeting resulted in the development of sixty recommendations to aid small business in the eighties.

With the economy in need of their particular kind of contribution, and with such governmental encouragement to beckon them on, entrepreneurs — as well as would-be entrepreneurs — may look toward the coming years with great eagerness and high hopes.

Why, then, do we hear so much about the so-called high "mortality rates" of small businesses?

Indeed, the figures seem to stack the odds against small retailers. For example, the Dun and Bradstreet figures published in *Your Business* (New York State Chamber of Commerce) indicate that survival depends far less on general business conditions than it does on the owner's personal business acumen and good fortune. Of all the reasons for failure that were listed in that study, the inexperience or incompetence of the owner accounted for over 90 percent. (See Table I-1.)

TABLE I-1. Causes of business failure in retail trade (percentage of total failures)

Inexperience, incompetence	92.2
Neglect	1.7
Fraud	1.4
Disaster	0.7
Reasons unknown	4.0

Another interesting finding was that, of those businesses involved in the study, only 1.5 percent failed in their first years. Most of the failures were two to five years old: Specifically, they constituted 52.7 percent of all failures and 58 percent of those in retail.

What does all this mean? Perhaps one conclusion is that, if a small business can survive its first three years, then its life expectancy improves with each passing year of its existence. Perhaps more important, though, those first few years depend largely on the individual abilities and resourcefulness of the owner. More than on anything else, it depends on personal preparedness.

And personal preparedness is what we try to offer in this book. Within its scope, you may benefit in a number of ways:

* If you seek *knowledge*, you may learn about the requirements for opening and operating a small store.
* If you seek *comprehension*, you may pick up the why's and how's.
* If you seek *analysis*, you may learn the relationships among the financing, the decision-making, the buying, and the other aspects of running a small store.
* If you seek *applications*, you may benefit from the practical work suggested at the end of each chapter.
* If you seek *evaluation*, you may obtain appraisals of your work from your instructor (if you are in a classroom situation).
* If you seek *synthesis*, you may apply all you learn in a hypothetical opening of your very own store.

Outside the scope of this book, however, you must prepare yourself in other ways. Here are some suggestions that may enhance your chances for success:

* Get several years of work experience in a store of moderate to large size.
* Thoroughly examine an actual small store operation that has become a success. Work in one for a while, or get to know an owner, to learn the problems and intricacies of individual ownership.
* Carefully examine any information that is available — pamphlets, textbooks, trade publications, and literature from the Department of Commerce and Small Business Administration.
* Discuss your business ideas in depth with a lawyer and accountant. What is the potential profit? Contingent liabilities? Government requirements? Capital needs? And so on.
* Perhaps most important, examine your personal response to problems, your ability to cope with daily stress, your maturity and general wherewithal, your motivation, and your experience. In brief, what personal qualifications can you bring to the business.

Finally, although you may complete all the assignments in this book with total understanding and skillful execution, bear in mind that there is a great difference between the classroom and the marketplace, between the book-work and the actual work. Your personal preparedness is the key factor to success. You must be ready to see things through.

How This Book
May Help You

Essentially, you have a case study in your hands. The case takes you through the steps of:

1. opening a store,
2. operating a store, and
3. evaluating a store's performance.

These are the three principal parts of the book.

Within each part, the chapters are organized so they fall in the same sequence that an actual entrepreneur would follow—from the initial planning through a full year of operation. But there is one exception: Chapter 6 should be Chapter 1, because in reality a would-be store owner needs professional services from the very outset. Yet since the subject might be a little "heavy" for an opening discussion, it takes a place at the end of Part I, where it might even be of greater benefit. After working your way through Chapters 1 through 5, you might better appreciate the real need for competent assistance and advice.

Within each chapter, four standardized units of organization draw together the general and the specific, the abstract and the concrete:

1. Introduction,
2. Managerial or Marketing Requirement,
3. Principles or Practices, and
4. Assignment (for *you* to solve).

These assignments in particular give you the opportunity to execute proven methods of planning and managing your own establishment. After completing these assignments, you will have made decisions on:

* acquiring a store,
* determining a suitable location,
* allocating your time and effort,
* maximizing profits,
* planning and conforming to merchandising policies,
* maintaining a cash flow,
* testing your managerial skills, and
* evaluating potential reward with the required time and effort.

In the process, you will also gain experience in gathering information from:

* "eyeball" observation,
* trade publications,
* library data,
* government figures, and
* the opinions of experts, professionals, and practitioners.

You will also come to realize that independent owners are generalists who play many roles. During a work week, store owners are involved in buying, receiving, marking, and selling merchandise. They are also concerned with financing the operation and with maintaining the physical plant (that is, the store itself). New store owners, especially those with considerable big store experience who are accustomed to directing and controlling specialists, are often unprepared for the manifold responsibilities of entrepreneurship.

So from the outset, understand clearly that operating a small store requires more than a willingness to work hard, more than a love of merchandising, and more than experience in a big store. You must bridge pitfalls with special techniques and accommodate yourself to conditions that are peculiar to small store operations.

The entire organization of the book is brought to bear on a case that we feel is particularly appropriate as a learning experience. You are called upon to play the role of an entrepreneur who intends to open a store for women's apparel and accessories.

THE CASE ITSELF

Why is the case so appropriate? The reason is that women's fashions comprise a unique product. Subject to relatively rapid change and completely dependent on consumer acceptance, women's clothing generally has less intrinsic value compared to such items as, say, an automobile or typewriter. The product's salability depends far less on serviceability than it does on the customer's search for a state of betterment—status, sexual desirability, improvement on nature, and so on. Hence the successful retailing of fashion requires sharper-than-average merchandising, managerial, and marketing skills. Success in such a line depends much more on the retailer's personal preparedness than in most other lines.

With your personal preparation in mind, then, your role throughout this book is as follows:

Your long-time career ambition has been to own and operate your own ladies' specialty store, dealing in apparel and some appropriate accessories, such as handbags, scarves, and a limited assortment of costume jewelry.

As you visualize the store, your potential customers, in the main, will be career women from 20 to 45 years old, who are interested in wearable, moderate- to better-priced merchandise. You are highly pleased to note the trend in department and specialty stores toward separate departments that cater to career-oriented women. In fact, you have been reading trade publications, noting newspaper advertisements, and gathering as much data as possible to support your position and to guide your future efforts.

Two weeks ago you decided to go full steam ahead and take immediate steps to reach your goal. Accordingly, you held discussions with your family and friends to determine the level of financial support you could expect from them. Your attitude is most affirmative because of the support you can depend on from those closest to you.

You are now in a position to evaluate your probable financial position. Your assessment is that with a starting capital of $70,000, you can open a small store of 2,000 to 3,000 square feet, stock the proper level of merchandise to put your best foot forward, and realize first year sales of between $250,000 to $300,000, a range that could yield a substantial profit. For capital, you have $15,000 of your own, you have been promised support of $30,000 from those nearest to you, and you need a commercial source to fund the additional $25,000.

You are now ready to work out judicious decisions to the challenges of starting your own store.

Good luck!

OPENING A STORE PART I

Financing the Operation

Money is the life blood of a business. The lack of it has resulted in the failure of thousands of businesspeople who have had everything else required for success. When planning to open a store, you must consider the necessity of having sufficient starter funds to:

INTRODUCTION

* pay for professional advice,
* establish credit facilities,
* pay rent in advance (current rent and security),
* purchase fixtures and equipment,
* procure merchandise for resale,
* promote the store (advertising and the like),
* install a telephone and other utilities,
* clean the premises,
* purchase business forms,
* open a checking account, and
* pay for miscellaneous fees and supplies.

Big companies employ full-time financial experts to arrange the inflow and outflow of money, so they can do the maximum amount of business with the minimum amount of cash. They also own the resources and means to raise cash that is not available to small businesspersons. Small businesspersons with limited resources must be aware of the possibility of being put out of business because of a temporary shortage of cash, even though the business may be perfectly sound. They must be able to show that the business can repay debts if given sufficient time.

MANAGERIAL REQUIREMENTS

To run a successful business, you must have *working capital*, that is, enough liquidity to permit the timely payment of required business expenditures, from the day a business starts. The start of a business "eats up" unusually large sums of money in an extremely short period. If the initial outflow depletes your cash supply, you stand in serious jeopardy of being forced out of business at the very start. So you have to start with enough cash to honor the terms of all investments, pay for expenses, and still maintain an adequate bank balance.

And you have to prove your credit-worthiness. As a case in point, the women's fashion markets sell merchandise on terms indicated by "8/10 EOM." These terms require payment on or before the tenth day of the month that follows. If the bill is paid on time, the retailer is entitled to a discount of 8 percent. (The trade discount rate varies in the accessory markets, such as 2 or 3 percent.) Invoices dated on the twenty-fifth of the month or later are considered dated the first day of the following month. For example, a bill dated August 25 is not payable until October 10 to qualify for the trade discount. The point is that manufacturers are not prone to ship merchandise on a paid-in-advance or cash-on-delivery basis. These methods of payments are unwieldly to handle, since manufacturers have the personnel and facilities only for the usual way to do business — on credit. To gain access to these credit facilities, you have to establish a credit rating; to get that, you have to file a statement of financial condition. If your financial condition is poor, you might never get that credit rating!

Prospective store owners with enough of their own cash do not have the initial problem of obtaining starting funds. So our concern is focused on what to do when you have to seek financial support from a third party. The assumption of the assignment later in this chapter is that you do, naturally, have to seek the necessary funds. It requires you to either obtain $25,000 or give up the idea of opening a store of the type and size you planned.

There are numerous ways of obtaining money for starting and operating a business. Borrowing money from a commercial source (a bank) is one possibility, especially if your business has a good track record. (Once again, of course, the assignment in this chapter assumes that, since you are just starting up, your business has *no* track record.) Relatives might be able and willing to help finance a new operation. Selling your investment idea to an outsider for a share of the profits, for a piece of the business, or on some other basis is also feasible. And you can always take in a partner, if you can find someone suitable. Another possible funding source is the Small Business Administration, a government agency that offers guarantees to banks, as well as direct loans under certain conditions to those in need. (SBA requirements are detailed in Appendix F.)

Borrowing from Commercial Sources

Let's concentrate on obtaining funds from a commercial bank, one that makes cash available for business purposes.

The Need for a Repayment Guarantee. Banks are not in the business of making loans for ventures. Opening a store is a venture. A bank reduces its chance of loss from a loan by requiring some form of adequate guarantee from the potential borrower. If the applicant has real estate, stock, or other assets of a value equal to the sum of the requested loan, and if there are no other

negative conditions concerning the applicant or the applicant's asset ownership, the bank would extend a loan.

What if you do *not* own assets to put up as collateral to guarantee
repayment? In this case, a third person (a *guarantor*) can become party to
a loan arrangement. An applicant without sufficient equity to guarantee
repayment, for example, can use a close friend or relative who is willing
and able to pledge the return of the loan. Obviously, if the borrower defaults
on the return of loan, the bank would then obtain repayment from the
guarantor.

Terms. The terms of a loan depend on:

1. the market cost of money (the given interest rate);
2. the mutually agreed manner of repayment (scheduled monthly
   payments or a lump sum at the end of the loan term); and
3. whether the loan is for a short or long term.

A bank's most usual type of loan extends for up to one year. Its terms
can provide for monthly payments for both interest and amortization
(that is, the monthly reduction of loan size). With the proper collateral and
safeguards for the interest rate that the bank charges, you can obtain longer-
term loans. The key consideration is that the bank must be able to renegoti-
ate its interest rate over the long term. Just imagine the plight of a bank that
has loans outstanding at 8 percent when bank depositors can earn 14
percent!

The Paperwork. Figure 1-1 is an example of a personal financial statement
and agreement that a bank requires in order to have enough information
on an applicant to decide on extending a loan.

Figure 1-2 is a financial statement and agreement that many banks
request at the end of each fiscal year. After three years of profitable operation, cooperating banks allow businesspersons *full-service accommodation*,
that is, loans up to a specified sum upon request. This type of loan does
not help you much when you are opening a store—it is true—but it is a
matter of planning for the future.

To open a checking account, an authorization must be properly executed and submitted to the bank so that its personnel have the authority
to honor all checks, drafts, or other demands against funds deposited by
a business firm. The forms appropriate to the various types of business
organization are shown as follows:

* Figure 1-3 — Single proprietorship (or assumed name)
* Figure 1-4 — Partnership
* Figure 1-5 — Corporation

A Matter of Creativity and Good Relations

Be creative. Try to think of techniques not discussed here that might suit
your individual situation. You can even influence a commercial bank by
reason of your unusual background, your reputation, your obvious business
acumen, and the percentage of starting money that you intend to put up.

As a matter of good business practice, a new owner should establish
a good working relationship with a commercial bank from the start. In a

FIGURE 1-1
Personal Financial Statement

PERSONAL FINANCIAL STATEMENT AND AGREEMENT
WITH EUROPEAN AMERICAN BANK & TRUST COMPANY

Name _____

Address _____

The undersigned, to induce you, from time to time, to extend credit to, or to rely for any purpose upon the financial responsibility of, the undersigned, furnishes, and represents to you to be true and to include all liabilities of the undersigned (direct or contingent), the following statement of the undersigned's financial condition and agrees that you may continue to consider the same to be at least as favorable as shown by said statement until otherwise notified in writing by the undersigned.

In consideration of any such extension of credit or reliance, the undersigned agrees with you that if (a) any of the information set forth in said statement shall prove to be false, or (b) the undersigned shall fail to notify you in writing of any material adverse change in the condition or affairs of the undersigned, or (c) any change occurs in the condition or affairs of the undersigned which, in your opinion, materially impairs the ability of the undersigned to pay all claims and demands against the undersigned, or (d) the undersigned shall suspend the transaction of the usual business of the undersigned or (e) the undersigned assigns any accounts or transfers or encumbers any assets without your written consent, or (f) the undersigned shall die, or (g) the undersigned shall become insolvent, or make a general assignment for the benefit of creditors, or a petition in bankruptcy, voluntary, or involuntary, or for reorganization, be filed, or a receiver be appointed or applied for, or order of attachment be issued or a judgment be rendered, against the undersigned, or (h) the undersigned shall fail to pay any obligation to you when same becomes due, or (i) the undersigned fails to produce for inspection upon request by you up-to-date books of accounts, statements, papers and records of the undersigned, then all obligations and liabilities of the undersigned to you, direct or contingent, now or hereafter arising, shall thereupon, unless you shall otherwise elect, become due and payable forthwith without any notice or demand.

The undersigned further agrees that you shall have, as security for the payment of all liabilities of the undersigned to you, direct or contingent, now existing or hereafter arising, a continuing lien upon and a right of set-off against any deposit or other account of the undersigned with you and a continuing lien upon all property of the undersigned, of any sort and description, which shall for any purpose (including safekeeping) be in or have come into your possession, custody or control.

Until the undersigned shall give you a new statement or notice in writing to the contrary, this statement shall be regarded as a representation and warranty on each occasion that the undersigned shall become obligated to you in any manner, or that you shall extend credit or make, renew, or extend a loan to the undersigned or shall purchase or discount any paper made or endorsed by the undersigned, that the following statement is, on each such occasion, true and specifically made and repeated for the purpose of inducing you on the faith thereof to advance credit, make a loan, grant a renewal or extension to the undersigned or purchase or discount any paper made or endorsed by the undersigned, or to have the undersigned become obligated to you in any manner, and that on each such occasion the actual net worth of the undersigned is no less than that shown in the following statement, and notwithstanding the receipt of such notice or of a new statement (except a statement on your form), on each such occasion the foregoing agreements, rights and remedies of yours shall be read into and become part of the said obligations of the undersigned.

The undersigned agrees that, if an attorney is used to obtain payment of or otherwise enforce any of the undersigned's obligations to you of any kind or nature and/or to enforce, declare, or adjudicate any rights or obligations under this agreement, whether by suit or by any other means whatsoever, an attorney's fee of 15% of the principal and interest then due by the undersigned to you shall be payable by the undersigned. You and the undersigned, in any litigation (whether or not arising out of, or relating to, this agreement or any of the matters contained herein) in which you and the undersigned shall be adverse parties, waive trial by jury, and the undersigned, in addition, waives the right to interpose any defense based upon any Statute of Limitations or any claim of laches and any set-off or counterclaim of any nature or description, and waives the performance of each and every condition precedent to which the undersigned might otherwise be entitled by law.

The foregoing shall be considered to supplement, and not to cancel or amend, in derogation of any rights which may be given to you thereby, the provisions of any agreements, promissory notes or other documents or instruments which may have been or may hereafter be made by the undersigned with or executed and delivered by the undersigned to you, and not to be cancelled or, adversely to you, amended by any such provisions.

STATEMENT AS OF THE _____ DAY OF _____, 19____.

ASSETS				LIABILITIES			
Cash (Schedule A) $				Notes Payable Banks (Schedule A) $			
Stocks and Bonds (Schedule B)				Notes Payable to Relatives			
Accounts and Notes Receivable:				Notes Payable to Others			
Due from relatives and friends				Accounts Payable			
Due from others — good				Federal & State Income Taxes Payable			
Doubtful				Other Accrued Taxes & Interest			
Real Estate Owned (Schedule C)				Mortgages Payable (Schedule C)			
Mortgages Owned (Schedule D)				Installment Contracts Payable			
Cash Surrender Value Life Ins. (Schedule E)				Loans against Life Insurance (Schedule E)			
Other assets (itemize):				Other Liabilities (itemize):			
				TOTAL LIABILITIES			
				NET WORTH			
TOTAL $				TOTAL $			
Amount of Assets Pledged $				Amount of Liabilities Secured $			

FIGURE 1-1. (con't)

(Please Complete All Schedules and Fill in All Blanks; Insert "None" if Appropriate)

Schedule A   CASH BALANCES AND BANK LOANS

Name of Bank	Statement Date		Method of Borrowing (Unsecured, Guaranty, Collateral)
	Cash Balance	Amount Owing	
Cash on Hand			
TOTALS AS PER STATEMENT			

Schedule B   STOCKS AND BONDS

Shares or Bonds	Name of Security	In Name of	Present Market Value	If Pledged State to Whom
	U. S. Governments, series —			

Schedule C   REAL ESTATE OWNED

Location, Type of Property and Date Acquired	Title in Name of	Cost	Recent Appraised Value	Mortgage	
				Amount	Due

Are there any other liens against any of the above property?

Are there any mortgage payments, interest or taxes in arrears?

Schedule D   REAL ESTATE MORTGAGES OWNED

Type of Lien (1st, 2nd, 3rd, etc.) Location and Type of Property	Mortgagee of Record	Original Amount	Present Amount	Maturity

Are there any principal payments, interest or taxes in arrears?   Are there any unrecorded assignments?

Schedule E   LIFE INSURANCE

Face Amount	Name of Company	Beneficiary	Type of Policy	Cash Value	Loans Against Policy

Are any of the above policies assigned except for loans as shown?

FIGURE 1-1. (con't)

Annual Income: Salary $_____ Fees or Commissions $_____ Other $ _____

Business or Occupation_____Name of Employer_____

Are you a partner or officer in any other business or venture ?_____

Age_____; No. of Dependents _____

Complete only if spouse will be contractually liable (co-maker, co-borrower)
Marital Status_____ Spouse's Name_____ (Married, unmarried, separated)

Are there any unsatisfied judgments or legal actions pending against you ?_____

Have you ever gone through bankruptcy or made a general assignment ?_____

As of the date of this financial statement, I had not pledged, assigned, hypothecated or transferred the title to any of my assets, except as noted on this form or on a supporting schedule, nor has any such action been taken since that date, except as follows (give details):

_____

_____

CONTINGENT LIABILITIES: As endorser or co-maker_____

On receivables discounted or sold_____As guarantor_____

On leases, mortgages or contracts_____Unsettled claims_____

Other (itemize)_____

The undersigned has carefully read the foregoing contracts, statements, and all printed and written matter therein, and agrees to all the provisions thereof, and hereby certifies to European American Bank & Trust Company that the figures contained in the foregoing statements are taken from the books and records of the undersigned; that the statements contained in every part of this document are known by the undersigned to be true and to give a correct showing of the financial condition of the undersigned; that the undersigned has no liabilities direct, indirect, or contingent, business or accommodation, except as set forth in said statement; that legal and equitable title to all assets therein set forth is in undersigned's sole name, except as may be therein otherwise noted.

Dated: _____ , 19 ___ .   _____

                                          _____

FIGURE 1-2.
Financial Statement and Agreement

BUSINESS FINANCIAL STATEMENT AND AGREEMENT
WITH EUROPEAN AMERICAN BANK & TRUST COMPANY

NAME (Title Under Charter or Articles) _____

ADDRESS _____

BUSINESS _____ Corporation ☐   Partnership ☐   Proprietorship ☐

The undersigned, to induce you, from time to time, to extend credit to, or to rely for any purpose upon the financial reponsibility of, the undersigned, furnishes, and represents to you to be true and to include all liabilities of the undersigned (direct or contingent), the following statement of the undersigned's financial condition as of the below date, and agrees that you may continue to consider the same to be at least as favorable as shown by said statement until otherwise notified in writing by the undersigned.

In consideration of any such extension of credit or reliance, the undersigned agrees with you that if (a) any of the information set forth in said statement shall prove to be false, or (b) the undersigned shall fail to notify you in writing of any material adverse change in the condition or affairs of the undersigned, or (c) any change occurs in the condition or affairs of the undersigned which, in your opinion, materially impairs the ability of the undersigned to pay all claims and demands against the undersigned, or (d) the undersigned shall suspend the transaction of the usual business of the undersigned, or (e) the undersigned assigns any accounts or transfers or encumbers any assets without your written consent, or (f) the undersigned shall die, or (g) the undersigned shall become insolvent, or make a general assignment for the benefit of creditors, or a petition in bankruptcy, voluntary or involuntary, or for reorganization, be filed, or a receiver be appointed or applied for, or order of attachment be issued or a judgment be rendered, against the undersigned, or (h) the undersigned shall fail to pay any obligation to you when same becomes due, or (i) the undersigned fails to produce for inspection upon request by you up-to-date books of accounts, statements, papers and records of the undersigned, then all obligations and liabilities of the undersigned to you, direct or contingent, now or hereafter arising, shall thereupon, unless you shall otherwise elect, become due and payable forthwith without any notice or demand.

The undersigned further agrees that you shall have, as security for the payment of all liabilities of the undersigned to you, direct or contingent, now existing or hereafter arising, a continuing lien upon and a right of set-off against any deposit or other account of the undersigned with you and a continuing lien upon all property of the undersigned, of any sort and description, which shall for any purpose (including safekeeping) be in or have come into your possession, custody or control.

Until the undersigned shall give you a new statement or notice in writing to the contrary, this statement shall be regarded as a representation and warranty on each occasion that the undersigned shall become obligated to you in any manner, or that you shall extend credit or make, renew, or extend a loan to the undersigned or shall purchase or discount any paper made or endorsed by the undersigned, that the following statement is, on each such occasion, true and specifically made and repeated for the purpose of inducing you on the faith thereof to advance credit, make a loan, grant a renewal or extension to the undersigned or purchase or discount any paper made or endorsed by the undersigned, or to have the undersigned become obligated to you in any manner, and that on each such occasion the actual net worth of the undersigned is no less than that shown in the following statement, and notwithstanding the receipt of such notice or of a new statement (except a statement on your form), on each such occasion the foregoing agreements, rights and remedies of yours shall be read into and become part of the said obligations of the undersigned.

The undersigned agrees that, if an attorney is retained to obtain payment of or otherwise enforce any of the undersigned's obligations to you of any kind or nature and/or to enforce, declare, or adjudicate any rights or obligations under this agreement, whether by suit or by any other means whatsoever, an attorney's fee of 20% of the principal and interest then due by the undersigned to you which is deemed by the undersigned to be reasonable shall be payable by the undersigned. The undersigned, in any litigation (whether or not arising out of, or relating to, this agreement or any of the matters contained herein) in which you and the undersigned shall be adverse parties, waive trial by jury, and the undersigned, in addition, waives the right to interpose any defense based upon any Statute of Limitations or any claim of laches and any set-off or counterclaim of any nature or description, and waives the performance of each and every condition precedent to which the undersigned might otherwise be entitled by law.

The foregoing shall be considered to supplement, and not to cancel or amend, in derogation of any rights which may be given to you thereby, the provisions of any agreements, promissory notes or other documents or instruments which may have been or may hereafter be made by the undersigned with or executed and delivered by the undersigned to you, and not to be cancelled or, adversely to you, amended by any such provisions.

FINANCIAL STATEMENT AS OF THE _____ DAY OF _____, 19_____.

ASSETS					LIABILITIES AND CAPITAL				
CURRENT:					**CURRENT:** (due within one year).				
Cash on hand and in banks					Notes Payable: Secured				
U. S. Government Securities					To Banks Unsecured				
Due from customers (for merchandise sold):					Notes sold through brokers				
Notes and Acceptances					To others for borrowed money				
Open Accounts (less Reserves)					Notes or Acceptances Payable—Trade				
(show details on Page 2)					Acceptances under Letters of Credit				
Due from controlled or affiliated concerns for current merchandise transactions only					Accounts Payable:				
					For merchandise				
Merchandise: (show details on Page 2)					Other				
Finished					Due to controlled or affiliated concerns				
In process					Due to directors, officers, and employees				
Raw					Deposits (when payable?)				
Other (itemize)					Accrued Expenses				
					Reserve for Federal Taxes				
FIXED: Total Current					Mortgages, Bonds, Long Term Notes				
Land and Buildings used in operations:					(due within a year)				
(how valued?)					Other (itemize)				
(list mortgages, if any, in liabilities)									
Machinery, Equipment and Fixtures									
Investments: (show details on Page 2)									
Controlled or Affiliated Concerns					Total Current				
Other Bonds or Stocks					**DEFERRED:** (due after one year)				
Cash Surrender Value Life Insurance					Mortgages Payable (due)				
Other (itemize)					Bonded Debt (due)				
Total Fixed					Other Deferred Debt				
DEFERRED AND MISCELLANEOUS:					**TOTAL LIABILITIES**				
Prepaid Expenses—Interest, Insurance, etc.					Other Reserves (Contingencies,				
Advances to controlled or affiliated concerns					Inventory, etc.)				
for other than current merchandise items					Deferred Income, Etc.				
Due from stockholders, directors, officers,					Capital Stock: Preferred*				
and employees					Common*				
Treasury Stock (do not incl. unissued stock)					Earned Surplus*				
Goodwill, Patents, Bond Discount, etc.					Capital Surplus*				
Other (itemize)					Net Worth				
TOTAL					**TOTAL**				

Have you any subsidiary or controlled companies? _____   If so, is above a consolidated statement? _____

(OVER)

FIGURE 1-2. (con't)

(Please Complete All Schedules and Fill in All Blanks; Insert "None" if Appropriate)

ACCOUNTS RECEIVABLE — CUSTOMERS:		NAMES OF LARGEST CUSTOMERS:

Not due ....
Past due   1 to   30 days ....
Past due   31 to   60 days ....
Past due   61 to   90 days ....
Past due   91 to 120 days ....
Over 120 days Past due ....
      Total ....
Less: Reserve for doubtful accounts ....
          Reserve for discounts ....
Total as per Statement (Page 1) ....

MERCHANDISE INVENTORY:

Merchandise on hand ....
      "   in warehouse ....
      "   consigned to others ....
      "   in transit ....

              Total ....
Less: Reserves (if any) ....
              Total as per Statement (Page 1) ..

As of statement date, what is amount of:
(1) Merchandise carried over from prior
        years or seasons? ....
(2) Unsalable or obsolete merchandise on
        hand? ....
(3) Merchandise consigned to you? ....
(4) Unpaid duty not included in liabilities?

(1) Does inventory represent physical count? .... If so, by whom? ....
(2) Describe in detail the basis of valuation ....
(3) State the extent of accountants' verification, if any ....
(4) Is merchandise consigned to you included in assets? ....
(5) Explain how contractors' accounts, if any, are handled in your statement ....
(6) At what time of year is inventory highest? .... lowest? ....
(7) Give date (or dates) on which corporation regularly takes inventory and closes books ....

INSURANCE:

Form	Carried on	Beneficiary	Assignee	Amount
Fire	Merchandise			
Fire	Buildings and Equipment			
Credit	Accounts and Notes Receivable			
Life	Endorsers, Executives, etc.			
Other Kinds				

CONTINGENT LIABILITIES AND COMMITMENTS:

Endorsed notes receivable, acceptances, or drafts discounted or sold ....
Accounts receivable pledged or assigned ....
Endorsements or guarantees for affiliated interests ....
Endorsements or guarantees for others ....
Unused portion of commercial letters of credit outstanding ....
If preferred dividends are cumulative, give amount in arrears, if any, at statement date ....
Amount of any unsettled claims or suits pending against company not appearing on books as liabilities ....
Amount of purchase commitments outstanding at statement date ....
Amount of unfilled sales orders at statement date ....
State any other contingent liabilities ....

FIGURE 1-2. (con't)

PROFIT AND LOSS ACCOUNT: for .... months ended .... 19 ......

Gross Sales	$			
Less: Returns, Allowances and Discounts				
Net Sales	$			
Less—Cost of Goods Sold:				
Beginning Inventory				
Add—Purchases				
If Manufacturer { Labor				
Add { Manufacturing Expense				
Total				
Less—Closing Inventory				
Total Cost of Goods Sold	$			
GROSS PROFIT	$			
Less—Selling Expense				
General and Administrative				
Provision for Bad Debts				
Reserve for Taxes (Excl. Fed. Taxes)				
Total Operating Expenses	$			
NET OPERATING PROFIT				
Add—Other Income				
Total Other Income	$			
Less—Other Expenses	$			
Total Other Expenses	$			
Less—Provision for Federal Taxes				
NET PROFIT	$			

Included Above—Depreciation Charges ....

         Executive Remuneration ....

Is above profit and loss statement on cash ☐ or accrual basis ☐

Are Federal taxes paid on cash ☐ or accrual basis ☐

SURPLUS RECONCILIATION				
Beginning Surplus	$			
Add—Profit				
Less—Dividends or Withdrawals				
Adjustments				
Closing Surplus	$			

BANK ACCOUNTS			
Names of Banks	Credit Lines Arranged	Amounts in use at statement date	On what Basis (endorsements, receivables, collateral, etc.)

(over)

FIGURE 1-2. (con't)

TRADE REFERENCES:

Names of Largest Creditors	Addresses	Amounts owing at statement date

OFFICERS, DIRECTORS, OR PARTNERS

Name	Office Held	Amount of General Partner-ship Interest	Amount of Special Partner-ship Interest	Special Partner-ship Agreement Expires	% of Ownership Preferred	Common

GENERAL INFORMATION:

Are branches or controlled companies financed entirely by you?..

If not, how do they borrow?..

Give amount outstanding at statement date ....

Are their loans included in this statement? ....

To what extent do officers of corporation endorse or guarantee obligations for other concerns or individuals?.............

Give amount of loans, if any, against cash surrender value of life insurance ....

To what extent, if any, have you pledged any assets during past year?...

Were any of the assets pledged at statement date?...................................If so, give details ....

What are your customary terms of sale...of purchase?.....................

Do you employ Certified Public Accountant(s) to audit your books regularly?...

Were books audited by Certified Public Accountant(s) at statement date? ....If so, please have appropriate certificate below signed.

SIGNATURE OF BORROWER

The undersigned has carefully read the foregoing contracts, statements, and all printed and written matter therein, and agrees to all the provisions thereof, and hereby certifies that the figures contained in the foregoing statements are taken from the books and records of the undersigned, that the statements contained on all sides of this sheet are known by the undersigned to be true and to give a correct showing of the financial condition of the undersigned; that the undersigned has no liabilities direct, indirect, or contingent, business or accommodation, except as set forth, in said statement; that legal and equitable title to all assets therein set forth is in undersigned's sole name, except as may be otherwise noted; and that the inventory of merchandise set forth in said statement has been verified by the undersigned, and that the accountants whose certificate is appended hereto are hereby authorized to furnish European American Bank & Trust Company, with any further information or details it desires concerning the financial condition of the undersigned.

Signed this................................day of.............................19_____.   Name...

By...

By...

ACCOUNTANT'S VERIFICATION

I/We have examined the balance sheet of _____ as of _____

and the related statement(s) of income and surplus for the _____ then ended. Our examination was made in accordance with generally

accepted auditing standards, and accordingly included such tests of the accounting records and such other auditing procedures as I/we considered necessary in the circumstances.

In my/our opinion, the accompanying balance sheet and statement(s) of income and surplus present fairly the financial position of the above at

and the results of its operations for the period then ended in conformity with generally accepted accounting principles

applied on a basis consistent with that of the preceding year.

....
Date signed

....
Certified Public Accountant(s)

FIGURE 1-3
Authorization – Facsimile Signature

AUTHORIZATION — FACSIMILE SIGNATURE

INDIVIDUAL AND ASSUMED NAME

TO EUROPEAN AMERICAN BANK & TRUST COMPANY

You are hereby requested, authorized and directed to honor all checks, drafts or other orders for the payment of money drawn on my account designated under my assumed business name of

(including those drawn to the individual order of any person or persons whose names appear thereon as signer or signers thereof) when bearing or purporting to bear the facsimile signature(s) of any .... of the following:

and your Bank (including its correspondent banks) shall be entitled to honor and to charge such account for all such checks, drafts or other orders for the payment of money, regardless of by whom or by what means the actual or purported facsimile signature or signatures thereon may have been affixed thereto, if such facsimile signature or signatures resemble the facsimile specimens from time to time filed with your bank by me or on my behalf.

All previous authorizations for the signing and honoring of checks, drafts, or other orders for the payment of money drawn on your Bank against said account are hereby continued in full force and effect as amplified hereby.

The undersigned agrees to and does hereby indemnify and hold the Bank harmless from any and all claims, loss, damage or expense it shall sustain or incur by reason of its acceptance of the authority herein granted, and its acts in reliance thereon.

In the event of any litigation in which the Bank and the undersigned are adverse parties arising out of or relating to this authorization and indemnity agreement or any of the provisions thereof, the Bank and the undersigned waive trial by jury and, additionally, the undersigned waives the right to interpose any set off or counterclaim of any nature or description.

The foregoing shall be governed and construed in accordance with the laws of the State of New York.

Dated:

....

FIGURE 1-4
Bank Account Agreement for Partnership

BANK ACCOUNT—PARTNERSHIP

Date.., 19..........

EUROPEAN AMERICAN BANK & TRUST COMPANY

Gentlemen:

The undersigned, co-partners, doing business under the name and style of

at   ,

in consideration of the opening and maintenance of a bank account of the said partnership by EUROPEAN AMERICAN BANK & TRUST COMPANY, hereinafter referred to as "Bank," certify that the said name is a trade name by which they are using in the conduct of an unincorporated business owned entirely by the undersigned as co-partners, and that they have complied with the applicable provisions of Section 130 of the New York State General Business Law, and the undersigned, jointly and severally, agree with said Bank that

1. The Bank be and hereby is designated as a depository of the partnership and it is hereby authorized to pay, cash or otherwise honor and charge to the partnership any and all checks, notes, drafts, bills of exchange, acceptances, orders, withdrawal tickets or other instruments for the payment of money or the withdrawal of funds, when signed, made, drawn, accepted or endorsed on behalf or in the name of the partnership by any of the following named partners or signatories, without counter-signature or co-signature except to the extent indicated as follows:

2. Said Bank is further authorized to pay, cash or otherwise honor and charge to the partnership any such instrument without regard to any notation on any part thereof indicating the effect, purpose or condition of its issuance, delivery, receipt or acceptance, and without regard to any alteration, defacement or erasure of such notation, and said Bank is expressly relieved of any duty on its part to pass upon the regularity of such notation, or to make any inquiry in respect thereof or of any alteration, defacement or erasure thereof. Said Bank may conclusively assume that the date of any such instrument, acceptance or endorsement is the true date of the making, drawing, acceptance or endorsement, as the case may be, completed in each instance by delivery on that date.

3. Said Bank is hereby authorized to pay, cash or otherwise honor and charge to the partnership any such instrument and any instrument payable to or held by the partnership when endorsed as aforesaid, and also to receive same for credit to the account of or in payment from the payee, endorsee or any other holder thereof, including any partner, agent or signatory of the partnership, without limitation of amount and without inquiry as to the circumstances of issue, negotiation or endorsement thereof or as to the disposition of the proceeds thereof, even if drawn, endorsed or payable to cash, bearer or to the individual order of any signing partner, agent or signatory, or tendered in payment of his individual obligation.

4. Endorsements on behalf of the partnership upon any and all commercial paper of any kind deposited by or on behalf of the partnership with the said Bank for credit or for collection or otherwise, may be made, affixed or imprinted (manually or by stamp impression) by any one of the foregoing partners or signatories or by any other person authorized or purporting to be authorized so to do, and in any case the endorsement may bear the name of the partnership alone without specifying the person who made, affixed or imprinted the same or his authority so to do.

5. Any   of the following partners are hereby authorized on behalf of this partnership under paragraph "5":

to borrow money and to obtain credit for this partnership from said Bank on such terms as may seem to (him) (them) advisable and to make and deliver notes, drafts, acceptances, instruments of guarantee, agreements and any other obligations of this partnership therefor in form satisfactory to said Bank, and as security therefor, to assign, pledge, deliver, withdraw, exchange or substitute stocks, bonds, mortgages, bills and accounts receivable, bills of lading, warehouse receipts, merchandise, insurance policies, certificates, savings passbooks or any other property of any nature and description held by and belonging to this partnership, with full authority to endorse, assign or guarantee the same in the name of the partnership; to execute and deliver general loan agreements, security agreements, financing statements and all instruments of assignment, transfer, hypothecation, mortgage, pledge and trust; to discount any bills receivable or other paper held by the partnership with full authority to indorse the same in the name of the partnership; to arrange with said Bank for time deposits (including certificates of deposit payable to bearer or order) on terms satisfactory to said Bank; to subordinate and assign any obligations and debts owed to the partnership by another or others, and in connection therewith, to execute and deliver instruments of subordination and assignment in form satisfactory to said Bank, to give any instructions to said Bank for the purchase, receipt, sale, delivery, exchange or other disposition of any stocks, bonds, certificates of deposit or other securities and foreign exchange or the proceeds thereof; to execute and deliver all instruments required by said Bank in connection with any of said matters.

FIGURE 1-4. (con't)

6. Notwithstanding any modification or termination of the power of any of the above named to represent the partnership, whether by expiration of the partnership agreement, by death or retirement of any partner, or the accession of one or more new partners, or otherwise, and notwithstanding any other notice thereof you may receive, this authority shall continue binding upon each of the undersigned individually and upon their legal representatives, and upon the partnership and its successors, until written notice to the contrary, signed by one of the undersigned or on his behalf by his duly authorized agent or representative, shall have been received by you at your branch where the account is maintained.

7. Each partner and/or signatory does hereby agree that this agreement is made under and governed and construed in accordance with the laws of the State of New York. Any provision hereof which may prove unenforceable under any law shall not effect the validity of any other provision hereof. The partnership and each partner and/or signatory agrees that actions arising out of this Agreement may be litigated under the laws of and submits to the jurisdiction of the courts of the State of New York, and that service of process by certified mail, return receipt requested, will be sufficient to confirm personal jurisdiction.

8. The undersigned agree to be bound by all the rules, regulations, conditions, limitations and agreements contained in any signature card, deposit ticket, check book, pass book, statement of account, receipt, instrument or other agreement received by this partnership from the Bank or delivered to the Bank by this partnership, with the same effect as if each and every term thereof were set forth in full herein and made a part hereof.

9. The following are the authentic signatures of the above named signatories of this partnership who are NOT partners thereof:

(Insert "None" if not applicable)   ....

....

....

10. The signatures below are in execution of this agreement and are the authentic signatures of all the partners.

....
             Name of Firm   *Address*

By .... residing at ....
             Partner

By .... residing at ....
             Partner

By .... residing at ....
             Partner

By .... residing at ....
             Partner

(All members of firm to sign)

FIGURE 1-5
Corporate Resolution

CORPORATE RESOLUTIONS

FOR THE ACCOUNT OF

____

DATED: ______________________________________

EAB
European American Bank

EAB 0255 Nov. 78
LR 3-78

FIGURE 1-5 (con't)

CERTIFIED COPY OF CORPORATE RESOLUTION BANK ACCOUNT —
LOAN AUTHORITY—SECURITY AGREEMENT

I, the undersigned, Secretary of ⬚

⬚ , a ⬚ corporation,

DO HEREBY CERTIFY that at a meeting of the Board of Directors of said corporation, duly held on the ⬚

day of ⬚ , 19 ⬚ , a quorum being present throughout, the following resolutions were unanimously

adopted and recorded in the minute books of said corporation, kept by me, and are in accord with and pursuant to the charter and by-laws of said corporation, and are now in full force and effect, to wit:

RESOLVED, that

1. EUROPEAN AMERICAN BANK & TRUST COMPANY, New York, N.Y. (Hereinafter referred to as Bank be and hereby is designated as a depository of this corporation, and any officer, agent or employee of this corporation hereby is authorized to deposit any of the funds of this corporation in said Bank, either at its head office or at any of its branches. Said Bank may at any time refuse to accept and/or may return by ordinary mail or otherwise, the whole or any part of a deposit.

2. Any persons then holding any of the following offices or any of the following named signatories, without counter-signature or co-signature except to the extent indicated as follows,

(Indicate below the titles only of the signing officers, without specifying the names of any such officers, and state the full names of the signatories who are not officers. If the signature of more than a single officer or signatory is required, then clearly indicate in what manner they are to sign, i.e. whether joint signatures or any other special combinations are required, as, for example, "President and Treasurer", or "any two officers".)

TITLE

⬚

are hereby authorized: To sign, make, draw, accept or indorse on behalf, or in the name, of this corporation any and all checks, notes, drafts, bills of exchange, acceptances, orders, withdrawal tickets or other instruments for the payment of money or the withdrawal of funds, including such as may bring about or increase an overdraft. Said Bank hereby is authorized to pay, cash or otherwise honor and charge to this corporation any such instrument and any instrument of any nature whatsoever payable to or held by this corporation when indorsed as aforesaid, and also to receive same for credit to the account of or in payment from the payee, indorsee or any other holder thereof (including any officer, agent or signatory of this corporation, and specifically including checks payable to this corporation, indorsed as aforesaid and deposited into the account of said officer, agent or signatory), without limitation of amount and without inquiry as to the circumstances of issue, negotiation or indorsement thereof or as to the disposition of the proceeds thereof, even if drawn, indorsed or payable to cash, bearer or to the individual order of any signing officer, agent or signatory, or other officer or agent, or tendered in payment of his individual obligations and without regard to any notation on any part thereof indicating the effect, purpose or condition of its issuance, delivery, receipt or acceptance and without regard to any alteration, defacement or erasure of such notation, and said Bank is expressly relieved of any duty on its part to pass upon the regularity of such notation, or to make any inquiry in respect thereof or in respect of any alteration, defacement or erasure thereof. Said Bank may conclusively assume that the date of any such instrument, acceptance or indorsement is the true date of the making, drawing, acceptance or indorsement, as the case may be, completed in each instance by delivery on that date. Checks drawn by this corporation payable to the order of and received by said Bank may be treated by said Bank for all purposes. in the absence of contrary written instructions, as payable to bearer or cash.

3. Any persons then holding any of the following offices or any of the following named signatories, without, counter-signature or co-signature. except to the extent indicated as follows,

(Indicate below the titles only of the signing officers, without specifying the names of any such officers, and state the full names of the signatories who are not officers. If the signature of more than a single officer or signatory is required, then clearly indicate in what manner they are to sign, i.e. whether joint signatures or any other special combinations are required, as, for example, "President and Treasurer", or "any two officers".)

TITLE

⬚

are hereby authorized:

To borrow money and to obtain credit for this corporation from said Bank on such terms as may seem to (him) (them) advisable and to make and deliver notes, drafts. acceptances and any other obligations of this corporation therefor, instruments of guarantee and of indemnity, agreements and contracts, all in form satisfactory to said Bank, and, as security therefor, to grant a security interest in and to assign, transfer. hypothecate. mortgage, pledge, trustee, withdraw, exchange and substitute any stocks, bonds, securities, mortgages, bills and accounts, bills of lading, warehouse receipts, goods, insurance policies, certificates, savings passbooks or any other property of every nature and description held by or belonging to this corporation, with full authority to indorse, assign or guarantee the same in the name of this corporation; to execute and deliver security agreements, financing statements and all instruments of assignment, transfer, hypothecation. mortgage. pledge and trust; to sell or discount with or without recourse any bills receivable or any other paper, whether or not negotiable, held by this corporation; to arrange with said Bank for time deposits (including certificates of deposit payable to bearer or order) on terms satisfactory to said Bank; to subordinate and assign any obligations and debts owed to this corporation by another or others, and in connection therewith, to execute and deliver instruments of subordination and assignment in form satisfactory to said Bank; to authorize and request said Bank to purchase, sell, deliver or exchange for the account of this corporation stocks, bonds, certificates of deposit or other securities. and foreign exchange or the proceeds thereof; to execute and deliver all instruments, agreements and contracts required by said Bank in connection with any matters herein contained; and to affix the corporate seal.

FIGURE 1-5. (con't)

4. Any and all instruments deposited by or on behalf of this corporation with said Bank for discount, credit, collection or otherwise, whether payable to or to the order of this corporation or any officer or signatory of this corporation, may be indorsed (by handwriting. stamp impression or by any other means) by any officer or signatory of this corporation, acting alone, or by any other person authorized or purporting to be authorized so to do, with or without specifying the person who made, affixed or imprinted such indorsement or his authority so to do.

5. This corporation hereby waives protest of any negotiable instruments deposited with or held by the Bank to which this corporation is a party, and this corporation hereby consents to any and every renewal or extension of time or other modifications which may be granted or made with respect to such negotiable instruments, and any such renewal or extension of time or other modification shall be deemed to have been granted or made with the full and express reservation by the Bank of all of its rights of recourse against this corporation in respect of such negotiable instruments.

6. This corporation agrees that any oral or written stop payment order must specify the precise account number and payee, date, amount and number of the item and be given by one authorized in Paragraph "2" hereof. This corporation agrees to indemnify and hold the Bank harmless from and against any and all claims and suits, whether groundless or otherwise, and from and against any and all liabilities, losses, damages, expenses and costs (including counsel fees) resulting from the Bank's non-payment of such item. This corporation further agrees that the Bank will in no way be responsible or liable (a) for certification or payment through error or inadvertence of post dated items or of items which this corporation has requested said Bank not to pay or for delay in executing such request, provided the Bank shall have used ordinary care as employed in the usage of trade in the banking industry, (b) if by reason of such certification or payment other items drawn, accepted or made by this corporation are dishonored by said Bank and returned unpaid, or (c) for dishonoring and returning items unpaid for any reason which, but for a stop payment order, would be applicable. Said Bank shall not be liable for loss in transit or otherwise of cancelled vouchers and/or statements, or loss resulting from failure to present or by reason of late presentation of any item.

7. This corporation does hereby give to the Bank a continuing lien for and security interest in the amount of any and all liabilities and obligations of this corporation to the Bank and claims of every nature and description of the Bank against this corporation, whether now existing or hereafter incurred, originally contracted with the Bank and/or with another or others and now or hereafter owing to or acquired in any manner by the Bank, whether contracted by this corporation alone or jointly and/or severally with another or others, absolute or contingent, secured or unsecured, matured or unmatured (all of which are hereafter collectively called "Obligations") upon any and all moneys, securities and any and all other property of this corporation and the proceeds thereof, now or hereafter actually or constructively held or received by or in transit in any manner to or from the Bank, its correspondents or agents from or for this corporation, whether for safekeeping, custody, pledge, transmission, collection or otherwise coming into the possession of the Bank in any way, or placed in any safe deposit box leased by the Bank to this corporation. The Bank is also hereby given a continuing lien and/or right of set-off for the amount of said Obligations upon any and all deposits (general or special) and credits of this corporation with, and any and all claims of this corporation against, the Bank at any time existing, and the Bank is hereby authorized at any time or times, without notice. to apply such deposits or credits, or any part thereof, to such Obligations and in such amounts as the Bank may elect, although said Obligations may be contingent or unmatured and whether any collateral therefor is deemed adequate or not. Corporation authorizes Bank to file a financing statement signed only by the Bank as secured party in all places where necessary to perfect Bank's security interest in all jurisdictions where such authorization is permitted by law.

8. Unless this corporation shall notify the Bank in writing within thirty calendar days of the delivery or mailing of any statement of account and cancelled vouchers of any claimed errors in such statement, or that this corporation's signature upon any such returned voucher was forged, or that any such voucher was made or drawn without the authority of this corporation or not in accordance with the signature arrangement set forth in Paragraph "2 (a)" hereof, or that it was raised or otherwise altered, or unless this corporation shall notify said Bank in writing within one year after the delivery or mailing of any such voucher that any indorsement was forged, improper, made without the authority of the indorsor or missing, said statement of account shall be considered correct for all purposes and said Bank shall not be liable for any payments made and charged to the account of this corporation or for any other errors in the statement of account as rendered to it. No legal proceeding or action shall be brought by this corporation against the Bank to recover any payment of any instrument upon which any signature or indorsement has been forged or was improper, or which was drawn, made, accepted or indorsed without the authority of this corporation or the indorsor or not in accordance with the signature arrangement stated in Paragraph "2" hereof, or which was raised or altered, or on which indorsement was missing unless (a) this corporation shall have given the written notice as provided hereinabove, and (b) such legal proceeding or action shall be commenced within one year after the date when such statement and cancelled vouchers were delivered or mailed to this corporation in the case of an unauthorized signature or any alteration on the face or back of the item and one or one and one-half years in the case of an unauthorized indorsement.

9. This corporation also agrees to be bound by all the rules. regulations, conditions, limitations and agreements contained in any signature card, deposit ticket, check book, passbook, statement of account, receipt, instrument or other agreement received by this corporation from the Bank or delivered to the Bank by this corporation, with the same effect as if each and every term thereof were set forth in full herein and made a part hereof.

10. In the event of any litigation in which the Bank and this corporation are adverse parties, the right to a trial by jury and to interpose any defense based upon any Statute of Limitations or any claims of laches, and any set-off or counterclaim of any nature or description, is hereby waived by this corporation. This corporation agrees that if an attorney is used, from time to time, to enforce, declare or adjudicate any of the provisions herein or any of the rights herein granted to the Bank or to obtain payment of said Obligations at maturity (expressed or declared) whether by suit or by any other means whatsoever, an attorney's fee of 15% of the principal and interest then due on account of said Obligations shall be added thereto and be payable by this corporation. The Bank shall not, by any act, delay, omission or otherwise, be deemed to have waived any of its rights or remedies hereunder unless such waiver be in writing, signed by the Bank, and then only to the extent therein set forth; failure of the Bank to insist on compliance with, or to exercise any right and/or remedy granted to it by, the resolutions and agreements set forth in this document or any of its rules, regulations, conditions limitations and agreements contained in any signature card, deposit ticket, check book, passbook, statement of account, receipt, notice. instrument or other agreement shall not be deemed a waiver thereof or a bar thereto on any other occasion nor shall same establish a course of conduct.

11. Any notice to the Bank shall be deemed effective only if sent to and received at the branch, division or department of the Bank conducting the transaction or transactions hereunder. Any notice to this corporation shall be deemed sufficient if sent to the last known address of this corporation appearing on the records of the Bank.

12. All the foregoing authorities shall be and continue in full force and effect until revoked or modified by written notice actually received by said Bank at its office wherein the account of this corporation is then maintained, setting forth a resolution to that effect stated to have been adopted by the Board of Directors of this corporation, and signed by one purporting to be the secretary or an assistant secretary of this corporation and bearing the purported seal of this corporation, provided, that such notice shall not be effective with respect to any exercise of said authorities prior to the receipt thereof nor with respect to any checks or other instruments for the payment of money or the withdrawal of funds dated on or prior to the date of such notice, but presented to the Bank after receipt of such notice and said Bank is hereby authorized at all times to rely upon the last notice, certificate or communication received by it, when so authenticated, as to any resolution of this corporation or as to the persons who from time to time may be officers or signatories of this corporation, or as to their respective specimen signatures and/or as to any other corporate matters, and said Bank shall be held harmless in such reliance, even though such resolution may have been changed.

13. The secretary (or any assistant secretary) of this corporation is hereby authorized to certify and deliver to said Bank copies of these resolutions, and that the signatures of the president (or any vice-president) and the secretary (or any assistant secretary) of this corporation at the foot of the certificate containing these resolutions shall constitute such certificate and resolutions an agreement by this corporation with said Bank (which may not be changed orally) with respect to all the matters set forth in said certificate and resolutions.

14. Any provision hereof which may prove unenforceable under any law shall not affect the validity of any other provision hereof. This agreement shall be governed by and construed in accordance with the laws of the State of New York.

FIGURE 1-5. (con't)

I FURTHER CERTIFY that the persons herein designated as officers of this corporation have been duly elected to and now hold the offices in this corporation set opposite their respective names, and that the following are the authentic, official signatures of the said respective officers and of the named signatories who are not corporate officers, to wit:

SIGNATURES   *Signatures*

_____   _____
      Name (Print or Type)   *President*

_____   _____
      Name (Print or Type)   *Vice-President*

_____   _____
      Name (Print or Type)   *Vice-President*

_____   _____
      Name (Print or Type)   *Secretary*

_____   _____
      Name (Print or Type)   *Assistant Secretary*

_____   _____
      Name (Print or Type)   *Treasurer*

_____   _____
      Name (Print or Type)   *Authorized Signature*

_____   _____
      Name (Print or Type)   *Authorized Signature*

_____   _____
      Name (Print or Type)   *Authorized Signature*

IN WITNESS WHEREOF, I have hereunto subscribed my name and affixed the seal of this corporation by order of the Board of Directors this _____ day of _____ , 19 _____

**AFFIX
CORPORATE
SEAL
HERE**

. . . . *Secretary.*

I, the undersigned President of the corporation above named, do hereby certify that the foregoing certificate is in all respects true and contains a true copy of the resolutions regularly adopted by the Board of Directors of said corporation in the manner therein stated and I do further acknowledge, on behalf of said corporation, that the foregoing resolutions also constitute an agreement by said corporation with said Bank in respect to the matters therein set forth.

Dated: _____ , 19 _____   _____
                                                     President

FIGURE 1-6.

20

Financing the Operation

Projected Profit and Loss Statement

For _____

Year Ending _____

	$	Percentage
Sales: Beginning inventory		100%
+Purchases		
=Available for sale		
–Ending inventory		
=Cost of goods sold		%
Gross Profit		%
Expenses: Rent		%
Utilities		%
Sales promotion		%
Freight-in and delivery		%
Insurance		%
Professional services		%
Interest on loan		%
Total Expenses		%
Net Profit		%

sense, a bank can be a long term "partner" of your business, one that can offer advice and that can be a resource for filling your business' financial needs.

1. Fill out the financial statement and agreement in Figure 1-2. **ASSIGNMENT**

2. Based on the type of organization you have selected, fill out *one* of the forms in Figures 1-3, 1-4, and 1-5.

3. Fill in your dollar and percentage estimates on the form in Figure 1-6, Projected Profit and Loss Statement for the first year's opera-operation.

4. With that information, visit a local commercial bank, see the appropriate employee, and apply for a loan of $25,000. (You should explain the purpose of your mission.)

5. Submit the original completed forms to your advisor (instructor) with a detailed explanation of the advice you received from the bank employee. The report should be in narrative form, typed, double-spaced, and in sufficient length to relate the complete information. Retain the copy for possible future use.

Visit a regional SBA office with the forms required for the assignment of this unit. Advise an SBA employee that you are seeking advice about how a governmental agency can help you obtain a $25,000 loan.

    Make a full report.

**OPTIONAL
ASSIGNMENT**

Financial Control

You have to carefully control your funds in a retail business for several reasons. One is the seasonal nature of retailing. Another is that you do not always realize cash receipts (cash inflow) at the same rate that you make cash expenditures (cash outflow). In other words, at times you temporarily have more going out than you have coming in. A cash balance fills this gap between receipts and expenditures. So you have to set aside a part of current assets and have it available in the form of cash to assure liquidity.

Figure 2-1 is a visualization of the inflow/outflow process. Cash, at the top center, flows out of the business to pay for operating expenses and merchandise. Cash returns to the business through cash receipts and accounts receivable from the sale of merchandise. As you can see, merchandise inventory is, in effect, turned into cash. *Turnover* is the name of the process by which cash is turned into merchandise and back again into cash in a given period. (This process is discussed more thoroughly in Chapter 8.)

The major objectives of financial management are to:

1. obtain money for business needs,
2. maintain and increase invested money through sound judgment and planning, and
3. generate income.

Estimating Capital Needs

Every store owner wants a beautiful place of business — a show-stopper, the talk of the town. Yet, realistically, your store could cost a great deal of money — often in excess of the planned capital investment. The construction

FIGURE 2-1.

23

The Inflow/Outflow Process

Financial Control

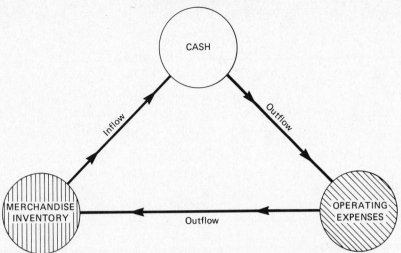

costs of a store have to stay within the limits of your financial capabilities, or you risk not having enough working capital to sustain the business during its early period of operation.

To operate comfortably and without financial pressure, you have to avoid such an early shortage of funds. You must therefore determine the financial outlay of capital well in advance of opening day. In so doing, be aware that an entrepreneur is most likely to underestimate financial need in this pre-planning period. So take advantage of the two tools that can make a big difference in arriving at a realistic estimate: a thorough research analysis of all cost factors and standard operating ratios, which we will discuss in this chapter.

As a first step, you have to prepare a financial planning worksheet in detail, to outline:

1. *start-up costs* — such as the cost of fixturing and decorating, and
2. *operating expenses for three months* — that is, the estimated expenses of running the business for a full business quarter.

Start-Up Costs. The cost of fixturing and decorating depends on a number of things: the type of operation, the segmented customer group, your own creativity. Physical plant costs are variable, depending on the quality of fixtures: Are the walls to be painted, paneled, or papered? What type of floor covering is required? Is the store self- or full-service? And so on.

Operating Expenses. After determining the total start-up costs, you have to formulate a working capital statement to estimate the cost of operation for three months. The components of working capital are:

1. a fund for customer credit,
2. a petty cash fund, and
3. three months operating expenses (see the income statement in Chapter 6).

A Statement of Start-Up Costs and Working Capital. The statement in Figure 2-2 clearly indicates the amount of investment needed to open a small store. It helps eliminate any unforeseen contingencies that may arise, and it enables

FIGURE 2-2.

24

Financial Control

Statement of Financial Requirements

Prepaid rent (one month)	$ 1,000
Vehicle	4,000
License, permits	500
Furniture and fixtures	7,500
Signs, display materials, decorating and lighting	3,000
Deposits	200
Prepaid insurance	500
Legal and accounting fees	1,000
Initial inventory	30,000
Advertising and promotion for opening	1,000
Salaries	1,000
Miscellaneous	500
Total start-up costs	$ 50,200

Operating expenses (estimated)	*Monthly*	
Inventory	$10,000	
Accounts receivable	2,000	
Owner's salary	800	
Salaries and commission	1,500	
Rent	1,000	
Advertising	300	
Maintenance and supplies	100	
Utilities	300	
Payment of loans	300	
Interest	100	
Insurance	100	
Taxes	100	
Petty cash	200	
Fund for customer credit	2,000	
Total monthly expenses	$18,800	
$18,800 × 3 months		$ 56,400
Total financial requirement		$106,600

the new store owner to make any changes in the planning before becoming committed to irreversible or costly decisions.

Cash Flow Forecast

An accurate cash flow projection enables many a small business to increase its operational performance, insure funds for extraordinary purchases, renovate the store when necessary, and insure capital funds for future growth. This projection is a necessary safeguard against future contingencies. Forecasting is not only essential to the daily operation of a business, it is also helpful when applying for credit or loans. The presentation of such reports can have a positive effect on those who represent sources of financial funding — banks and factors.

The most basic and comprehensive method of predicting the amount and the time of future needs for funds is through the preparation of a *cash* gauges the impact of the firm's plans on the receipts and expenditures of cash. The basic aim of this forecast is to predict when cash will come into the firm and when payments of cash will have to be made, as well as the quantities coming in and going out.

In a ready-to-wear store, monthly sales vary, and the merchandise must be stocked to accommodate sales patterns. It is therefore difficult to operate at a constant retail inventory level. Facing seasonal variations, you need advance planning to insure a constant and adequate flow of available capital for buying merchandise and paying all operating expenses.

How do you predict what you will need and when?

Stock/Sales Ratio. This ratio is essential to cash budget planning. A successful retail operation needs an adequate opening inventory. "Adequate" means that the inventory must have enough depth and assortment to fill customers' varied needs over a given period (say, a month), as well as to leave a closing inventory for that period. The question is, How much inventory is adequate?

The stock/sales ratio helps a new store owner to answer that question. This ratio reflects the relationship between the estimated sales and the amount of inventory needed to maintain that sales level. In effect, it tells the owner that, if you want to maintain "such-and-such" level of sales, you must have "so-much" inventory on hand. The value of inventory is expressed as a multiple of sales, that is, as 3, 4, 6, or some other number of times the amount of sales. For example, if you estimate sales for the month to be $10,000, and if you know from past experience that you need, say, 4 times the sales volume in inventory, then you know that you will need $40,000 in inventory to fill orders and to have a closing inventory for the month. The ratio is calculated as follows:

$$\text{Stock/sales ratio} = \frac{\text{Retail stock (first day of the month)}}{\text{Sales for the period (that month)}}$$

These ratios may vary from month to month, depending on consumer buying patterns and accepted industry figures. So how do you know which ratio is the right one?

The Sales and Inventory Distribution Graph. The graph in Figure 2-3 shows monthly variations in sales and their effect on cash inflow and outflow. Using industry averaged ratios and assuming a total estimated first year sales of $250,000, the graph shows three factors:

1. averaged stock/sales ratios,
2. recommended stock/sale ratios (revised), and
3. sales distribution by month (as a percentage of total sales).

These industry figures are yardsticks of performance. They are based on stores doing business in the million-dollar range, and so they may be too high for stores in the $100,000 to $500,000 class. The variation between the top and middle lines in the graph are therefore due to differences in store size, in available capital, and in traffic flow. Small stores would be well advised to carry the level of inventory as shown in the middle line of the graph with the lower ratios.

To predict each month's inventory, just use the estimated sales percentage for each month, which is based on industry standards of when consumers buy.

FIGURE 2-3.

The Effect of Monthly Variations in Sales on Cash Inflow/Outflow Process

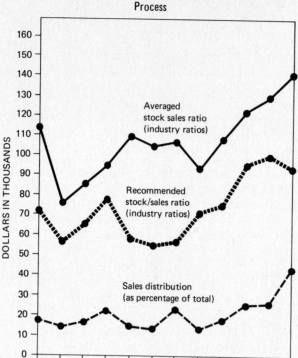

Example: The sales percentage for January is 7.2; that is, 7.2 percent of the year's sales are made in January. So 7.2 percent becomes $18,000 ($250,000 × 7.2). By applying the industry stock/sale ratio of 6.3 (top line), the projected opening inventory becomes $113,400 (6.3 × $18,000).

But, perhaps because of prevailing economic conditions, the application of a somewhat lower stock/sales ratio is recommended. As a case in point, the projected sales for February are $14,000 ($250,000 × 5.6). By multiplying the projected sales of $14,000 by the recommended stock/sale ratio of 4 (middle line), the estimated stock position is $56,000, as opposed the industry average ratio of 5.6 or $78,400 (top line). By using the more conservative figure, you reduce your capital need by $22,400, thereby controlling working capital more efficiently and allowing the remaining cash to be used for other purposes.

An estimated cash budget, as shown in Figure 2-4, enables the entrepreneur to be constantly aware of financial needs and business trends.

Initially, such a cash budget statement should be prepared for a period of three months and later for a fiscal period of one year. These two statements provide both a short- and long-term view of operations, and they allow time to prepare in advance any necessary financial adjustments.

Using Credit

Trade Credit. The timely or advance payment of invoices (anticipation, discussed in Chapter 10) is one way to increase profits, by taking advantage of

FIGURE 2-4.

CASH BUDGET
For Three Months Ending August 30, 19XX

Line	Expected Cash Receipts	June	July	August	Basis of Projection
1.	Cash sales	$10,000	$12,500	$15,000	Sales forecast
2.	Collections on accounts receivable	2,200	2,000	2,500	Based on industrial averages
3.	Other income	—	—	—	List if applicable
4.	Total cash receipts	$12,200	$14,500	$17,500	Sum of lines 1, 2, and 3.
	Expected Cash Payments				
5.	Merchandise purchased	$ 8,500	$10,000	$ 9,000	Estimated purchases
6.	Payroll	2,500	2,500	2,800	Sales help
7.	Maintenance	—	250	—	Store upkeep
8.	Advertising	250	400	400	Sale ads
9.	Commissions	330	400	450	Anticipated sales
10.	Administrative expense	500	500	500	General office expenses
11.	Loan repayments	—	—	1,500	Repayment of loan for period
12.	Interest expense	80	50	50	Estimate
13.	Other payments	625	200	200	Utilities, taxes, insurance, etc.
14.	Total cash payments	$12,785	$14,300	$14,900	Sum of lines 5 through 13.
15.	Expected cash balance at beginning of month	$ 500	$ 1,415	$ 1,615	Last month's ending cash balance
16.	Cash increase (decrease)	(585)	200	2,600	Line 4 minus line 14
17.	Expected cash balance at end of month	(85)	1,615	4,215	Line 15 plus line 16
18.	Desired cash balance	1,500	1,500	1,500	Your policy
19.	Short-term loans needed	1,500	—	—	Line 18 minus line 17, if line 18 is larger
20.	Cash available for short-term investment	—	115	2,715	Line 17 minus line 18, if line 17 is larger

trade discounts (see Chapter 1). These are optional practices, based on your business' financial ability.

Credit Cards. For you as a small store retailer to be competitive with larger stores, you have to consider extending credit to customers. There are three ways to accommodate this consumer need:

1. *Carrying accounts receivable:* Just remember that the capital you tie up could be used to yield more turnover and to increase profits.

2. *Arranging to accept national credit cards:* Many small retailers arrange for this alternative. Although credit cards reduce the margin of profit, they generally increase the cash flow, and you do not have to dun slow-paying customers and possibly create ill will.

3. *Factoring the accounts receivables through banks or factors:* This is an accepted practice among small store owners, who sell their accounts receivables and thereby obtain cash immediately following sales.

Discuss the extension of credit to consumers with an accountant, so that the effect of each method can be weighed to determine its cost and the extent to which it affects profit.

Pre-planning is the essence of good financial management. A retailer who anticipates problems rather than reacts to them is able to accept sudden and unexpected profitable opportunities. Start-up cost calculations and cash budget charts show the financial and manufacturing community that you are knowledgeable in business practices and techniques, as well as that you should be respected when applying for a loan or credit. Good financial control of a business also enables you to reap many benefits of an efficiently run venture, such as:

* a good credit standing,
* growth potential,
* ease of borrowing,
* better flow of merchandise,
* investment funds, and
* better use of working capital.

Of the many hats that a small business entrepreneur wears in supervising an operation—those of buyer, personnel supervisor, and others—the role of financial controller obliges you to assume the financial responsibility of making expeditious use of capital funds. While you should be enthusiastic, creative, and daring in the role of buyer, you should be objective in the spending of the firm's funds. Successful merchandising and an efficient operation are dependent upon this objectivity.

You have accumulated $75,000 to invest in the store you intend to open.

1. Prepare a statement of financial requirement to insure enough for initial investment and working capital for the first three months' operation. Design your own form, but refer to Figure 2-2. Include the corollary forms in Figures 2-5 and 2-6: Estimating Starting Costs and Estimated Monthly Expenses.

2. Assume a sales projection of $300,000 for the first year, as detailed in Figure 2-7:
   a. establish an opening inventory for each month based on the industry recommended stock/sales ratio (use Figure 2-8);
   b. establish an opening inventory for each month based on the more conservative ratios;
   c. analyze how your working capital is affected by the use of stock/sales ratios (do you have more or less for each month?);
   d. graph the stock/sale ratios you prepared for the answer to c on the assignment form.

3. To encourage sales and to provide a cash flow, you intend to offer customer credit facilities.
   a. obtain information from banks and national credit agencies (American Express, Diner's Club, and the like), and conclude how and why either or both types can be utilized by your operation. (Use Figure 2-9.)

4. Submit all the completed statements to your accountant (instructor) for analysis and verification.

FIGURE 2-5.

Estimated Starting Costs

	Planned	Actual
Inventory		
Fixtures and Equipment		
Decorations		
Legal and professional fees		
Utility deposits		
Pre-opening advertising		
Cash contingency fund		
Insurance		
Supplies		
Pre-paid rent		
Miscellaneous		
Total start-up costs		

FIGURE 2-6.

Estimated Monthly Expenses

	Monthly	3 months
Salaries		
Rent		
Utilities		
Inventory replenishment		
Advertising		
Supplies		
Insurance		
Maintenance		
Professional fees		
Delivery expense		
Loan interest		
Subscriptions, dues		
Miscellaneous		
Total operating expenses		

Analysis:

FIGURE 2-7. Anticipated Sales Volume: $300,000

	J	F	M	A	M	J	Jy	A	S	O	N	D
Sales distribution percentage	7.2	5.5	6.6	7.8	7.4	6.9	8.3	6.9	7.2	9	9.2	17.7
Industry stock/sale ratios	6.3	5.6	5	4.8	5.9	5.8	4.9	5.1	5.7	5.4	5.5	3.1
Recommended stock/sale ratios	5	4	4	4	3	3	2.5	4	4	4	4	2

FIGURE 2-8.

Month	$ Sales Distribution	Monthly Industry $ Inventory	Monthly Recommended $ Inventory	Differences in Dollars
Jan.				
Feb.				
Mar.				
April				
May				
June				
July				
Aug.				
Sept.				
Oct.				
Nov.				
Dec.				

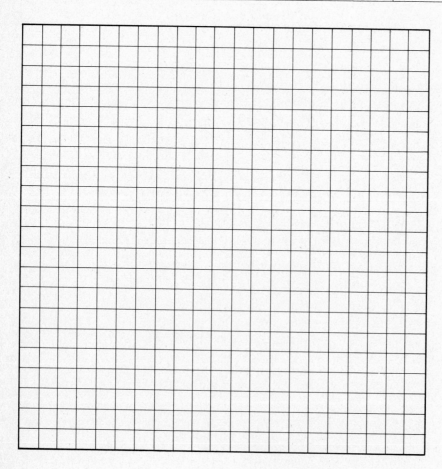

32

FIGURE 2-9.

Credit Card Analysis

Bank credit cards

    Date   *Resource*   *Conditions and Cost Factors*

1. _____

_____

_____

2. _____

_____

_____

3. _____

_____

_____

National Credit Cards

    Date   *Resource*   *Conditions and Cost Factors*

1. _____

_____

_____

_____

2. _____

_____

_____

3. _____

_____

_____

Comments: _____

_____

_____

_____

Location 3

The "right" location is essential for the success of a retail store. Retail transactions are initiated by consumers who have the option of going to any store that offers the greatest satisfaction. In such a highly competitive environment, a retailer has to stock consumer-wanted merchandise in a consumer-convenient location. Both these conditions have to be satisfied before an owner can stimulate patronage. The only exception to convenience is when the retailer can offer something in its place — unique value, product, price, service, ambience, or some other consumer benefit — that motivates people to buy despite the inconvenience. In addition, a small store has only a limited ability to draw traffic. Yet it must try to meet competition with a restricted stock assortment, shallow stock depth, and limited price ranges.

Small store entrepreneurs therefore have to offset these negative conditions by capitalizing on a small store's advantages: They can stock merchandise for a narrow and clearly defined customer group. They can offer personalized service. They can establish customer relationships that support strong patronage loyalty. Perhaps most important, they have to have the right location.

Arriving at the right location involves three decisions:

1. the most favorable trading area, or community,
2. the most favorable site within the area, and
3. the rental cost compared to potential sales.

Trading Area. The term "location" has two meanings — a trading area and a specific site in the area. The *trading area* is the surrounding area or community from which most of a store's trade is drawn. This area has to contain enough potential customers with the appropriate characteristics of income, age, profession or job, and with the buying habits that suit the store's

INTRODUCTION

products. Every retailer, regardless of size, must therefore segment a market

and identify a group of people to be served.

The site. After determining the most suitable trading area, the next step is to select a specific site within it.

Rent. A high-traffic location commands high rent, and a low-traffic one can be leased for a relatively low cost.

The dilemma is, which combination of factors makes for the most appropriate place to do business within the limits of available capital, planned sales, and the cost of doing business? A careful investigation of all the aspects of location — general and specific — can lead to the most appropriate site, an extremely important decision in starting a solid business. (Another method of site selection is, of course, the purchase of a going store, a circumstance that is not within the range of this book.) Gathering adequate information takes some time, effort, and analytical ability. It also obliges you to discuss the data you accumulate, along with your conclusions, with an accountant or business advisor.

Researching the Trading Area

The most basic question is whether a trading area is capable of supporting the proposed store. The first step is therefore to assess the selected market's ability to yield sales for already established stores. This sort of research can lead to several important conclusions:

* the ability of the location to support the proposed store;
* the market share owned by established stores, their level of competition, and the proposed store's probable ability to meet the assessed strength of competition; and
* the estimated ability and willingness of the market to buy particular types of merchandise.

With reasonable care, you can also develop evaluations that you can apply to questions about other trading areas' current adequacy and growth potential.

Several sources and information-gathering methods enable researchers to arrive at meaningful conclusions.

Preliminary Research

Buying Power Index. For preliminary data, a well-stocked library should contain several sources of generalized information. *Sales Management*, a business periodical, compiles data that can be used to appraise an area's ability to support retail activities. These studies (called "Buying Power Index" and prepared annually by the editors of the publication) include three demographic and economic characteristics of areas:

1. population,
2. effective buying income, and
3. retail sales.

This information, although valuable, does not permit you to precisely

evaluate narrow trading areas or strength of current and future competitors. But they can serve as the logical approach to research; you can establish a premise, obtain introductory material, and then follow through with specific data.

The Standard Industrial Classification. Published by the Office of Management Control, this manual contains a system of classifying most of the basic economic data of the nation. It provides a sound definitional basis for the collection of business data by government agencies. Each business activity is divided into groups and identified by code numbers. Although this information is too general for the purpose of small-store ownership research, the SIC codes are used by *County Business Patterns* and the *Dun and Bradstreet Reference Book*, both of which can supply detailed information about firms in more specific areas, about the level of competition, and about other pertinent information.

Fairchild's Financial Manual of Retail. Published annually, this source contains data about major store ownership, financial details (sales of the past five years), record of profit, and executive personnel.

Sheldon's Retail Directory. This directory lists department, specialty, and chain stores of a wide range of trading areas in every state. It also includes personnel lists that enable a reader to estimate ball-park yearly sales figures for selected stores.

Observational Research

More specific information involves some shoe-leather effort and "eye-ball" observation. The following are suggested methods:

1. *A walking tour* of the residential area of a selected location. Note the type of homes, cars, and atmosphere of the area. What is probable income range of the residents? Are there other clues as to which type of merchandise would meet with the greatest acceptance?

2. Speak to residents to determine their views about:
   a. the present and future population mix,
   b. current and future area growth,
   c. opinions, attitudes, and beliefs of residents, and
   d. planned community projects that have economic meaning.

3. Investigate the level of retail saturation or undersaturation. To determine these important factors, ask questions about:
   a. the number of stores that sell similar lines of merchandise,
   b. the number of empty stores,
   c. previous and current retail employment rates,
   d. sales per square foot of selling area of stores (Chamber of Commerce, local trade organization, local real estate organization), and
   e. general information from the personnel of the local bank and local small business association.

4. Take a head count of customers passing and entering stores. This sampling should be done over an extended period. Here are a couple of suggestions:
   a. Counts should be taken during store-open hours on six con-

traffic is abnormally high.

b. Observe traffic of specific departments that stock the same or similar merchandise of the proposed store.

5. Examine newspaper advertisements to evaluate the type of goods featured by retailers for fashion prestige and promotional purposes. This technique can give evidence of:

a. the strengths and weaknesses of competition,

b. merchandising opportunities, and

c. customer attitudes about fashion merchandise.

6. Take the license plate numbers of cars in the parking areas. Although time-consuming, of course, this method identifies customer characteristics of: where they live, income range, and mobility. (This information must be obtained from a local license bureau.)

PRINCIPLES OR PRACTICES

Since the beginning of recorded history, retailers have tended to cluster together in groups of competing and/or complementary stores. Clustering is a way to serve customers' needs best by minimizing purchase effort. So wherever people reside or frequent in sufficient numbers, a retail market of stores develop in a cluster.

Following World War II, the mass exodus to suburbia caused retailers to respond to the needs of newly developed communities. Department stores extended their operations by opening branch stores. Discount and mass operations appeared with unparalled rapidity. Chains extended their number of units, many specialty shops becoming chains. Every retailer to some degree was affected by unprecedented and continued population movement. Over the years, the rapid shift of markets resulted in an environment in which retail business is now conducted in virtually every trading area within and outside of municipal boundary lines. In fact, many geographic boundary lines between city and suburbia have been blurred and flow into each other.

These events result in the formation of four major types of retail cluster institutions:

1. the central business district,

2. the regional shopping center,

3. the community shopping center, and

4. the neighborhood shopping center.

Location Characteristics

Wherever most Americans live and/or frequent, retail sites and their characteristics fall into a number of commonly encountered classes, which should be weighed as part of your investigation of a particular site:

Downtown Core — located in a central business area; high rental zone; limited parking facilities; pedestrian traffic; big store competition.

Downtown Frame — outer part of the urban environment; relatively low rental; best suited for dealers in autos, lumber, hardware, and building materials.

Strip Development (Radial Site) — usually situated along major traffic areas connecting central business districts and residential areas; best suited for

convenience goods; prone to "deterioration" due to a lack of long-range planning.

Interceptor Ring —outer loop of an urban area, frequently at the outer section of two or more principal thoroughfares; usually service stations and thirty or forty stores; possibly an important site due to its nearness to residential section and traffic.

Peripheral Site —outreach of city; adjacent to highway or access road; high traffic; usually beyond zone of municipal taxes; "unplanned" buildings; generally well suited for a mass merchandising operation.

Isolated Location —lack of other retail stores; low rental; most appropriate for local convenience store or discount operation.

External Site —along traffic artery between communities; depends on highway traffic; low rental; sometimes as part of cluster of stores.

Mall and Shopping Center —clusters of stores that can be included in the fore-mentioned sites; most often dominated by two or more major outlets, large branch units of a department store or national chain operation; high customer traffic; planned parking area; high rental; in-premise competition; mall enclosed and arranged so that ambience encourages leisurely shopping.

Site Criteria

After considering a trading area's importance and the type, there are the final criteria for selection of the specific site.

Number and Quality of Customers. The first qualitative aspect is the number and quality of potential customers who pass the site. High traffic in itself does not necessarily mean many potential customers. Traffic flow can even have a negative effect on a site where people are in a hurry or have no place to park a car. As an example, thousands of people pass by stores in major railroad terminals, but how many are inclined to buy a dress or suit in such an environment?

An additional consideration is that some sites have an uneven traffic flow. A store operated in an office building in a business area would be closed on Saturdays and have no business during the evenings. Its best traffic would be during the hours from noon to 2 p.m., with additional consumer interest after 5 p.m.

Although these examples involve high-traffic sites, for certain products the value of a traffic count must be weighed against consumer motivational factors: Is it the right time and the right place to purchase given products? [The relationship between location, atmosphere, and consumer motivation is explained in the next chapter.]

A retail axiom is that competition attracts greater traffic—provided, naturally, that the competition is equal and fair. People are prone to shop in sites that have several stores carrying similar lines so they can make comparisons and decide on value. And indeed, shopping centers often have tenants who are in direct competition with each other, but the total of retail business generated is far greater for each than if they did not coexist.

Conversely, what is undesirable is a neighboring store that is incompatible with your manner of doing business, your merchandise, or any other condition that adversely affects business. For example, a specialty shop that sells moderate to better merchandise would be ill-positioned next to a butcher shop. A bridal shop abutted by a pizza parlor would not be conducive to better business. And, to use an extreme, what apparel store would want a graveyard for cars as a next-door neighbor? On the other hand, price-maintaining apparel store owners would prefer neighboring stores that carry shoes, children's wear, or any other merchandise that attracts the type of customer they serve. Good interrelationships among neighboring stores, depend to a great degree on product compatability, on the manner in which business is conducted, and on the customer groups for whom merchandise is intended.

As a consumer convenience, give serious thought to parking facilities. In some main street suburban areas, stores have been forced out of business due to the lack of parking space. In the absence of space convenient for potential customers, what appears to be a highly desirous site could be a poor risk. How much space is required is relative to a particular site, to the time and frequency of shopping hours, and to the manner in which business is conducted — all rather broad guidelines. Although there are no precise guidelines, a rule of thumb is that a specialty shop requires four to five spaces per 1,000 square feet of store space.

Lease Commitment Terms

Once a site is selected, the final arrangement is the signing of a lease for a given term. (It goes without saying that a lease should not be signed until it has been examined and explained by an attorney.) The most common forms of leases are:

1. *Flat amount for a year* — a fixed amount to be paid each month.
2. *A straight percentage* — stipulates that a percentage of sales or profit shall be paid.
3. *A percentage with a guaranteed minimum* — the tenant pays on the same basis as a percentage lease except that the landlord is guaranteed a minimum sum regardless of sales or profit.

The limit of affordable rent for a specialty shop (as noted in Chapter 1) is 9 percent of net sales. So certain desired sites may be beyond your proposed store's capacity to operate successfully. In the final analysis, picking the most desirable site must be done only after comparing the cost of rent with potential net sales. If the "numbers" necessitate the selection of an "80 percent" location, for example, you must realize the necessity to create a store that has the value of uniqueness for potential customers, such as:

* unusual personal service,
* merchandise that targets consumer needs,
* the arrangement of merchandise that pleases consumers,

including dramatic window displays,

* fashion shows with prophetic merchandise, or
* pleasant store ambience.

Location is a primary and critical concern. First you must identify your consumer group target and trading area, as well as determine that they satisfy each other. Once the trading area requirement is satisfied, you can

decide on a particular site. But your decisions should be based on the most thorough research efforts — the weighing of all plus and minus factors.

Figures 3-1 to 3-3 are standard leases for commercial property. Following the twenty-fifth clause in Figure 3-2 is space for additional clauses, such as rent as a percentage of sales or profit, sublease terms, or any variation of the standard lease clauses.

Start an investigation to determine the availability of a site that responds most nearly to the store you intend to open. Select two alternatives: read your local newspaper real estate offerings and solicit the help of a real estate agent. Your efforts should include:

Newspaper Advertisements

1. Select two ads that relate best to locations that you feel are most appropriate.
2. Visit both sites:
   a. Analyze the qualitative aspects of location and site, as discussed in the chapter.
   b. Compare rental costs with your proposed net sales, and determine if they are in line with your financial capability.
   c. Obtain information about lease conditions, such as: the required lease term and renewal option(s); restrictions of merchandise to be stocked; fuel cost adjustment; type and size of store signs, including any other references to displays; outer store costs, such as cleaning of hallways, area maintenance costs, or other cost responsibilities that would increase the cost of rent.
   d. Write a detailed report of your findings so that your advisors, accountant, and lawyer can analyze them and give you advice.

Real Estate Company Offering

1. Visit a real estate company in a location that you feel you want to establish your proposed store.
2. Advise the agent of your requirements, type of store, size, and the rent you can afford.
3. Obtain a list of sites that the agent suggests.
4. Visit *one* site, and conclude whether the agent is the proper person to support your search.

Figures 3-4 and 3-5 provide a suitable form to be discussed with your advisors. Your conclusions about the real estate agent's value will be the subject of an oral report to your advisors (that is, to the class and/or instructor).

FIGURE 3-1.

STANDARD FORM OF STORE LEASE
The Real Estate Board of New York, Inc.

𝕬𝕘𝕣𝕖𝕖𝕞𝕖𝕟𝕥 𝖔𝖋 𝕷𝖊𝖆𝖘𝖊, made as of this   day of   19   , between

party of the first part, hereinafter referred to as LANDLORD, and

party of the second part, hereinafter referred to as TENANT,

𝖂𝖎𝖙𝖓𝖊𝖘𝖘𝖊𝖙𝖍: Landlord hereby leases to Tenant and Tenant hereby hires from Landlord

in the building known as
in the Borough of   , City of New York, for the term of

(or until such term shall sooner cease and expire as hereinafter provided) to commence on the
    day of   nineteen hundred and   , and to end on the
    day of   nineteen hundred and
both dates inclusive, at an annual rental rate of

which Tenant agrees to pay in lawful money of the United States which shall be legal tender in payment of all debts and dues, public and private, at the time of payment, in equal monthly installments in advance on the first day of each month during said term, at the office of Landlord or such other place as Landlord may designate, without any set off or deduction whatsoever, except that Tenant shall pay the first   monthly installment(s) on the execution hereof (unless this lease be a renewal).

In the event that, at the commencement of the term of this lease, or thereafter, Tenant shall be in default in the payment of rent to Landlord pursuant to the terms of another lease with Landlord or with Landlord's predecessor in interest, Landlord may at Landlord's option and without notice to Tenant add the amount of such arrearages to any monthly installment of rent payable hereunder and the same shall be payable to Landlord as additional rent.

The parties hereto, for themselves, their heirs, distributees, executors, administrators, legal representatives, successors and assigns, hereby covenant as follows:

Rent   1. Tenant shall pay the rent as above and as hereinafter provided.
Occupancy   2. Tenant shall use and occupy demised premises for

and for no other purpose. Tenant shall at all times conduct its business in a high grade and reputable manner and shall keep show windows and signs in a neat and clean condition.

Alterations: 3. Tenant shall make no changes in or to the demised premises of any nature without Landlord's prior written consent. Subject to the prior written consent of Landlord, and to the provisions of this article, Tenant at Tenant's expense, may make alterations, installations, additions or improvements which are non-structural and which do not affect utility services or plumbing and electrical lines, in or to the interior of the demised premises by using contractors or mechanics first approved by Landlord. All fixtures and all paneling, partitions, railings and like installations, installed in the premises at any time, either by Tenant or by Landlord in Tenant's behalf, shall, upon installation, become the property of Landlord and shall remain upon and be surrendered with the demised premises unless Landlord, by notice to Tenant no later than twenty days prior to the date fixed as the termination of this lease, elects to relinquish Landlord's right thereto and to have them removed by Tenant, in which event, the same shall be removed from the premises by Tenant prior to the expiration of the lease, at Tenant's expense. Nothing in this article shall be construed to give Landlord title to or to prevent Tenant's removal of trade fixtures, moveable office furniture and equipment, but upon removal of any such from the premises or upon removal of other installations as may be required by Landlord, Tenant shall immediately and at its expense, repair and restore the premises to the condition existing prior to installation and repair any damage to the demised premises or the building due to such removal. All property permitted or required to be removed by Tenant at the end of the term remaining in the premises after Tenant's removal shall be deemed abandoned and may, at the election of Landlord, either be retained as Landlord's property or may be removed from the premises by Landlord at Tenant's expense. Tenant shall, before making any alterations, additions, installations or improvements, at its expense, obtain all permits, approvals and certificates required by any governmental or quasi-governmental bodies and (upon completion) certificates of final approval thereof and shall deliver promptly duplicates of all such permits, approvals and certificates to Landlord and Tenant agrees to carry and will cause Tenant's contractors and sub-contractors to carry such workman's compensation, general liability, personal and property damage insurance as Landlord may require. If any mechanic's lien is filed against the demised premises, or the building of which the same forms a part, for work claimed to have been done for, or materials furnished to, Tenant, whether or not done pursuant to this article, the same shall be discharged by Tenant within ten days thereafter, at Tenant's expense, by filing the bond required by law.

Repairs: 4. Landlord shall maintain and repair the public portions of the building, both exterior and interior, except that if Landlord allows Tenant to erect on the outside of the building a sign or signs, or a hoist, lift or sidewalk elevator for the exclusive use of Tenant, Tenant shall maintain such exterior installations in good appearance and shall cause the same to be operated in a good and workmanlike manner and shall make all repairs thereto necessary to keep same in good order and condition, at Tenant's own cost and expense, and shall cause the same to be covered by the insurance provided for hereafter in Article 8. Tenant shall, throughout the term of this lease, take good care of the demised premises and the fixtures and appurtenances therein and at its sole cost and expense, make all non-structural repairs thereto as and when needed to preserve them in good working order and condition, reasonable wear and tear, obsolescence and damage from the elements, fire or other casualty, excepted. Notwithstanding the foregoing, all damage or injury to the demised premises or to any other part of the building, or to its fixtures, equipment and appurtenances, whether requiring structural or non-structural repairs, caused by or resulting from carelessness, omission, neglect or improper conduct of Tenant, its servants, employees, invitees or licensees, shall be repaired promptly by Tenant at its sole cost and expense, to the satisfaction of Landlord reasonably exercised. Tenant shall also repair all damage to the building and the demised premises caused by the moving of Tenant's fixtures, furniture or equipment. All the aforesaid repairs shall be of quality or class equal to the original work or construction. If Tenant fails after ten days notice to proceed with due diligence to make repairs required to be made by Tenant, the same may be made by Landlord at the expense of Tenant and the expenses thereof incurred by Landlord shall be collectible as additional rent after rendition of a bill or statement therefor. If the demised premises be or become infested with vermin, Tenant shall at Tenant's expense, cause the same to be exterminated from time to time to the satisfaction of Landlord. Tenant shall give Landlord prompt notice of any defective conditions in any plumbing, heating system or electrical lines located in, servicing or passing through the demised premises and following such notice, Landlord shall remedy the condition with due diligence but at the expense of Tenant if repairs are necessitated by damage or injury attributable to Tenant, Tenant's servants, agents, employees, invitees or licensees as aforesaid. Except as specifically provided in Article 9 or elsewhere in this lease, there shall be no allowance to the Tenant for the diminution of rental value and no liability on the part of Landlord by reason of inconvenience, annoyance or injury to business arising from Landlord, Tenant or others making or failing to make any repairs, alterations, additions or improvements in or to any portion of the building or the demised premises or in and to the fixtures, appurtenances or equipment thereof. The provisions of this article 4 with respect to the making of repairs shall not apply in the case of fire or other casualty which are dealt with in article 9 hereof.

FIGURE 3-1. (con't)

character of electric service shall in no wise make Landlord liable or responsible to Tenant, for any loss, damages or expenses which Tenant may sustain.

Access to Premises: 13. Landlord or Landlord's agents shall have the right (but shall not be obligated) to enter the demised premises in any emergency at any time, and, at other reasonable times, to examine the same and to make such repairs, replacements and improvements as Landlord may deem necessary and reasonably desirable to the demised premises or to any other portion of the building or which Landlord may elect to perform following Tenant's failure to make repairs or perform any work which Tenant is obligated to perform under this lease, or for the purpose of complying with laws, regulations and other directions of governmental authorities. Tenant shall permit Landlord to use and maintain and replace pipes and conduits in and through the demised premises and to erect new pipes and conduits therein. Landlord may, during the progress of any work in the demised premises, take all necessary materials and equipment into said premises without the same constituting an eviction nor shall the Tenant be entitled to any abatement of rent while such work is in progress nor to any damages by reason of loss or interruption of business or otherwise. Throughout the term hereof Landlord shall have the right to enter the demised premises at reasonable hours for the purpose of showing the same to prospective purchasers or mortgagees of the building, and during the last six months of the term for the purpose of showing the same to prospective tenants and may, during said six months period, place upon the premises the usual notices "To Let" and "For Sale" which notices Tenant shall permit to remain thereon without molestation. If Tenant is not present to open and permit an entry into the premises, Landlord or Landlord's agents may enter the same whenever such entry may be necessary or permissible by master key or forcibly and provided reasonable care is exercised to safeguard Tenant's property and such entry shall not render Landlord or its agents liable therefor, nor in any event shall the obligations of Tenant hereunder be affected. If during the last month of the term Tenant shall have removed all or substantially all of Tenant's property therefrom, Landlord may immediately enter, alter, renovate or redecorate the demised premises without limitation or abatement of rent, or incurring liability to Tenant for any compensation and such act shall have no effect on this lease or Tenant's obligations hereunder. Landlord shall have the right at any time, without the same constituting an eviction and without incurring liability to Tenant therefor to change the arrangement and/or location of public entrances, passageways, doors, doorways, corridors, elevators, stairs, toilets, or other public parts of the building and to change the name, number or designation by which the building may be known.

Vault, Vault Space, Area: 14. No Vaults, vault space or area, whether or not enclosed or covered, not within the property line of the building is leased hereunder, anything contained in or indicated on any sketch, blue print or plan, or anything contained elsewhere in this lease to the contrary notwithstanding. Landlord makes no representation as to the location of the property line of the building. All vaults and vault space and all such areas not within the property line of the building, which Tenant may be permitted to use and/or occupy, is to be used and/or occupied under a revocable license, and if any such license be revoked, or if the amount of such space or area be diminished or required by any federal, state or municipal authority or public utility, Landlord shall not be subject to any liability nor shall Tenant be entitled to any compensation or diminution or abatement of rent, nor shall such revocation, diminution or requisition be deemed constructive or actual eviction. Any tax, fee or charge of municipal authorities for such vault or area shall be paid by Tenant.

Occupancy: 15. Tenant will not at any time use or occupy the demised premises in violation of the certificate of occupancy issued for the building of which the demised premises are a part. Tenant has inspected the premises and accepts them as is, subject to the riders annexed hereto with respect to Landlord's work, if any. In any event, Landlord makes no representation as to the condition of the premises and Tenant agrees to accept the same subject to violations whether or not of record.

Bankruptcy: 16. (a) If at the date fixed as the commencement of the term of this lease or if at any time during the term hereby demised there shall be filed by or against Tenant in any court pursuant to any statute either of the United States or of any state, a petition in bankruptcy or insolvency or for reorganization or for the appointment of a receiver or trustee of all or a portion of Tenant's property, and within 60 days thereof, Tenant fails to secure a dismissal thereof, or if Tenant make an assignment for the benefit of creditors or petition for or enter into an arrangement, this lease, at the option of Landlord, exercised within a reasonable time after notice of the happening of any one or more of such events, may be cancelled and terminated by written notice to the Tenant (but if any of such events occur prior to the commencement date, this lease shall be ipso facto cancelled and terminated) and whether such cancellation and termination occur prior to or during the term, neither Tenant nor any person claiming through or under Tenant by virtue of any statute or of any order of any court, shall be entitled to possession or to remain in possession of the premises demised but shall forthwith quit and surrender the premises, and Landlord, in addition to the other rights and remedies Landlord has by virtue of any other provision herein or elsewhere in this lease contained or by virtue of any statute or rule of law, may retain as liquidated damages, any rent, security deposit or moneys received by him from Tenant or others in behalf of Tenant. If this lease shall be assigned in accordance with its terms, the provisions of this Article 16 shall be applicable only to the party then owning Tenant's interest in this lease.

(b) It is stipulated and agreed that in the event of the termination of this lease pursuant to (a) hereof, Landlord shall forthwith, notwithstanding any other provisions of this lease to the contrary, be entitled to recover from Tenant as and for liquidated damages an amount equal to the difference between the rent reserved hereunder for the unexpired portion of the term demised and the fair and reasonable rental value of the demised premises for the same period. In the computation of such damages the difference between any instalment of rent becoming due hereunder after the date of termination and the fair and reasonable rental value of the demised premises for the period for which such instalment was payable shall be discounted to the date of termination at the rate of four per cent (4%) per annum. If such premises or any part thereof be re-let by the Landlord for the unexpired term of said lease, or any part thereof, before presentation of proof of such liquidated damages to any court, commission or tribunal, the amount of rent reserved upon such re-letting shall be deemed to be the fair and reasonable rental value for the part or the whole of the premises so re-let during the term of the re-letting. Nothing herein contained shall limit or prejudice the right of the Landlord to prove for and obtain as liquidated damages by reason of such termination, an amount equal to the maximum allowed by any statute or rule of law in effect at the time when, and governing the proceedings in which, such damages are to be proved, whether or not such amount be greater, equal to, or less than the amount of the difference referred to above.

Default 17. (1) If Tenant defaults in fulfilling any of the covenants of this lease other than the covenants for the payment of rent or additional rent; or if the demised premises become vacant or deserted; or if the demised premises are damaged by reason of negligence or carelessness of Tenant, its agents, employees or invitees; or if any execution or attachment shall be issued against Tenant or any of Tenant's property whereupon the demised premises shall be taken or occupied by someone other than Tenant; or if Tenant shall make default with respect to any other lease between Landlord and Tenant; or if Tenant shall fail to move into or take possession of the premises within fifteen (15) days after the commencement of the term of this lease, of which fact Landlord shall be the sole judge; then, in any one or more of such events, upon Landlord serving a written five (5) days notice upon Tenant specifying the nature of said default and upon the expiration of said five (5) days, if Tenant shall have failed to comply with or remedy such default, or if the said default or omission complained of shall be of a nature that the same cannot be completely cured or remedied within said five (5) day period, and if Tenant shall not have diligently commenced curing such default within such five (5) day period, and shall not thereafter with reasonable diligence and in good faith proceed to remedy or cure such default, then Landlord may serve a written three (3) days' notice of cancellation of this lease upon Tenant, and upon the expiration of said three (3) days, this lease and the term thereunder shall end and expire as fully and completely as if the expiration of such three (3) day period were the day herein definitely fixed for the end and expiration of this lease and the term thereof and Tenant shall then quit and surrender the demised premises to Landlord but Tenant shall remain liable as hereinafter provided.

(2) If the notice provided for in (1) hereof shall have been given, and the term shall expire as aforesaid: or if Tenant shall make default in the payment of the rent reserved herein or any item of additional rent herein mentioned or any part of either or in making any other payment herein required; then and in any of such events Landlord may without notice, re-enter the demised premises either by force or otherwise, and dispossess Tenant by summary proceedings or otherwise, and the legal representative of Tenant or other occupant of demised premises and remove their effects and hold the premises as if this lease had not been made, and Tenant hereby waives the service of notice of intention to re-enter or to institute legal proceedings to that end. If Tenant shall make default hereunder prior to the date fixed as the commencement of any renewal or extension of this lease, Landlord may cancel and terminate such renewal or extension agreement by written notice.

Remedies of Landlord and Waiver of Redemption: 18. In case of any such default, re-entry, expiration and/or dispossess by summary proceedings or otherwise, (a) the rent shall become due thereupon and be paid up to the time of such re-entry, dispossess and/or expiration, together with such expenses as Landlord may incur for legal expenses, attorneys' fees, brokerage, and/or putting the demised premises in good order, or for preparing the same for re-rental; (b) Landlord may re-let the premises or any part or parts thereof, either in the name of Landlord or otherwise, for a term or terms, which may at Landlord's option be less than or exceed the period which would otherwise have constituted the balance of the term of this lease and may grant concessions or free rent or charge a higher rental than that in this lease, and/or (c) Tenant or the legal representatives of Tenant shall also pay Landlord as liquidated damages for the failure of Tenant to observe and perform said Tenant's covenants herein contained, any deficiency between the rent hereby reserved and/or covenanted to be paid and the net amount, if any, of the rents collected on account of the lease or leases of the demised premises for each month of the period which would otherwise have constituted the balance of the term of this lease. The failure of Landlord to re-let the premises or any part or parts thereof shall not release or affect Tenant's liability for damages. In computing such liquidated damages there shall be added to the said deficiency such expenses as Landlord may incur in connection with re-letting, such as legal expenses, attorneys' fees, brokerage, advertising and for keeping the demised premises in good order or for preparing the same for re-letting. Any such liquidated damages shall be paid in monthly installments by Tenant on the rent day specified in this lease and any suit brought to collect the amount of the deficiency for any month shall not prejudice in any way the rights of Landlord to collect the deficiency for any subsequent month by a similar proceeding. Landlord, in putting the demised premises in good order or preparing the same for re-rental may, at Landlord's option, make such alterations, repairs, replacements, and/or decorations in the demised premises as Landlord, in Landlord's sole judgment, considers advisable and necessary for the purpose of re-letting the demised premises, and the making of such alterations, repairs, replacements, and/or decorations shall not operate or be construed to release Tenant from liability hereunder as aforesaid. Landlord shall in no event be liable in any way whatsoever for failure to re-let the demised premises, or in the event that the demised premises are re-let, for failure to collect the rent thereof under such re-letting, and in no event shall Tenant be entitled to receive any excess, if any, of such net rent collected over the sums payable by Tenant to Landlord hereunder. In the event of a breach or threatened breach by Tenant of any of the covenants or provisions hereof, Landlord shall have the right of injunction and the right to invoke any remedy allowed at law or in equity as if re-entry, summary proceedings and other remedies were not herein provided for. Mention in this lease of any particular remedy, shall not preclude Landlord from any other remedy, in law or in equity. Tenant hereby expressly waives any and all rights of redemption granted by or under any present or future laws in the event of Tenant being evicted or dispossessed for any cause, or in the event of Landlord obtaining possession of demised premises, by reason of the violation by Tenant of any of the covenants and conditions of this lease, or otherwise.

FIGURE 3-1. (con't)

Fees and Expenses

19. If tenant shall default in the observance or performance of any term or covenant on tenant's part to be observed or performed under or by virtue of any of the terms or provisions in any article of this lease, then, unless otherwise provided elsewhere in this lease, landlord may immediately or at any time thereafter and without notice perform the obligation of tenant thereunder, and if landlord, in connection therewith or in connection with any default by tenant in the covenant to pay rent hereunder, makes any expenditures or incurs any obligations for the payment of money, including but not limited to attorney's fees, in instituting, prosecuting or defending any action or proceeding, such sums so paid or obligations incurred with interest and costs shall be deemed to be additional rent hereunder and shall be paid by tenant to landlord within five (5) days of rendition of any bill or statement to tenant therefor, and if tenant's lease term shall have expired at the time of making of such expenditures or incurring of such obligations, such sums shall be recoverable by landlord as damages.

No Representations by Landlord:

20. Neither Landlord nor Landlord's agents have made any representations or promises with respect to the physical condition of the building, the land upon which it is erected or the demised premises, the rents, leases, expenses of operation or any other matter or thing affecting or related to the premises except as herein expressly set forth and no rights, easements or licenses are acquired by Tenant by implication or otherwise except as expressly set forth in the provisions of this lease. Tenant has inspected the building and the demised premises and is thoroughly acquainted with their condition, and agrees to take the same "as is" and acknowledges that the taking of possession of the demised premises by Tenant shall be conclusive evidence that the said premises and the building of which the same form a part were in good and satisfactory condition at the time such possession was so taken, except as to latent defects. All understandings and agreements heretofore made between the parties hereto are merged in this contract, which alone fully and completely expresses the agreement between Landlord and Tenant and any executory agreement hereafter made shall be ineffective to change, modify, discharge or effect an abandonment of it in whole or in part, unless such executory agreement is in writing and signed by the party against whom enforcement of the change, modification, discharge or abandonment is sought.

End of Term:

21. Upon the expiration or other termination of the term of this lease, Tenant shall quit and surrender to Landlord the demised premises, broom clean, in good order and condition, ordinary wear excepted, and Tenant shall remove all its property. Tenant's obligation to observe or perform this covenant shall survive the expiration or other termination of this lease. If the last day of the term of this lease or any renewal thereof, falls on Sunday, this lease shall expire at noon on the preceding Saturday unless it be a legal holiday in which case it shall expire at noon on the preceding business day.

Quiet Enjoyment:

22. Landlord covenants and agrees with Tenant that upon Tenant paying the rent and additional rent and observing and performing all the terms, covenants and conditions, on Tenant's part to be observed and performed, Tenant may peaceably and quietly enjoy the premises hereby demised, subject, nevertheless, to the terms and conditions of this lease including, but not limited to, Article 33 hereof and to the ground leases, underlying leases and mortgages hereinbefore mentioned.

Failure to Give Possession:

23. If Landlord is unable to give possession of the demised premises on the date of the commencement of the term hereof, because of the holding-over or retention of possession of any tenant, undertenant or occupants, or if the premises are located in a building being constructed, because such building has not been sufficiently completed to make the premises ready for occupancy or because of the fact that a certificate of occupancy has not been procured or for any other reason, Landlord shall not be subject to any liability for failure to give possession on said date and the validity of the lease shall not be impaired under such circumstances, nor shall the same be construed in any wise to extend the term of this lease, but the rent payable hereunder shall be abated (provided Tenant is not responsible for the inability to obtain possession) until after Landlord shall have given Tenant written notice that the premises are substantially ready for Tenant's occupancy. If permission is given to Tenant to enter into the possession of the demised premises or to occupy premises other than the demised premises prior to the date specified as the commencement of the term of this lease, Tenant covenants and agrees that such occupancy shall be deemed to be under all the terms, covenants, conditions and provisions of this lease, except as to the covenant to pay rent. The provisions of this article are intended to constitute "an express provision to the contrary" within the meaning of Section 223-a of the New York Real Property Law.

No Waiver:

24. The failure of Landlord to seek redress for violation of, or to insist upon the strict performance of any covenant or condition of this lease or of any of the Rules or Regulations set forth or hereafter adopted by Landlord, shall not prevent a subsequent act which would have originally constituted a violation from having all the force and effect of an original violation. The receipt by Landlord of rent with knowledge of the breach of any covenant of this lease shall not be deemed a waiver of such breach and no provision of this lease shall be deemed to have been waived by Landlord unless such waiver be in writing signed by Landlord. No payment by Tenant or receipt by Landlord of a lesser amount than the monthly rent herein stipulated shall be deemed to be other than on account of the earliest stipulated rent, nor shall any endorsement or statement of any check or any letter accompanying any check or payment as rent be deemed an accord and satisfaction, and Landlord may accept such check or payment without prejudice to Landlord's right to recover the balance of such rent or pursue any other remedy in this lease provided. No act or thing done by Landlord or Landlord's agents during the term hereby demised shall be deemed an acceptance of a surrender of said premises and no agreement to accept such surrender shall be valid unless in writing signed by Landlord. No employee of Landlord or Landlord's agent shall have any power to accept the keys of said premises prior to the termination of the lease and the delivery of keys to any such agent or employee shall not operate as a termination of the lease or a surrender of the premises.

☛ Space to be filled in or deleted.

Waiver of Trial by Jury:

25. It is mutually agreed by and between Landlord and Tenant that the respective parties hereto shall and they hereby do waive trial by jury in any action, proceeding or counterclaim brought by either of the parties hereto against the other (except for personal injury or property damage) on any matters whatsoever arising out of or in any way connected with this lease, the relationship of Landlord and Tenant, Tenant's use of or occupancy of said premises, and any emergency statutory or any other statutory remedy. It is further mutually agreed that in the event Landlord commences any summary proceeding for possession of the premises, Tenant will not interpose any counterclaim of whatever nature or description in any such proceeding.

Inability to Perform:

26. This lease and the obligation of Tenant to pay rent hereunder and perform all of the other covenants and agreements hereunder on part of Tenant to be performed shall in no wise be affected, impaired or excused because Landlord is unable to fulfill any of its obligations under this lease or to supply or is delayed in supplying any service expressly or impliedly to be supplied or is unable to make, or is delayed in making any repair, additions, alterations or decorations or is unable to supply or is delayed in supplying any equipment or fixtures if Landlord is prevented or delayed from so doing by reason of strike or labor troubles or any cause whatsoever including, but not limited to, government preemption in connection with a National Emergency or by reason of any rule, order or regulation of any department or subdivision thereof of any government agency or by reason of the conditions of supply and demand which have been or are affected by war or other emergency.

Bills and Notices:

27. Except as otherwise in this lease provided, a bill, statement, notice or communication which Landlord may desire or be required to give to Tenant, shall be deemed sufficiently given or rendered if, in writing, delivered to Tenant personally or sent by registered or certified mail addressed to Tenant at the building of which the demised premises form a part or at the last known residence address or business address of Tenant or left at any of the aforesaid premises addressed to Tenant, and the time of the rendition of such bill or statement and of the giving of such notice or communication shall be deemed to be the time when the same is delivered to Tenant, mailed, or left at the premises as herein provided. Any notice by Tenant to Landlord must be served by registered or certified mail addressed to Landlord at the address first hereinabove given or at such other address as Landlord shall designate by written notice.

Water Charges:

28. If Tenant requires, uses or consumes water for any purpose in addition to ordinary lavatory purposes (of which fact Tenant constitutes Landlord to be the sole judge) Landlord may install a water meter and thereby measure Tenant's water consumption for all purposes. Tenant shall pay Landlord for the cost of the meter and the cost of the installation thereof and throughout the duration of Tenant's occupancy Tenant shall keep said meter and installation equipment in good working order and repair at Tenant's own cost and expense in default of which Landlord may cause such meter and equipment to be replaced or repaired and collect the cost thereof from Tenant. Tenant agrees to pay for water consumed, as shown on said meter as and when bills are rendered, and on default in making such payment Landlord may pay such charges and collect the same from Tenant. Tenant covenants and agrees to pay the sewer rent, charge or any other tax, rent, levy or charge which now or hereafter is assessed, imposed or a lien upon the demised premises or the realty of which they are part pursuant to law, order or regulation made or issued in connection with the use, consumption, maintenance or supply of water, water system or sewage or sewage connection or system. The bill rendered by Landlord shall be payable by Tenant as additional rent. If the building or the demised premises or any part thereof be supplied with water through a meter through which water is also supplied to other premises Tenant shall pay to Landlord as additional rent, on the first day of each month, ☛ % ($) of the total meter charges, as Tenant's portion. Independently of and in addition to any of the remedies reserved to Landlord hereinabove or elsewhere in this lease, Landlord may sue for and collect any monies to be paid by Tenant or paid by Landlord for any of the reasons or purposes hereinabove set forth.

Sprinklers:

29. Anything elsewhere in this lease to the contrary notwithstanding, if the New York Board of Fire Underwriters or the New York Fire Insurance Exchange or any bureau, department or official of the federal, state or city government require or recommend the installation of a sprinkler system or that any changes, modifications, alterations, or additional sprinkler heads or other equipment be made or supplied in an existing sprinkler system by reason of Tenant's business, or the location of partitions, trade fixtures, or other contents of the demised premises, or for any other reason, or if any such sprinkler system installations, changes, modifications, alterations, additional sprinkler heads or other such equipment, become necessary to prevent the imposition of a penalty or charge against the full allowance for a sprinkler system in the fire insurance rate set by any said Exchange or by any fire insurance company, Tenant shall, at Tenant's expense, promptly make such sprinkler system installations, changes, modifications, alterations, and supply additional sprinkler heads or other equipment as required whether the work involved shall be structural or non-structural in nature. Tenant shall pay to Landlord as additional rent the ☛ sum of $, on the first day of each month during the term of this lease, as Tenant's portion of the contract price for sprinkler supervisory service.

Heat, Cleaning:

30. As long as Tenant is not in default under any of the covenants of this lease Landlord shall, if and insofar as existing facilities permit furnish heat to the demised premises, when and as required by law, on business days from 8:00 a.m. to 6:00 p.m. and on Saturdays from 8:00 a.m. to 1:00 p.m. Tenant shall at Tenant's expense, keep demised premises clean and in order, to the satisfaction of Landlord, and if demised premises are situated on the street floor, Tenant shall, at Tenant's own expense, make all repairs and replacements to the sidewalks and curbs adjacent thereto, made necessary by Tenant's use or occupancy of the demised premises, or negligence, and keep said sidewalks and curbs free from snow, ice, dirt and rubbish. Tenant shall pay to Landlord the cost of removal of any of Tenant's refuse and rubbish from the building. Bills for the same shall be rendered by Landlord to Tenant at such times

FIGURE 3-1. (con't)

as Landlord may elect and shall be due and payable when rendered, and the amount of such bills shall be deemed to be, and be paid as, additional rent. Tenant shall, however, have the option of independently contracting for the removal of such rubbish and refuse in the event that Tenant does not wish to have same done by employees of Landlord. Under such circumstances, however, the removal of such refuse and rubbish by others shall be subject to such rules and regulations as, in the judgment of Landlord, are necessary for the proper operation of the building. Landlord reserves the right to stop the service of the steam, sprinkler system, plumbing and electric systems when necessary, by reason of accident, or of repairs, alterations or improvements, in the judgment of Landlord desirable or necessary to be made, until such repairs, alterations or improvements shall have been completed, and shall further have no responsibility or liability for failure to supply steam, elevator, sprinkler, plumbing and electric service, when prevented from so doing by strikes or accidents or by any cause beyond Landlord's reasonable control, or by orders or regulations of any Federal, State or Municipal Authority or failure of coal, oil or other suitable fuel supply, or inability by the exercise of reasonable diligence to obtain coal, oil or other suitable fuel.

Security **31.** Tenant has deposited with Landlord the sum of $ _____ as security for the faithful performance and observance by Tenant of the terms, provisions and conditions of this lease; it is agreed that in the event Tenant defaults in respect of any of the terms, provisions and conditions of this lease, including, but not limited to, the payment of rent and additional rent, Landlord may use, apply or retain the whole or any part of the security so deposited to the extent required for the payment of any rent and additional rent or any other sum as to which Tenant is in default or for any sum which Landlord may expend or may be required to expend by reason of Tenant's default in respect of any of the terms, covenants and conditions of this lease, including but not limited to, any damages or deficiency in the re-letting of the premises, whether such damages or deficiency accrued before or after summary proceedings or other re-entry by Landlord. In the event that Tenant shall fully and faithfully comply with all of the terms, provisions, covenants and conditions of this lease, the security shall be returned to Tenant after the date fixed as the end of the Lease and after delivery of entire possession of the demised premises to Landlord. In the event of a sale of the land and building or leasing of the building, of which the demised premises form a part, Landlord shall have the right to transfer the security to the vendee or lessee and Landlord shall thereupon be released by Tenant from all liability for the return of such security; and Tenant agrees to look to the new Landlord solely for the return of said security; and it is agreed that the provisions hereof shall apply to every transfer or assignment made of the security to a new Landlord. Tenant further covenants that it will not assign or encumber or attempt to assign or encumber the monies deposited herein as security and that neither Landlord nor its successors or assigns shall be bound by any such assignment, encumbrance, attempted assignment or attempted encumbrance.

Captions: **32.** The Captions are inserted only as a matter of convenience and for reference and in no way define, limit or describe the scope of this lease nor the intent of any provision thereof.

Definitions: **33.** The term "Landlord" as used in this lease means only the owner, or the mortgagee in possession, for the time being of the land and building (or the owner of a lease of the building or of the land and building) of which the demised premises form a part, so that in the event of any sale or sales of said land and building or of said lease, or in the event of a lease of said building, or of the land and building, the said Landlord shall be and hereby is

◣ Space to be filled in or deleted.

entirely freed and relieved of all covenants and obligations of Landlord hereunder, and it shall be deemed and construed without further agreement between the parties or their successors in interest, or between the parties and the purchaser, at any such sale, or the said lessee of the building, or of the land and building, that the purchaser or the lessee of the building, or of the land and building, that the purchaser or the lessee of the building has assumed and agreed to carry out any and all covenants and obligations of Landlord hereunder. The words "re-enter" and "re-entry" as used in this lease are not restricted to their technical legal meaning. The term "business days" as used in this lease shall exclude Saturdays (except such portion thereof as is covered by specific hours in Article 30 hereof), Sundays and all days observed by the State or Federal Government as legal holidays.

Adjacent **34.** If an excavation shall be made upon land adjacent
Excavation— to the demised premises, or shall be authorized to be
Shoring: made, Tenant shall afford to the person causing or authorized to cause such excavation, license to enter upon the demised premises for the purpose of doing such work as said person shall deem necessary to preserve the wall or the building of which demised premises form a part from injury or damage and to support the same by proper foundations without any claim for damages or indemnity against Landlord, or diminution or abatement of rent.

Rules and **35.** Tenant and Tenant's servants, employees, agents,
Regulations: visitors, and licensees shall observe faithfully, and comply strictly with, the Rules and Regulations and such other and further reasonable Rules and Regulations as Landlord or Landlord's agents may from time to time adopt. Notice of any additional rules or regulations shall be given in such manner as Landlord may elect. In case Tenant disputes the reasonableness of any additional Rule or Regulation hereafter made or adopted by Landlord or Landlord's agents, the parties hereto agree to submit the question of the reasonableness of such Rule or Regulation for decision to the New York office of the American Arbitration Association, whose determination shall be final and conclusive upon the parties hereto. The right to dispute the reasonableness of any additional Rule or Regulation upon Tenant's part shall be deemed waived unless the same shall be asserted by service of a notice, in writing upon Landlord within ten (10) days after the giving of notice thereof. Nothing in this lease contained shall be construed to impose upon Landlord any duty or obligation to enforce the Rules and Regulations or terms, covenants or conditions in any other lease, as against any other tenant and Landlord shall not be liable to Tenant for violation of the same by any other tenant, its servants, employees, agents, visitors or licensees.

Glass: **36.** Landlord shall replace, at the expense of Tenant, any and all plate and other glass damaged or broken from any cause whatsoever in and about the demised premises. Landlord may insure, and keep insured, at Tenant's expense, all plate and other glass in the demised premises for and in the name of Landlord. Bills for the premiums therefor shall be rendered by Landlord to Tenant at such times as Landlord may elect, and shall be due from, and payable by, Tenant when rendered, and the amount thereof shall be deemed to be, and paid as, additional rent.

Successors **37:** The covenants, conditions and agreements contained
and Assigns: in this lease shall bind and inure to the benefit of Landlord and Tenant and their respective heirs, distributees, executors, administrators, successors, and except as otherwise provided in this lease, their assigns.

𝔍𝔫 𝔚𝔦𝔱𝔫𝔢𝔰𝔰 𝔚𝔥𝔢𝔯𝔢𝔬𝔣, Landlord and Tenant have respectively signed and sealed this lease as of the day and year first above written.

Witness for Landlord:

.... ☷ CORP. SEAL

.... [L. S.]

Witness for Tenant:

.... [L. S.]

.... ☷ CORP. SEAL

FIGURE 3-2.

RULES AND REGULATIONS

1. The sidewalks, entrances, passages, courts, elevators, stairways, or halls shall not be obstructed by any Tenant or used for any purpose other than ingress and egress to and from the demised premises, and if said premises are situate on the ground floor the Tenant thereof shall keep the sidewalks and curbs directly in front of said premises clean and free from ice, snow, etc. Nothing shall be thrown out of windows or doors or down passages of building.

2. Movement of goods in or out of the premises and building shall only be effected through entrances and elevators designated for that purpose. No hand trucks, carts, etc. shall be used in the building unless equipped with rubber tires and side guards.

3. No awnings or other projections shall be attached to the outside walls of the building and no curtains, blinds, shades, or screens shall be used without the prior written consent of the Landlord.

4. The skylights, windows, and doors that reflect or admit light and air into the halls, or other public places in the building shall not be covered or obstructed by any Tenant, nor shall any thing be placed on the windowsills.

5. The water and wash closets and other plumbing fixtures shall not be used for any purposes other than those for which they were constructed, and no rubbish, rags, or other substances shall be thrown therein. All damages resulting from any misuse of the fixtures shall be borne by the Tenant who, or whose employees, agents, visitors or licensees, shall have caused the same.

6. No Tenant shall mark, paint, drill into, or in any way deface any part of the demised premises or the building of which they form a part. No boring, cutting or stringing of wires shall be permitted, except with the prior written consent of the Landlord, and as the Landlord may direct. No Tenant shall lay linoleum, or other similar floor covering, so that the same shall come in direct contact with the floor of the demised premises, and, if linoleum or other covering is used an interlining of builder's deadening felt shall be first affixed to the floor, by a paste or other material, soluble in water, the use of cement or other adhesive being expressly prohibited.

7. No Tenant shall make, or permit to be made, any unseemly or disturbing noises or disturb or interfere with occupants of this or neighboring premises or those having business with them whether by the use of any instrument, radio, talking machine, unmusical noise, whistling, singing, or otherwise.

8. No Tenant, nor any of Tenant's employees, agents, visitors or licensees, shall at any time bring or keep upon the demised premises any inflammable, combustible or explosive fluid, chemical or substance, or allow any unusual or objectionable odors to be produced upon the demised premises, or permit animals or birds to be brought or kept on the premises.

9. No machine may be operated on the premises without the written consent of the Landlord; machinery shall be placed in approved settings to absorb or prevent any noise or annoyance.

10. No Tenant shall place a load upon any floor of the building exceeding the floor load per square foot area which such floor was designed to carry, and all floor loads shall be evenly distributed. All removals, or the carrying in or out of any safes, freight, furniture or bulky matter of any description must take place during the hours which the Landlord or Landlord's agent may determine from time to time. The Landlord reserves the right to prescribe the weight and position of all safes, which must be placed so as to distribute the weight. The Landlord reserves the right to inspect all freight to be brought into the building and to exclude from the building all freight which violates any of these Rules and Regulations or this lease. Safes and machinery may not be put on elevators.

11. Canvassing, soliciting and peddling in the building is prohibited and each Tenant shall co-operate to prevent the same.

12. No water cooler, air conditioning unit or system or other apparatus shall be installed or used by any Tenant without the written consent of Landlord.

State of New York, County of   ss.:

On this   day of   , 19   , before me

personally came

to me known and known to me to be the individual   described
in and who executed the foregoing instrument   and acknowledged to me that   he   executed the same.

State of New York, County of   ss.:

On this   day of   , 19   , before me
personally came   ,
to me known, who being by me duly sworn, did depose and say
that he resides in   ;
that he is the   of

the corporation described in and which executed the foregoing
instrument; that he knows the seal of said corporation; that
the seal affixed to said instrument is such corporate seal; that
it was so affixed by order of the Board of Directors of said
corporation, and that he signed his name thereto by like order.

   In Consideration of the letting of the premises within mentioned to the within named Tenant and the sum of $1.00 paid to the undersigned by the within named Landlord, the undersigned hereby covenants and agrees, to and with the Landlord and the Landlord's successors and assigns, that if default shall at any time be made by the said Tenant in the payment of the rent and the performance of the covenants contained in the within lease, on the Tenant's part to be paid and performed, that the undersigned will well and truly pay the said rent, or any arrears thereof, that may remain due unto the said Landlord, and also pay all damages that may arise in consequence of the non-performance of said covenants, or either of them, without requiring notice of any such default from the said Landlord. The undersigned hereby waives all right to trial by jury in any action or proceeding hereinafter instituted by the Landlord, to which the undersigned may be a party.

   In Witness Whereof, the undersigned ha   set   hand   and seal   this   day of
                , 19

WITNESS

---L. S.

TO

Lease

Dated
Premises
Rent per Year
Rent per Month
Term
From
To

FIGURE 3-2. (con't)

Rules and Regulations

23rd.   Tenant and Tenant's employees, agents and visitors shall comply strictly with the Rules and Regulations set forth on the back of this lease, and such other and further reasonable Rules and Regulations as Landlord or Landlord's agents may from time to time adopt. Landlord shall not be liable to Tenant for violation of any of said Rules or Regulations, or the breach of any covenant or condition in any lease, by any other tenant in the building.

Window Cleaning

24th.   Tenant will not clean, nor require, permit, suffer or allow any window in the demised premises to be cleaned, from the outside in violation of Section 202 of the Labor Law or of the rules of the Board of Standards and Appeals, or of any other board or body having or asserting jurisdiction.

Possession

25th.   Landlord shall not be liable for failure to give possession of the premises upon commencement date by reason of the fact that premises are not ready for occupancy, or due to a prior Tenant wrongfully holding over or any other person wrongfully in possession or for any other reason; in such event the rent shall not commence until possession is given or is available, but the term herein shall not be extended.

Headings

The marginal headings are inserted only as a matter of convenience and in no way define the scope of this lease or the intent of any provision thereof.

Quiet Enjoyment

Landlord covenants that the said Tenant on paying the said rent, and performing all the covenants aforesaid, shall and may peacefully and quietly have, hold and enjoy the said demised premises for the term aforesaid, provided however, that this covenant shall be conditioned upon the retention of title to the premises by Landlord.

And it is mutually understood and agreed that the covenants and agreements contained in the within lease shall be binding upon the parties hereto and upon their respective successors, heirs, executors and administrators.

In Witness Whereof, Landlord and Tenant have respectively signed and sealed this lease as of the day and year first above written.

Signed, sealed and delivered

in the presence of

....L. S.

....L. S.

....L. S.

FIGURE 3-2. (con't)

A 256—Lease—Offices or Lofts: 4-78.

JULIUS BLUMBERG, INC., LAW BLANK PUBLISHERS
80 EXCHANGE PLACE AT BROADWAY, NEW YORK

This Agreement made this   day of   19   between

as Landlord

and

as Tenant

WITNESSETH: The Landlord hereby leases to Tenant and Tenant hereby hires from Landlord

in the building known as

for the term of   to commence on the   day of   19

and to end on the   day of   19   , upon the conditions and covenants following:

Rent

1st.   Tenant shall pay the annual rent of

said rent to be paid in equal monthly payments in advance on the   day of each and every month during the term aforesaid, as follows:

Occupancy

2nd.   Tenant shall use and occupy demised premises for no purpose other than

Repairs

Alterations

3rd.   Tenant shall take good care of the premises and fixtures, make good any injury or breakage done by Tenant or Tenant's agents, employees or visitors, and shall quit and surrender said premises, at the end of said term, in as good condition as the reasonable use thereof will permit; shall not make any additions, alterations or improvements in said premises, or permit any additional lock or fastening on any door, without the written consent of Landlord; and all alterations, partitions, additions, or improvements, which may be made by either of the parties hereto upon the premises, shall be the property of Landlord, and shall remain upon and be surrendered with the premises, as a part thereof, at the termination of this lease, without disturbance, molestation or injury.

Requirements of Law

4th.   Tenant shall promptly execute and comply with all statutes, ordinances, rules, orders, regulations and requirements of the Federal, State and City Government and of any and all their Departments and Bureaus applicable to said premises, for the correction, prevention, and abatement of nuisances or other grievances, in, upon, or connected with said premises during said term; and shall also promptly comply with and execute all rules, orders and regulations of the New York Board of Fire Underwriters for the prevention of fires at Tenant's own cost and expense.

Assignment

5th.   Tenant, successors, heirs, executors or administrators shall not assign this agreement, or underlet or underlease the premises, or any part thereof, without Landlord's prior consent in writing, which consent shall not be unreasonably withheld; or occupy, or permit or suffer the same to be occupied for any business or purpose deemed disreputable or extra-hazardous on account of fire, under the penalty of damages and forfeiture, and in the event of a breach thereof, the term herein shall immediately cease and determine at the option of Landlord as if it were the expiration of the original term.

Destruction

6th.   In case of damage, by fire or other action of the elements, to the building in which the leased premises are located, without the fault of Tenant or of Tenant's agent or employees, if the damage is so extensive as to amount practically to the total destruction of the leased premises or of the building, or if Landlord shall within a reasonable time decide not to rebuild, this lease shall cease and come to an end, and the rent shall be apportioned to the time of the damage. In all other cases where the leased premises are damaged by fire without the fault of Tenant or of Tenant's agents or employees, Landlord shall repair the damage with reasonable dispatch after notice of damage, and if the damage has rendered the premises untenantable, in whole or in part, there shall be an apportionment of the rent until the damage has been repaired. In determining what constitutes reasonable dispatch consideration shall be given to delays caused by strikes, adjustment of insurance and other causes beyond Landlord's control.

Access to Premises

7th.   Tenant agrees that Landlord and Landlord's agents and other representatives shall have the right to enter into and upon said premises, or any part thereof, at all reasonable hours for the purpose of examining the same, or for making such repairs, alterations, additions or improvements therein as may be necessary or deemed advisable by Landlord. Tenant also agrees to permit Landlord or Landlord's agents to show the premises to persons wishing to hire or purchase the same; and Tenant further agrees that during the 6 months next preceding the expiration of the term hereby granted, Landlord or Landlord's agents shall have the right to place notices on the front of said premises, or any part thereof, offering the premises "To Let" or "For Sale", and Tenant hereby agrees to permit the same to remain thereon without hindrance or molestation.

Lease Not In Effect

8th.   If, before the commencement of the term, Tenant takes the benefit of any insolvent act, or if a Receiver or Trustee be appointed for Tenant's property, or if the estate of Tenant hereunder be transferred or pass to or devolve upon any other person or corporation, or if Tenant shall default in the performance of any agreement by Tenant contained in any other lease to Tenant by Landlord or by any corporation of which an officer of Landlord is a Director, this lease shall thereby, at the option of Landlord, be terminated and in that case, neither Tenant nor anybody claiming under Tenant shall be entitled to go into possession of the demised premises. If after the commencement of the term, any of the events mentioned above in this subdivision shall occur, or if Tenant shall make default in fulfilling any of the covenants of this lease or the rules and regulations, other than the covenants for the payment of rent or "additional rent" or if the demised premises become vacant or deserted, Landlord may give to Tenant ten days' notice of intention to end the term of this lease, and thereupon at the expiration of said ten days' (if said condition which was the basis of said notice shall continue to exist) the term under this lease shall expire as fully and completely as if that day were the date herein definitely fixed for the expiration of the term and Tenant will then quit and surrender the demised premises to Landlord, but Tenant shall remain liable as hereinafter provided.

Defaults

10 Day Notice

Remedies

If Tenant shall make default in the payment of the rent reserved hereunder, or any item of "additional rent" herein mentioned, or any part of either or in making any other payment herein provided for, or if the notice last above provided for shall have been given and if the condition which was the basis of said notice shall exist at the expiration of said ten days' period, Landlord may immediately, or at any time thereafter, re-enter the demised premises and remove all persons and all or any property therefrom, either by summary dispossess proceedings, or by any suitable action or proceeding at law, or by force or otherwise, without being liable to indictment, prosecution or damages therefor, and re-possess and enjoy said premises together with all additions, alterations and improvements. In any such case or in the event that this lease be "terminated" before the commencement of the term, as above provided, Landlord may either re-let the demised premises or any part or parts thereof for Landlord's own account, or may, at Landlord's option, re-let the demised premises or any part or parts thereof as the agent of Tenant, and receive the rents therefor,

FIGURE 3-2.

Re-Letting applying the same first to the payment of such expenses as Landlord may have incurred, and then to the fulfillment of the covenants of Tenant herein, and the balance, if any, at the expiration of the term first above provided for, shall be paid to Tenant. Landlord may rent the premises for a term extending beyond the term hereby granted without releasing Tenant from any liability. In the event that the term of this lease shall expire as above in this subdivision 8th provided, or terminate by summary proceedings or otherwise, and if Landlord shall not re-let the demised premises for Landlord's own account, then, whether or not the premises be re-let, Tenant shall remain liable for, and Tenant hereby agrees to pay to Landlord, until the time when this lease would have expired but for such termination or expiration, the equivalent of the amount of all of the rent and "additional rent" reserved herein, less the avails of reletting, if any, and the same shall be due and payable by Tenant to Landlord on the several rent days above specified, that is, upon each of such rent days Tenant shall pay to Landlord the amount of deficiency then existing. Tenant hereby expressly waives any and all right of redemption in case Tenant shall be dispossessed by judgment or warrant of any court or judge, and Tenant waives and will waive all right to trial by jury in any summary proceedings hereafter instituted by Landlord against Tenant in respect to the demised premises or any action to recover rent or damages hereunder. In the event of a breach or threatened breach by Tenant of any of the covenants or provisions hereof, Landlord shall have the right of injunction and the right to invoke any remedy allowed at law or in equity, as if re-entry, summary proceedings and other remedies were not herein provided for. The words "re-enter" and "re-entry" as used in this lease are not restricted to their technical legal meaning.

Cumulative Remedies

Services 9th. As long as Tenant is not in default under any of the covenants of this lease, Landlord shall, excepting on Sundays and Holidays, provide the following services, if and insofar as the existing facilities permit: (a) furnish heat to the premises on business days from 8 A.M. to 6 P.M. when and as required by law; (b) OPERATE elevators, or permit self-operated elevators to be used, on business days from 8 A.M. to 6 P.M. except Saturdays when the hours shall be from 8 A.M. to 1 P.M.

Signs 10th. No sign, advertisement, notice or other lettering shall be exhibited, inscribed, painted or affixed by Tenant on any part of the premises or building without the prior written approval and consent of Landlord. Should Landlord deem it necessary to remove the same in order to paint, alter, or remodel any part of the building, Landlord may remove and replace same at Landlord's expense.

Cleaning 11th. Tenant shall, at Tenant's expense, keep the demised premises clean and in order to the satisfaction of Landlord. Tenant shall pay to Landlord the cost of removal of Tenant's refuse and waste, upon presentation of bills therefor and the amount of such bills shall be paid as additional rent.

Liability 12th. Landlord is exempt from any and all liability for any damage or injury to person or property caused by or resulting from steam, electricity, gas, water, rain, ice or snow, or any leak or flow from or into any part of said building or from any damage or injury resulting or arising from any other cause or happening whatsoever unless said damage or injury be caused by or be due to the negligence of Landlord.

Subordination 13th. That this instrument shall not be a lien against said premises in respect to any mortgages that are now on or that hereafter may be placed against said premises, and that the recording of such mortgage or mortgages shall have preference and precedence and be superior and prior in lien of this lease, irrespective of the date of recording and Tenant agrees to execute any such instrument without cost, which may be deemed necessary or desirable to further effect the subordination of this lease to any such mortgage or mortgages, and a refusal to execute such instrument shall entitle Landlord, or Landlord's assigns and legal representatives to the option of cancelling this lease without incurring any expense or damage and the term hereby granted is expressly limited accordingly.

Security 14th. Tenant has this day deposited with Landlord the sum of $ as security for the full and faithful performance by Tenant of all the terms, covenants and conditions of this lease upon Tenant's part to be performed, which said sum shall be returned to Tenant after the time fixed as the expiration of the term herein, provided Tenant has fully and faithfully carried out all of said terms, covenants and conditions on Tenant's part to be performed. In the event of a bona fide sale, subject to this lease, Landlord shall have the right to transfer the security to the vendee for the benefit of Tenant and Landlord shall be considered released by Tenant from all liability for the return of such security; and Tenant agrees to look to the new Landlord solely for the return of the said security, and it is agreed that this shall apply to every transfer or assignment made of the security to a new Landlord. That the security deposited under this lease shall not be mortgaged, assigned or encumbered by Tenant without the written consent of Landlord.

Sprinklers 15th. If there now is or shall be installed in the building a "sprinkler system", and such system or any of its appliances shall be damaged or injured or not in proper working order by reason of any act or omission of Tenant, Tenant's agents, servants, employees, licensees or visitors, Tenant shall forthwith restore the same to good working condition at its own expense; and if the New York Board of Fire Underwriters or the New York Fire Insurance Exchange or any bureau, department or official of the state or city government, require or recommend that any changes, modifications, alterations or additional sprinkler heads or other equipment be made or supplied by reason of Tenant's business, or the location of partitions, trade fixtures, or other contents of the demised premises, or for any other reason, or if any such changes, modifications, alterations, additional sprinkler heads or other equipment, become necessary to prevent the imposition of a penalty or charge against the full allowance for a sprinkler system in the fire insurance rate as fixed by said Exchange, or by any Fire Insurance Company, Tenant shall, at Tenant's expense, promptly make and supply such changes, modifications, alterations, additional sprinkler heads or other equipment. Tenant shall pay to Landlord as additional rent the sum of $ on the rent day of each month during the term of this lease, as Tenant's portion of the contract price for sprinkler supervisory service.

Water Sewer 16th Tenant shall pay to Landlord the rent or charge, which may, during the demised term, be assessed or imposed for the water used or consumed in or on the said premises, whether determined by meter or otherwise, as soon as and when the same may be assessed or imposed, and will also pay the expenses for the setting of a water meter in the said premises should the latter be required. Tenant shall pay Tenant's proportionate part of the sewer rent or charge imposed upon the building. All such rents or charges or expenses shall be paid as additional rent and shall be added to the next month's rent thereafter to become due.

Fire Insurance 17th. Tenant will not, nor will Tenant permit undertenants or other persons to do anything in said premises, or bring anything into said premises, or permit anything to be brought into said premises or to be kept therein, which will in any way increase the rate of fire insurance on said demised premises, nor use the demised premises or any part thereof, nor suffer or permit their use for any business or purpose which would cause an increase in the rate of fire insurance on said building, and Tenant agrees to pay on demand any such increase as additional rent.

No Waiver 18th. The failure of Landlord to insist upon a strict performance of any of the terms, conditions and covenants herein, shall not be deemed a waiver of any rights or remedies that Landlord may have, and shall not be deemed a waiver of any subsequent breach or default in the terms, conditions and covenants herein contained. This instrument may not be changed, modified or discharged orally.

Condemnation 19th. That should the land whereon said building stands or any part thereof be condemned for public use, then in that event, upon the taking of the same for such public use, this lease, at the option of Landlord, shall become null and void, and the term cease and come to an end upon the date when the same shall be taken and the rent shall be apportioned as of said date. No part of any award, however, shall belong to Tenant.

Fixtures 20th. If after default in payment of rent or violation of any other provision of this lease, or upon the expiration of this lease, Tenant moves out or is dispossessed and fails to remove any trade fixtures or other property prior to such said default, removal, expiration of lease, or prior to the issuance of the final order or execution of the warrant, then and in that event, the said fixtures and property shall be deemed abandoned by Tenant and shall become the property of Landlord.

Inability To Perform 21st. This lease and the obligation of Tenant to pay rent hereunder and perform all of the other covenants and agreements hereunder on part of Tenant to be performed shall in nowise be affected, impaired or excused because Landlord is unable to supply or is delayed in supplying any service expressly or impliedly to be supplied or is unable to make, or is delayed in making any repairs, additions, alterations or decorations or is unable to supply or is delayed in supplying any equipment or fixtures if Landlord is prevented or delayed from so doing by reason of governmental preemption in connection with any National Emergency declared by the President of the United States or in connection with any rule, order or regulation of any department or subdivision thereof of any governmental agency or by reason of the condition of supply and demand which have been or are affected by war or other emergency.

No Diminution of Rent 22nd. No diminution or abatement of rent, or other compensation, shall be claimed or allowed for inconvenience or discomfort arising from the making of repairs or improvements to the building or to its appliances, nor for any space taken to comply with any law, ordinance or order of a governmental authority. In respect to the various "services," if any, herein expressly or impliedly agreed to be furnished by Landlord to Tenant, it is agreed that there shall be no diminution or abatement of the rent, or any other compensation, for interruption or curtailment of such "service" when such interruption or curtailment shall be due to accident, alterations or repairs desirable or necessary to be made or to inability or difficulty in securing supplies or labor for the maintenance of such "service" or to some other cause, not gross negligence on the part of Landlord. No such interruption or curtailment of any such "service" shall be deemed a constructive eviction. Landlord shall not be required to furnish, and Tenant shall not be entitled to receive, any of such "services" during any period wherein Tenant shall be in default in respect to the payment of rent. Neither shall there be any abatement or diminution of rent because of making of repairs, improvements or decorations to the demised premises after the date above fixed for the commencement of the term, it being understood that rent shall, in any event, commence to run at such date so above fixed.

FIGURE 3-3.

ACKNOWLEDGMENTS

CORPORATE LANDLORD
STATE OF NEW YORK, } ss.:
    County of

On this   day of   , 19   , before me

personally came
to me known, who being by me duly sworn, did depose and say that he resides

in   ;

that he is the   of

the corporation described in and which executed the foregoing instrument, as LANDLORD; that he knows the seal of said corporation; that the seal affixed to said instrument is such corporate seal; that it was so affixed by order of the Board of Directors of said corporation, and that he signed his name thereto by like order.

....

CORPORATE TENANT
STATE OF NEW YORK, } ss.:
    County of

On this   day of   , 19   , before me

personally came
to me known, who being by me duly sworn, did depose and say that he resides

in   ;

that he is the   of

the corporation described in and which executed the foregoing instrument, as TENANT; that he knows the seal of said corporation; that the seal affixed to said instrument is such corporate seal; that it was so affixed by order of the Board of Directors of said corporation, and that he signed his name thereto by like order.

....

INDIVIDUAL LANDLORD
STATE OF NEW YORK, } ss.:
    County of

On this   day of   , 19   , before me

personally came
                                                                   ,
to me known and known to me to be the individual   described in and who, as LANDLORD, executed the foregoing instrument and acknowledged to me that he   executed the same.

....

INDIVIDUAL TENANT
STATE OF NEW YORK, } ss.:
    County of

On this   day of   , 19   , before me

personally came
                                                                   ,
to me known and known to me to be the individual   described in and who, as TENANT, executed the foregoing instrument and acknowledged to me that he   executed the same.

....

 IMPORTANT — PLEASE READ

RULES AND REGULATIONS ATTACHED TO AND MADE A PART OF THIS LEASE IN ACCORDANCE WITH ARTICLE 35.

1. The sidewalks, entrances, driveways, passages, courts, elevators, vestibules, stairways, corridors or halls shall not be obstructed or encumbered by any Tenant or used for any purpose other than for ingress to and egress from the demised premises and for delivery of merchandise and equipment in a prompt and efficient manner using elevators and passageways designated for such delivery by Landlord. There shall not be used in any space, or in the public hall of the building, either by any tenant or by jobbers, or others in the delivery or receipt of merchandise, any hand trucks except those equipped by rubber tires and safeguards. If said premises are situate on the ground floor of the building Tenant thereof shall further, at Tenant's expense, keep the sidewalks and curb in front of said premises clean and free from ice, snow, etc.

2. The water and wash closets and plumbing fixtures shall not be used for any purposes other than those for which they were designed or constructed and no sweepings, rubbish, rags, acids or other substances shall be deposited therein, and the expense of any breakage, stoppage, or damage resulting from the violation of this rule shall be borne by the Tenant who, or whose clerks, agents, employees or visitors, shall have caused it.

3. No carpet, rug or other article shall be hung or shaken out of any window of the building; and no Tenant shall sweep or throw or permit to be swept or thrown from the demised premises any dirt or other substances into any of the corridors or halls, elevators, or out of the doors or windows or stairways of the building, and Tenant shall not use, keep or permit to be used or kept any foul or noxious gas or substance in the demised premises, or permit or suffer the demised premises to be occupied or used in a manner offensive or objectionable to Landlord or other occupants of the building by reason of noise, odors and/or vibrations or interfere in any way with other Tenants or those having business therein, nor shall any animals or birds be kept in or about the building. Smoking or carrying lighted cigars or cigarettes in the elevators of the building is prohibited.

4. No awnings or other projections shall be attached to the outside walls of the building without the prior written consent of Landlord.

5. No sign, advertisement, notice or other lettering shall be exhibited, inscribed, painted or affixed by any Tenant on any part of the outside of the demised premises or the building or on the inside of the demised premises if the same is visible from the outside of the premises without the prior written consent of Landlord, except that the name of Tenant may appear on the entrance door of the premises. In the event of the violation of the foregoing by any Tenant, Landlord may remove same without any liability, and may charge the expense incurred by such removal to Tenant or Tenants violating this rule. Landlord shall have the right to prohibit any advertising by Tenant which, in Landlord's opinion, impairs the reputation or desirability of the building of which the demised premises are a part. Signs on interior doors and directory tablet shall be inscribed, painted or affixed for each Tenant by Landlord at the expense of such Tenant and shall be of a size, color and style acceptable to Landlord.

6. No Tenant shall mark, paint, drill into, or in any way deface any part of the demised premises or the building of which they form a part. No boring, cutting or stringing of wires shall be permitted, except with the prior written consent of Landlord, and as Landlord may direct. No Tenant shall lay linoleum, or other similar floor covering, so that the same shall come in direct contact with the floor of the demised premises, and, if linoleum or other similar floor covering is desired to be used an interlining of builder's deadening felt shall be first affixed to the floor, by a paste or other material, soluble in water, the use of cement or other similar adhesive material being expressly prohibited.

7. No additional locks or bolts of any kind shall be placed upon any of the doors or windows by any Tenant, nor shall any changes be made in existing locks or mechanism thereof. Each Tenant must, upon the termination of his Tenancy, restore to the Landlord all keys of stores, offices and toilet rooms, either furnished to, or otherwise procured by, such Tenant, and in the event of the loss of any keys, so furnished, such Tenant shall pay to Landlord the cost thereof.

8. Freight, furniture, business equipment, merchandise and bulky matter of any description shall be delivered to and removed from the premises only on the freight elevators and through the service entrances and corridors, and only during hours and in a manner approved by Landlord. Landlord reserves the right to inspect all freight to be brought into the building and to exclude from the building all freight which violates any of these Rules and Regulations or the lease of which these Rules and Regulations are a part.

9. No Tenant shall obtain for use upon the demised premises ice, drinking water, towel and other similar services, or accept barbering or bootblacking services in the demised premises, except from persons authorized by the Landlord, and at hours and under regulations fixed by Landlord. Canvassing, soliciting and peddling in the building is prohibited and each Tenant shall co-operate to prevent the same.

10. Landlord reserves the right to exclude from the building between the hours of 6 P.M. and 8 A.M. and at all hours on Sundays, and legal holidays all persons who do not present a pass to the building signed by Landlord. Landlord will furnish passes to persons for whom any Tenant requests same in writing. Each Tenant shall be responsible for all persons for whom he requests such pass and shall be liable to Landlord for all acts of such persons.

11. Landlord shall have the right to prohibit any advertising by any Tenant which, in Landlord's opinion, tends to impair the reputation of the building or its desirability as a building for offices, and upon written notice from Landlord, Tenant shall refrain from or discontinue such advertising.

12. Tenant shall not bring or permit to be brought or kept in or on the demised premises, any inflammable, combustible or explosive fluid, material, chemical or substance, or cause or permit any odors of cooking or other processes, or any unusual or other objectionable odors to permeate in or eminate from the demised premises.

Address

Premises   TO

STANDARD FORM OF
Store Lease

The Real Estate Board of New York, Inc.
©Copyright 1973. All Rights Reserved.
Reproduction in whole or in part prohibited.

Dated   , 19

Rent per Year

Rent per Month

Term
From
To

Drawn by .... Checked by ....
Entered by .... Approved by ....

FIGURE 3-3. (con't)

Window Cleaning: 5. Tenant will not clean nor require, permit, suffer or allow any window in the demised premises to be cleaned from the outside in violation of Section 202 of the New York State Labor Law or any other applicable law or of the Rules of the Board of Standards and Appeals, or of any other Board or body having or asserting jurisdiction.

Requirements of Law, Fire Insurance, Floor Load: 6. Prior to the commencement of the lease term, if Tenant is then in possession, and at all times thereafter, Tenant, at Tenant's sole cost and expense, shall promptly comply with all present and future laws, orders and regulations of all state, federal, municipal and local governments, departments, commissions and boards and any direction of any public officer pursuant to law, and all orders, rules and regulations of the New York Board of Fire Underwriters or any similar body which shall impose any violation, order or duty upon Landlord or Tenant with respect to the demised premises whether or not arising out of Tenant's use or manner of use thereof, or with respect to the building if arising out of Tenant's use or manner of use of the premises or the building (including the use permitted under the lease). Except as provided in Article 29 hereof, nothing herein shall require Tenant to make structural repairs or alterations unless Tenant has by its manner of use of the demised premises or method of operation therein, violated any such laws, ordinances, orders, rules, regulations or requirements with respect thereto. Tenant may, after securing Landlord to Landlord's satisfaction against all damages, interest, penalties and expenses, including, but not limited to, reasonable attorneys' fees, by cash deposit or by surety bond in an amount and in a company satisfactory to Landlord, contest and appeal any such laws, ordinances, orders, rules, regulations or requirements provided same is done with all reasonable promptness and provided such appeal shall not subject Landlord to prosecution for a criminal offense or constitute a default under any lease or mortgage under which Landlord may be obligated, or cause the demised premises or any part thereof to be condemned or vacated. Tenant shall not do or permit any act or thing to be done in or to the demised premises which is contrary to law, or which will invalidate or be in conflict with public liability, fire or other policies of insurance at any time carried by or for the benefit of Landlord with respect to the demised premises or the building of which the demised premises form a part, or which shall or might subject Landlord to any liability or responsibility to any person or for property damage, nor shall Tenant keep anything in the demised premises except as now or hereafter permitted by the Fire Department, Board of Fire Underwriters, Fire Insurance Rating Organization or other authority having jurisdiction, and then only in such manner and such quantity so as not to increase the rate for fire insurance applicable to the building, nor use the premises in a manner which will increase the insurance rate for the building or any property located therein over that in effect prior to the commencement of Tenant's occupancy. Tenant shall pay all costs, expenses, fines, penalties or damages, which may be imposed upon Landlord by reason of Tenant's failure to comply with the provisions of this article and if by reason of such failure the fire insurance rate shall, at the beginning of this lease or at any time thereafter, be higher than it otherwise would be, then Tenant shall reimburse Landlord, as additional rent hereunder, for that portion of all fire insurance premiums thereafter paid by Landlord which shall have been charged because of such failure by Tenant, and shall make such reimbursement upon the first day of the month following such outlay by Landlord. In any action or proceeding wherein Landlord and Tenant are parties a schedule or "make-up" of rate for the building or demised premises issued by the New York Fire Insurance Exchange, or other body making fire insurance rates applicable to said premises shall be conclusive evidence of the facts therein stated and of the several items and charges in the fire insurance rate then applicable to said premises. Tenant shall not place a load upon any floor of the demised premises exceeding the floor load per square foot area which it was designed to carry and which is allowed by law. Landlord reserves the right to prescribe the weight and position of all safes, business machines and mechanical equipment. Such installations shall be placed and maintained by Tenant, at Tenant's expense, in settings sufficient, in Landlord's judgment, to absorb and prevent vibration, noise and annoyance.

Subordination: 7. This lease is subject and subordinate to all ground or underlying leases and to all mortgages which may now or hereafter affect such leases or the real property of which demised premises are a part and to all renewals, modifications, consolidations, replacements and extensions of any such underlying leases and mortgages. This clause shall be self-operative and no further instrument of subordination shall be required by any ground or underlying lessee or by any mortgagee, affecting any lease or the real property of which the demised premises are a part. In confirmation of such subordination, Tenant shall execute promptly any certificate that Landlord may request.

Tenant's Liability Insurance, Property Loss, Damage, Indemnity: 8. Landlord or its agents shall not be liable for any damage to property of Tenant or of others entrusted to employees of the building, nor for loss of or damage to any property of Tenant by theft or otherwise, nor for any injury or damage to persons or property resulting from any cause of whatsoever nature, unless caused by or due to the negligence of Landlord, its agents, servants or employees; nor shall Landlord or its agents be liable for any such damage caused by other tenants or persons in, upon or about said building or caused by operations in construction of any private, public or quasi public work. Tenant agrees, at Tenant's sole cost and expense, to maintain general public liability insurance in standard form in favor of Landlord and Tenant against claims for bodily injury or death or property damage occurring in or upon the demised premises, effective from the date Tenant enters into possession and during the term of this lease. Such insurance shall be in an amount and with carriers acceptable to the Landlord. Such policy or policies shall be delivered to the Landlord. On Tenant's default in obtaining or delivering any such policy or policies or failure to pay the charges therefor, Landlord may secure or pay the charges for any such policy or policies and charge the Tenant as additional rent therefor. If at any time any windows of the demised premises are temporarily closed, darkened or bricked up (or permanently closed, darkened or bricked up, if required by law) for any reason whatsoever including, but not limited to Landlord's own acts, Landlord shall not be liable for any damage Tenant may sustain thereby and Tenant shall not be entitled to any compensation therefor nor abatement or diminution of rent nor shall the same release Tenant from its obligations hereunder nor constitute an eviction. Tenant shall not move any safe, heavy machinery, heavy equipment, bulky matter, or fixtures into or out of the building without Landlord's

prior written consent. If such safe, machinery, equipment, bulky matter or fixtures requires special handling, all work in connection therewith shall comply with the Administrative Code of the City of New York and all other laws and regulations applicable thereto and shall be done during such hours as Landlord may designate. Tenant shall indemnify and save harmless Landlord against and from all liabilities, obligations, damages, penalties, claims, costs and expenses for which Landlord shall not be reimbursed by insurance, including reasonable attorneys fees, paid, suffered or incurred as a result of any breach by Tenant, Tenant's agents, contractors, employees, invitees, or licensees, of any covenant or condition of this lease, or the carelessness, negligence or improper conduct of the Tenant, Tenant's agents, contractors, employees, invitees or licensees. Tenant's liability under this lease extends to the acts and omissions of any subtenant, and any agent, contractor, employee, invitee or licensee of any sub-tenant. In case any action or proceeding is brought against Landlord by reason of any such claim, Tenant, upon written notice from Landlord, will, at Tenant's expense, resist or defend such action or proceeding by counsel approved by Landlord in writing, such approval not to be unreasonably withheld.

Destruction, Fire and Other Casualty: 9. (a) If the demised premises or any part thereof shall be damaged by fire or other casualty, Tenant shall give immediate notice thereof to Landlord and this lease shall continue in full force and effect except as hereinafter set forth. (b) If the demised premises are partially damaged or rendered partially unusable by fire or other casualty, the damages thereto shall be repaired by and at the expense of Landlord and the rent, until such repair shall be substantially completed, shall be apportioned from the day following the casualty according to the part of the premises which is usable. (c) If the demised premises are totally damaged or rendered wholly unusable by fire or other casualty, then the rent shall be proportionately paid up to the time of the casualty and thenceforth shall cease until the date when the premises shall have been repaired and restored by Landlord, subject to Landlord's right to elect not to restore the same as hereinafter provided. (d) If the demised premises are rendered wholly unusable or (whether or not the demised premises are damaged in whole or in part) if the building shall be so damaged that Landlord shall decide to demolish it or to rebuild it, then, in any of such events, Landlord may elect to terminate this lease by written notice to Tenant given within 90 days after such fire or casualty specifying a date for the expiration of the lease, which date shall not be more than 60 days after the giving of such notice, and upon the date specified in such notice the term of this lease shall expire as fully and completely as if such date were the date set forth above for the termination of this lease and Tenant shall forthwith quit, surrender and vacate the premises without prejudice however, to Landlord's rights and remedies against Tenant under the lease provisions in effect prior to such termination, and any rent owing shall be paid up to such date and any payments of rent made by Tenant which were on account of any period subsequent to such date shall be returned to Tenant. Unless Landlord shall serve a termination notice as provided for herein, Landlord shall make the repairs and restorations under the conditions of (b) and (c) hereof, with all reasonable expedition subject to delays due to adjustment of insurance claims, labor troubles and causes beyond Landlord's control. After any such casualty, Tenant shall cooperate with Landlord's restoration by removing from the premises as promptly as reasonably possible, all of Tenant's salvageable inventory and movable equipment, furniture, and other property. Tenant's liability for rent shall resume five (5) days after written notice from Landlord that the premises are substantially ready for Tenant's occupancy. (e) Nothing contained hereinabove shall relieve Tenant from liability that may exist as a result of damage from fire or other casualty. Notwithstanding the foregoing, each party shall look first to any insurance in its favor before making any claim against the other party for recovery for loss or damage resulting from fire or other casualty, and to the extent that such insurance is in force and collectible and to the extent permitted by law, Landlord and Tenant each hereby releases and waives all right of recovery against the other or any one claiming through or under each of them by way of subrogation or otherwise. The foregoing release and waiver shall be in force only if both releasors' insurance policies contain a clause providing that such a release or waiver shall not invalidate the insurance and also, provided that such a policy can be obtained without additional premiums. Tenant acknowledges that Landlord will not carry insurance on Tenant's furniture and/or furnishings or any fixtures or equipment, improvements, or appurtenances removable by Tenant and agrees that Landlord will not be obligated to repair any damage thereto or replace the same. (f) Tenant hereby waives the provisions of Section 227 of the Real Property Law and agrees that the provisions of this article shall govern and control in lieu thereof.

Eminent Domain: 10. If the whole or any part of the demised premises shall be acquired or condemned by Eminent Domain for any public or quasi public use or purpose, then and in that event, the term of this lease shall cease and terminate from the date of title vesting in such proceeding and Tenant shall have no claim for the value of any unexpired term of said lease.

Assignment, Mortgage, Etc.: 11. Tenant, for itself, its heirs, distributees, executors, administrators, legal representatives, successors and assigns, expressly covenants that it shall not assign, mortgage or encumber this agreement, nor underlet, or suffer or permit the demised premises or any part thereof to be used by others, without the prior written consent of Landlord in each instance. If this lease be assigned, or if the demised premises or any part thereof be underlet or occupied by anybody other than Tenant, Landlord may, after default by Tenant, collect rent from the assignee, under-tenant or occupant, and apply the net amount collected to the rent herein reserved, but no such assignment, underletting, occupancy or collection shall be deemed a waiver of this covenant, or the acceptance of the assignee, under-tenant or occupant as tenant, or a release of Tenant from the further performance by Tenant of covenants on the part of Tenant herein contained. The consent by Landlord to an assignment or underletting shall not in any wise be construed to relieve Tenant from obtaining the express consent in writing of Landlord to any further assignment or underletting.

Electric Current: 12. Rates and conditions in respect to submetering or rent inclusion, as the case may be, to be added in RIDER attached hereto. Tenant covenants and agrees that at all times its use of electric current shall not exceed the capacity of existing feeders to the building or the risers or wiring installation and Tenant may not use any electrical equipment which, in Landlord's opinion, reasonably exercised, will overload such installations or interfere with the use thereof by other tenants of the building. The change at any time of the

FIGURE 3-4

Analysis of Two Proposed Store Sites

Date of Visit _____

Site A

Location Aspects

_____

_____

_____

_____

_____

_____

_____

_____

Site Aspects

_____

_____

_____

_____

_____

_____

_____

_____

Rental Terms

_____

_____

_____

_____

_____

_____

_____

FIGURE 3-5

Analysis of Two Proposed Store Sites

Date of Visit _____

Site B

Location Aspects

_____
_____
_____
_____
_____
_____
_____
_____

Site Aspects

_____
_____
_____
_____
_____
_____
_____
_____
_____
_____

Rental Terms

_____
_____
_____
_____
_____
_____
_____
_____

Store Layout and Ambience (and Space Usage)

CHAPTER 4

A store's layout and ambience has a strong relationship to retail efficiency and effectiveness. The physical plant is where sales are "manufactured." So every square foot must be planned to produce its share of the total store volume and to support sales, within the constraints of:

INTRODUCTION

* physical size,
* physical shape,
* required shipping and receiving facilities, and
* structural and utility features.

Although retailing is essentially the buying and selling of merchandise, store layout and ambience are key factors in attracting potential customers, as well as in discouraging those with no interest in a store's merchandise. In the final analysis, the foundation of success or failure depends on the retail "package"—how well it brings customers and merchandise together.

The maximum use of space is, at best, a subjective topic that may take some experimentation before you arrive at a "solution." Most retailers make periodic changes—of fixtures, of reserve and storage space, of aisles, and of other physical aspects—to update physical arrangements for greater customer and employee convenience and for better store efficiency. Although there are guidelines, there are no pat answers on how to utilize space to greatest advantage.

To go one step further, what appears to be an exciting and customer-satisfying layout today, can be dated and inefficient tomorrow. Since currency is a retail demand, layout and ambience, like fashion merchandise, depend on the latest developments and consumer acceptance.

Within the boundaries of your available capital and your estimates of consumer shopping attitudes, you should plan store space and atmosphere to:

* maximize sales,
* save time and energy, and
* discourage theft and retail shortage (errors of omission and commission).

The store's location and its physical characteristics, critical aspects of the retail mix, go hand in glove with merchandising policies, services, and communications — all of which add up to a retail "personality."

Exterior Appearance

Whether or not a shopper decides to stop, look, and enter a store can be attributed in no small degree to its exterior: the combination of its architectural details, of its window treatment, and of its entrance.

Entrance. An accessible entrance aids in generating traffic. Most malls have eliminated traditional entrances and replaced them with air doors or with electric mechanisms that automatically open and close. Glass doors are widely used to allow customers to view a store's interior from the outside, a motivating factor to the first stage of consumer purchase behavior — to enter the store's premises.

Window Display. Windows are an integral part of a small store's sales promotion efforts since they communicate immediate and prominent messages to consumers about the store's image and the type of merchandise it carries. The three most important purposes of window display are:

1. *Promotional:* to influence the purchase of merchandise.
2. *Institutional:* to create a favorable store image.
3. *Community Value:* to generate goodwill and build a community position for the store.

Interior Layout

A customer may enter a store by reason of the first attraction, an exterior that promises buying value. The next attraction should be an artful and consumer-satisfying display of wanted fashions, arranged so that merchandise can be purchased with minimum effort.

Guidelines. A store's interior is arranged by the merchandising guidelines of:

1. ease of traffic flow (customer movement),
2. economical maintenance of layout,
3. presentation of merchandise,
4. sales and profit per square feet, and
5. accessibility of merchandise to customers.

The particular type of layout in a given situation depends on the amount of available space, on its shape and structural elements (such as girders), or on utility requirements. Someone without the appropriate experience would do well to engage the services of an architect or interior designer. The need for a properly "packaged" product is too critical to leave to chance or inexperience.

Selling and Nonselling Areas. The total interior arrangement needs to provide for both selling (merchandising) and nonselling (operations) areas. The total share should cover the retailing requirements of:

Merchandising:

1. location of regular selling departments,
2. temporary special sales merchandise,
3. other nonpermanent merchandise displays,
4. auxiliary functions of selling (such as dressing rooms, alteration area), and
5. reserve stock room.

Operations:

1. receiving and marking,
2. office space, and
3. housekeeping supplies.

The relationship between selling and nonselling space is related to retail store size: a large-scale operation requires a greater share of space for non-selling activities than a small store. In terms of average percentages, a department store allots approximately 60 percent for selling, but a small store uses about 75 to 80 percent for the same purpose.

Since rent is based on total space, each square foot must yield enough of a dollar sales volume so that the store's nonproductive (nonselling) space requirement does not add up to a disproportionate cost of your retail operation. A layout requirement of first magnitude is therefore to group merchandise in the *most* productive and customer-convenient areas. In simple terms, merchandise should be grouped in direct relationship to its importance.

Figure 4-1 shows the sections of a typical small store as they relate to traffic density and therefore to their selling importance. Apparently the rear of a store is the weakest selling area, and therefore it is most appropriate for nonselling areas; the owner's office, the receiving and marking room, the alteration room, the reserve stock room, and dressing rooms. Since these different areas of a selling flow have different values of traffic and sales production, merchandise that is currently in greatest consumer demand should be allocated prime space in adequate proportion to its salability.

What's "adequate"? Table 4-1 is a chart of industry-prepared ratios to determine space allocation for major fashion merchandise classifications. Based on these recommended figures, a store that does a yearly volume of,

TABLE 4-1. Industry-Prepared Ratios for Space Allocation

Category	Sales Per Square Foot of Selling Space for Selected Categories	Net Sales Percentage of Total Store
Dresses	$100	40%
Sportswear	$125	50%
Accessories	$110	10%

FIGURE 4-1.

56

Store Layout and
Ambience

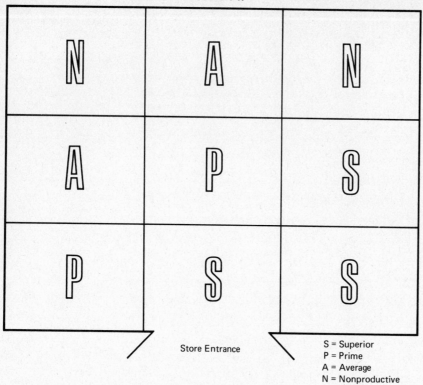

Store Entrance

S = Superior
P = Prime
A = Average
N = Nonproductive

say, $250,000 would estimate its yearly dress sales at $100,000 ($25,000 × 0.40 = $100,000). The dress department (or classification) would then be allotted 1,000 square feet, on the basis of:

Sales per square foot = $100

$100,000 divided by $100 = 1,000 square feet.

A second method is to multiply the total amount of selling space by the anticipated percentage of volume for each category. For example, let's say that the total selling space is 2,000 square feet and that the percentage of total sales volume for dresses is 40 percent. In such a case, the amount of space needed for dresses would be 800 square feet (2,000 × 0.40 = 800).

Other considerations affect the location of selling departments, or sections, in a specialty store. They are:

1. department sales and profit,
2. pleasing appearance,
3. convenience of customers, and
4. ease of selling.

Department Sales and Profit. Because the various sections of a store have varying degrees of selling importance, the most productive space should be allocated to departments with the highest ratio of sales. Yet exceptions may be made for the sake of expediency or possibly merchandising advantage. Conceivably a special purpose could dictate the use of your most valuable space for merchandise that does not sell particularly well, on the assumption that highlighting certain merchandise has institutional or long-term value.

Pleasing Appearance. In planning the location of merchandise departments, you have to create a pleasant ambience. Fashion-conscious women prefer to shop in stores in which the merchandise arrangement and decor combine the values of utility and sense appeal, again for institutional or long-term value. The color coordination of stock, good housekeeping, attractive decorations, and artfully prepared displays all add up to an atmosphere conducive to continued customer patronage. Even the store's odor can be so important that some stores use atomizers to spray perfume for a pleasant odor.

Convenience of Customers. Layout should be planned so that customers can shop easily and conveniently. Traffic aisles should be wide enough to prevent traffic jams, and merchandise should be within easy reach of shoppers. Displays should show merchandise to its best advantage, on attractive mannikins and appropriately accessorized. To offset customers' natural tendency to use the right side to walk through a store, use striking displays or merchandise in high demand to divert them to the left side. In this way, you balance traffic flow.

Ease of Selling. The layout and the arrangement of merchandise should also lend themselves to increasing customer purchases and to decreasing selling and operating costs. The location of fitting rooms and the cash register can save the time of customers and employees alike, offer customers the best service, and make it most convenient to finalize sales transactions.

Your salespeople can make more sales per customer by suggesting things "to go with" whatever the customer has just bought. The "to go with" technique enhances the probability of multiple sales even more, however, when the merchandise is prominently exposed along the way as the customer comes up to the selling desk — where the sale is written up.

Layout Plans

Of the many plans to facilitate the flow of traffic, the most frequently used are:

1. the grid plan, and
2. the free flow plan.

Grid Layout. The most frequently used retail layout is the grid plan. Designed primarily for efficiency, it actually serves as a barrier to free customer movement. Yet it ensures maximum shopper exposure to selected merchandise, as well as the greatest security. The grid flow plan literally forces customers to follow a planned traffic pattern. Supermarkets and most department store main floors are prime examples of grid plan usage. Figure 4-2 is an example of how a grid plan controls customer traffic flow.

Free Flow. Small stores and boutiques use the free flow plan to give customers the greatest freedom of movement and the widest immediate choice of merchandise. In this sense, the method can be said to be consumer-oriented. This looser arrangement, with its easier access to merchandise, allows the customer greater freedom to determine the compatibility of different classifications of merchandise. It thus encourages multiple unit sales. Many department stores have incorporated free flow plan method into fashion department layouts, to simulate the ambience of a small store or boutique.

FIGURE 4-2. Grid Layout

58

Store Layout and
Ambience

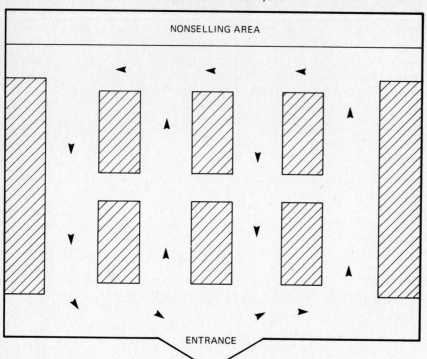

NONSELLING AREA

ENTRANCE

Free Flow

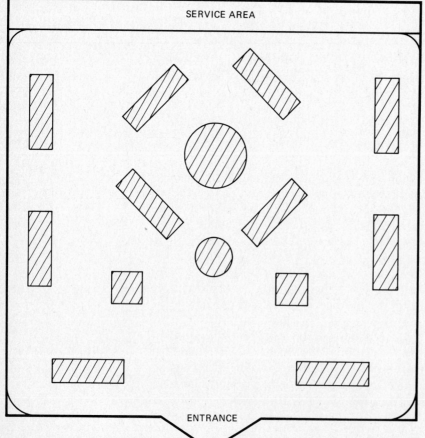

SERVICE AREA

ENTRANCE

Retailing includes operational functions that require approximately 20 to 25 percent of a small store's total space, a considerable cost of doing business. Although these functions contribute indirectly to profit, they demand adequate managerial consideration and efficient performance because they also have a strong relationship to customer store loyalty. So for the purposes of space allocation, the following auxiliaries of retailing, which are performed either by the owner or by an employee, must be carefully laid out:

1. receiving and marking,
2. alteration department, and
3. law-away and stock room facilities.

Receiving and Marking. An important phase of merchandising is the receiving and marking of goods, the efficiency of which depends on:

1. careful inspection of merchandise quality,
2. verification of quantity and details of orders,
3. correct pricing and ticketing, and
4. the prompt movement of goods from the receiving area to the selling floor.

Prior to accepting merchandise from the carrier, either you or a responsible employee should inspect the package for damages, for the correct weight, and for charges, in the presence of the delivery person. Many shipping clerks, intentionally or not, tend to overcharge on shipments. Checking weight and charges can save the small store owner a considerable amount of money over a period of time. If a package is damaged, you or your receiving clerk should refuse to accept it or demand a receipt that acknowledges the damage.

After the merchandise has been accepted, its quality and quantity should be verified. There are three basic methods of checking incoming merchandise:

a. the blind check method,
b. direct check method, and
c. the semiblind check method.

In the *blind check method*, merchandise is received and listed without reference to an invoice or order copy. This method forces the receiving clerk (or owner) to inspect the merchandise immediately.

In the *direct check method* (the most widely used), merchandise is checked directly against the invoice (which may be in the package or received in the mail prior to the receipt of merchandise) and against the buyer's order copy. This method is faster than the blind check approach, and any discrepancies between the merchandise shipped and what was ordered can be discerned quickly and accurately.

The *semiblind check method*, entails only the use of the buyer's order copy in checking the merchandise.

Once the merchandise has been properly checked with any of these methods, it is priced, marked, and ticketed. The marking of merchandise can be done by hand or by machine. A number of firms (such as the Dennison Manufacturing Co., the Monarch Manufacturing Co., and others) either lease or sell marking machines. By using a machine rather than marking goods by hand, you can:

* ticket goods in a uniform manner,
* present legible price tickets,
* offer understandable price tickets,
* use price tickets as a selling aid, and
* facilitate the recording of merchandise events (unit control).

Alteration Department. A proper fit is an important criterion of selling efficiency in fashion merchandise. If a garment does not fit to a customer's satisfaction, you can very possibly lose the sale — and the customer! So although an alteration department is rarely a profit-making activity and can be a cost of considerable proportion, it is a service that merits inclusion in a small store's operation.

Even within the budget of a small store, however, several alternatives are available. The first and obvious option, if financially feasible, is to hire a good seamstress. Second, possibly you might arrange for a seamstress or tailor to work on the premises as an independent agent in business for herself or himself. This approach relieves you, the owner, of an expense while still offering a needed service. A third possibility — another way to offer service without assuming a financial burden — is to arrange for a nearby tailor shop to handle alterations. Finally, an arrangement can be made with a piece worker to be available on specified days.

Not uncommonly the alteration department is housed in the same area as the receiving and marking department. This location ensures the presence of someone in the area at all times for security purposes.

Lay-Away and Stockroom Facilities. Since the scarcity of space is a constant problem in a small store, you can make provisions for space to be used for multiple purposes, such as for both lay-aways and reserve stock. By properly utilizing stock space, you can avoid a cluttered, overstocked appearance in the store. At the same time, you can offer a lay-away program, which could accommodate customers who cannot afford to pay cash or who do not have credit cards.

Ambience

Although ambience as it relates to customer segmentation is discussed in Chapter 5, it is of sufficient importance to require reinforcement here. A store atmosphere — created through the use of color, fixtures, and other design features — relaxes a consumer and effects affirmative purchase behavior. Ambience is so important and, sometimes, so tricky, that putting together all the elements for a pleasing and functional store may require professional services, available at approximately 7 percent of the total cost of interior design costs.

Fixturing. The type of fixtures usually varies with a store's merchandising policies. As the owner of a better (higher-priced) store, you would probably purchase fewer but more expressive fixtures, while a lower-priced store operator usually prefers less costly but more functional ones. Your decor, your finances, and the store image you desire also influence the type of fixtures selected. (Note that fixtures can be purchased new or used.) Whatever your circumstances, use movable fixtures, which allow for later rearrangement. Sometime in the future, you will need a new look, a different utilization of space, or the accommodation of a change in store traffic.

Lighting. Lighting plays such an important part in creating a store's atmosphere, that it should be planned with lighting consultants. The current trend is toward flexible lighting: fluorescent lights for basic lighting, and incandescent lights for emphasis. Spotlights, lights on movable tracks, and colored lights are all used as merchandising tools to highlight areas of special interest. Note that local electric power companies often provide free lighting plans to small retailers.

Color. In store design, color is used for merchandising and atmosphere. Color may be soft or bold, and it may act as a divider between departments. Most major companies use color as a psychological tool to increase productivity and efficiency.

Leasing of Equipment. Leasing equipment is becoming an important means of fixturing small stores. Although more expensive initially, in the long run leasing may be actually less costly. By not investing in store design fixtures and lighting, you keep capital on hand for daily business operations. Additionally, leased equipment can be exchanged for updated fixtures without a heavy outlay of cash. If such an exchange does not seem likely, then leasing terms can be arranged so that the leasing costs are applied against the sale price, if you decide later to purchase leased equipment. A store owner either who has limited capital or who wishes to use it to other advantage may find leasing financially advantageous.

PRINCIPLES OR PRACTICES

Store layout is a complex subject. The layout that *best* accommodates merchandising and operational needs varies from store to store. Yet what is not variable is that every square foot must be productive, either as a sales area or as a supporting function. Location requirements call for the arrangement of selling, nonselling, and service areas to obtain maximum merchandise presentation, customer flow, sales, and profit.

Consumers tend to characterize stores when they have buying needs. A store's exterior, its interior, its services, and other retail requirements must all suit customers' expectations, because how they feel about a store directly affects where they shop. As an axiom, "Customers shop where they are comfortable."

The onus on retailers is therefore to provide a physical plant that responds to the consumer's quest for shopping ease, pleasure, and ultimate satisfaction. At the same time, the retailer has to make the best use of space for the total retail effort, to maximize profit.

ASSIGNMENT

1. Visit a ladies' dress department in at least three stores. Using the layout analysis in Figure 4-3, identify:
   a. the type of retailer (such as department store, specialty shop, discount operation, and so on),
   b. the layout of each department,
   c. the location of the department within the store,
   d. the physical characteristics of the department (lighting, display, storage, and the like), and
   e. submit a floor plan sketch of each department along with this information.
2. Compare two types of retail establishments: a department store and a specialty store. Contrast them in terms of *store* layout, specifically their interior and window displays. Make up a summary chart (Figure 4-4) of your comparisons, and write up a narrative suggesting the operating strategies of the two establishments. Finally, explain how they respond to the needs of your intended store.

FIGURE 4-3.

Layout Analysis

1. Type of outlet:

   a. _____

   _____

   b. _____

   _____

   c. _____

   _____

2. The layout:

   a. _____

   _____

   b. _____

   _____

   c. _____

   _____

3. Location of department within the store:

   a. _____

   _____

   b. _____

   _____

   c. _____

   _____

4. Physical characteristics of department:

   a. _____

   _____

   b. _____

   _____

   c. _____

   _____

5. Simple sketch of each department utilizing above information:

FIGURE 4-4.

Comparative Analysis

	Department store	Specialty store
Store Layout		
Interior		
Window display		
Summary		

Customer Segmentation— 5
Retailing Mix

The relationship between market segmentation and location is so critical (as discussed in Chapter 3), that your planning must start with a determination of *who* is to be served.

On this basic determination all your other retail strategies are formulated. Retail segmentation is done in terms of geography. In other words, *where* are the people located *who* exhibit the consumption and buying behavior that favors the goals of your intended store? Having established the *who* and *where* by answering that question, your next step is to develop strategies to deal with the *what* and *how* aspects.

INTRODUCTION

All these questions compose the *retailing mix*, which, if properly designed and employed, can produce two effects:

1. the ability to compete, as well as
2. an affirmative response from the segmented consumer group.

The broad elements of the retailing mix are:

1. location and ambience,
2. merchandising policies, and
3. services and communications.

MANAGERIAL REQUIREMENTS

Location and Ambience

Since location was discussed in Chapter 3, we may confine our attention to ambience in this section. Further, since the creation of ambience was treated

64

in Chapter 5, we may devote this section to its relationship to motivating consumers to make the purchase decision.

Opening a new store to customers can be compared to two people meeting for the first time. In either case, each party has standards for the other, and these role expectations can cause attitudes that might affect the future relationship. Although a store is inanimate, its exterior and interior arrangements can communicate such effective messages as, "This is where you should shop . . . This is the type of merchandise you need."

The Exterior. A store's exterior is a customer's first point of contact. The architecture — the physical set-up — should, if possible, be designed so that it is esthetically attractive and so that it creates the most favorable image. For example, the sign's size, shape, color and type of lettering should all be in harmony with the nonpersonal "package" of strategies, by which you create a store image.

The exterior windows of a small store can serve as a most effective and economical sales promotion "workhorse," since they work twenty-four hours a day, seven days a week. Many apparel chain stores in shopping centers, for example, do minimal or no advertising. They depend instead wholly on location, traffic, and effective exterior windows to obtain a local share of fashion business in highly competitive environments. Perceptive retailers take advantage of exterior windows by arranging their styles in the most artistic manner. Their aim is to influence consumer reactions in two ways: (1) to create an impulse purchase, and (2), in the longer-range view, to convince shoppers that their stores can satisfy a fashion need.

The Interior. Interior display, as already noted, depends a great deal on your store's layout. In other words, how well does your utilization of space anticipate consumer needs? Interior display is so important, in fact, that it merits a summary and reinforcement of its previous treatment, from another point of view. Interior display should be regarded as the partner of exterior display and advertising. What consumers do not see in exterior windows and newspaper advertisements can be promoted by interior visual presentations: How is the merchandise arranged? How is it placed in stock? How are styles highlighted? And how are they accessorized?

The purposes of interior display can be summarized as follows:

1. to create a favorable shopping atmosphere,
2. to help customers locate merchandise seen in advertisements or exterior windows,
3. to help salespeople sell merchandise,
4. to contribute ideas for suggestive selling (additional and/or high-priced merchandise), and
5. to set a mood to support a promotional theme.

An appropriate atmosphere, naturally, depends on the segment of the market that you have selected to serve. Yet it also depends on what that group has reason to expect from your retailing mix, as compared with that of your competition.

Merchandising Policies

The most fundamental activities of retailing are the buying and selling of merchandise. The qualitative aspects of what type of merchandise is to be handled? In what quantity? When should it be stocked? How is it to be sold? As a principle, a stock should be "balanced"; that is, it should have an assortment and depth appropriate to your customers' demand.

The merchandising of a small store has unique limitations regarding its space, its buying power, and the number of potential customers. In essence, a small retail operation is a specialty store that carries a narrow range of merchandise at a limited number of price points. A prospective merchant, with these conditions in mind, should plan a stock composition according to certain guidelines:

1. Merchandise assortments (style variations) must be targeted to "most-wanted" consumer preferences.
2. Merchandise depth (how many of each) should be related to a carefully projected rate of sale.
3. Buying "mistakes"—merchandise that is marked down for disposal —should be held to a minimum because:
   a. the store's limited traffic impedes fast disposal, and
   b. high markdowns reduce your planned profit.

If a targeted stock is to meet demand and reflect a concern for fashion, the merchandise plan should take into account the benefits of national brands versus exclusivity.

National Brands. Whether or not to carry nationally branded merchandise (when it is available to you, a small store retailer) is a two-sided question. For some stores, brands have recognized advantages: ample markup, known quality, proven specifications, resource responsibility, and favorable disposition towards them by some customers. Yet there are two factors on the negative side: first, to obtain a brand, you must have in-depth purchase, that is, a purchase of a quantity required by the manufacturer. Second, national brands are widely distributed, with strong stock concentration by department stores and other large-scale retailers. So too much brand merchandise could make your already limited assortment of merchandise contract even more, placing your small store in unequal competition—small versus big.

The decision to handle nationally branded merchandise requires careful weighing of the pros and cons.

Exclusivity of Merchandise. Every store would like to have merchandise of high consumer acceptance on an exclusive basis, and in fact all stores—big or small—can enjoy some form of exclusivity, depending on their buying power or their level of merchandising creativity.

Some manufacturers grant various types of exclusivity to stores that can meet certain conditions. The "exclusivity" might assume the form of:

1. confinement of the line within a specified trading area,
2. exclusive representation of given styles (part of a line), or
3. delivery time lead, which gives temporary exclusivity.

These advantages, by far, are given to powerful retailers that have trading area influence, and they give manufacturers the opportunity to use large store relationships for marketing advantages.

The individual small store owner, on the other hand, has an extremely limited opportunity for carrying an exclusive line of nationally known merchandise. Yet even the less powerful retailer—with a keen eye and a hand on the pulse of the trade—can select merchandise from the lines of newcomers or from those who are not distributed widely. Exclusivity or imagery can also be gained through awareness and know-how: the way that individual components of stock (dresses, sweaters, and so on) compliment each other in styles, colors, silhouette, and details. This, too, can be a form of exclusivity, a reflection of taste. This fashion keenness—pinpointing merchandise to consumer preferences—can go a long way toward establishing the recognition among consumers that your store is different and worthy of their patronage. Exclusivity can be attained simply through your expression of fashion creativity.

Pricing

Insofar as your customers' average income level is one of the yardsticks for their identification, a fundamental retail policy is to stock merchandise at certain price levels to attract particular customers. With a limited range of prices, a small store does well to confine its price points to what is referred to as *price zones*—the levels of greatest consumer interest. In this manner, you can target stock to the fastest moving merchandise. You can also eliminate broad assortments and make your stock investment work to its best advantage. This tack limits consumer choices, true, but it helps to build store character, one of the major reasons why some customers prefer to shop in small shops with a particular fashion viewpoint.

Services and Communication

One of the inherent specialty shop advantages is the availability of personal service, a consumer–retailer relationship that has deteriorated in most other sectors of retailing. Knowing that customers shop where they are comfortable, as a store owner you should expend every effort to make personal selling service a competitive "tool."

Other services that can be offered are garment alteration, refunds, delivery, gift wrapping, and fashion trend information.

Communicating your store's image and advantages to customers is an area in which a specialty shop can shine. Although newspapers in metropolitan centers are expensive, they are not required by a store that operates in a confined trading area. With few exceptions, local publications serve small stores just as effectively as newspapers with wide circulations. Other communication forms are:

* *Fashion shows*—in and outside of the premises that create sales and relations with consumers.
* *Publicity*—an unpaid form of sales promotion to create a favorable store image. Again, local publications can be utilized for the purpose.
* *Telephone*—to sell, service, and establish a person-to-person relationship.
* *Direct mail*—an excellent technique to sell merchandise and to build store character.
* *Shopping bags, merchandise boxes, and wrapping paper*—seemingly minor items of sales promotion. Artistically created logo and color-attractive selling paraphernalia are valuable adjuncts of a well conceived sales promotion program.

FIGURE 5-1.

68

Customer Segmentation –
Retailing Mix

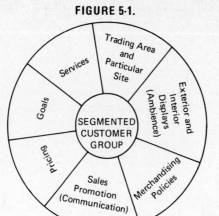

So what, then, is the "retailing mix"? Initially, even before the opening of a store, it entails planned strategies to:

PRINCIPLES

* be competitive,
* develop store character,
* attract customers,
* stock appropriate merchandise, and
* maintain customer relationships.

Since store planning includes the entire range of marketing activities, a small store, like all other business enterprises, is a marketing structure. An essential part of the marketing process is merchandising: planning, buying, and selling. So classically retail marketing also consists of transportation, storage, financing, risk bearing, and obtaining and analyzing marketing information.

This whole line of thought leads to a more precise definition of the meaning of retailing: that is, an activity that includes all merchandising activities, plus the operational and financial functions required to place goods into the hands of the ultimate consumer. Figure 5-1 includes the elements of the retailing mix.

Markups. In this diagram, pricing, although actually a part of merchandising policies, is shown as a separate unit because of its importance. The price at which merchandise is sold must cover the cost of doing business and still yield a satisfactory return to the owner. So you must exercise skill in pricing each unit of merchandise by applying an adequate *markup*, which is the difference between the merchandise cost and its retail price.

The retail system is an accounting method that is discussed in Chapter 8. In this system, all merchandise is carried at retail values, and all merchandising activities are related to and evaluated against retail sales results. Its formula for planning markup is:

$$\text{Markup} = \frac{\text{Expenses + Operating profit + Reductions}}{\text{Sales + Reductions}}$$

where Reductions = markdowns and shortages (which equal the differences between *book* inventory and *actual* stock.)
For example:

$$46.6\% \text{ markup} = \frac{\$70,000 + \$20,000 + \$6,000}{200,000 + 6,000}$$

1. Visit two small independently owned stores that most nearly approximate the one you propose to open. Before you make your visits, select their recent advertisements, if available.

   a. Observe the customers of the stores. Analyze them to develop an averaged profile that you believe identifies their income, age group(s), and any other pertinent characteristics. (See Figures 5-2 and 5-3.)

   b. Review the stock of three classifications of merchandise (such as sweaters, jackets, dresses, and the like). Determine the price points of greatest importance. Do you think they are supportive of store goals?

   c. Determine the stores' forms of communication, and comment on how they relate to their retail mix.

   d. Finally, give your thoughts on how the exterior and the interior of the stores create an atmosphere to influence consumer impulse buying or at least to present a favorable image.

2. Submit the forms in Figures 5-2 and 5-3 to your advisor (instructor). Attach any collected material to support your analysis: newspaper ads, shopping bags, store flyers, and so on.

FIGURE 5-2.

Store Analysis

Date _____

Store _____

Location _____

1. *Customer Profile:*

_____

_____

_____

_____

_____

_____

_____

_____

_____

_____

2. *Merchandise Analysis* (by Classification):

A _____	B _____	C _____
Merchandise Available	Merchandise Available	Merchandise Available
from _____ to _____	from _____ to _____	from _____ to _____
Retail Prices _____	Retail Prices _____	Retail Prices _____
of most _____	of most _____	of most _____
importance _____	importance _____	importance _____
_____	_____	_____

Comments:

_____

_____

_____

_____

_____

_____

FIGURE 5-2. (con't)

Communication Analysis: (attach evidence, if possible, as supporting data)

_____

_____

_____

_____

_____

_____

_____

_____

Exterior and Interior Analysis:

_____

_____

_____

_____

_____

_____

_____

_____

_____

Additional Comments:

_____

_____

_____

_____

_____

_____

_____

FIGURE 5-3.

Store Analysis

Date _____

Store _____

Location _____

1. *Customer Profile:*

_____

_____

_____

_____

_____

_____

_____

_____

_____

2. *Merchandise Analysis* (by Classification):

A _____	B _____	C _____
Merchandise Available	Merchandise Available	Merchandise Available
from _____ to _____	from _____ to _____	from _____ to _____
Retail Prices _____	Retail Prices _____	Retail Prices _____
of most _____	of most _____	of most _____
importance _____	importance _____	importance _____
_____	_____	_____

Comments:

_____

_____

_____

_____

_____

_____

_____

FIGURE 5-3. (con't)

Communication Analysis: (attach evidence, if possible, as supporting data)

_____

_____

_____

_____

_____

_____

_____

_____

_____

Exterior and Interior Analysis:

_____

_____

_____

_____

_____

_____

_____

_____

_____

_____

Additional Comments:

_____

_____

_____

_____

_____

_____

The Need for Professional Advice CHAPTER 6

Due to the competitive nature of retailing, prospective small store owners must seek objective professional advice to validate their plans and thus ensure the greatest possible chance of success. At the very start of a small business venture, therefore, you must prepare a solid foundation through proper planning and the setting of goals, both of which are tantamount to using a roadmap to arrive at your destination. The major goal of prospective store owners is to achieve success within the limitations of their available capital and their personal attributes. So logically your initial plan should provide for seeking professional advice on legal requirements, on standards of business performance, or business contingencies, and on your readiness to assume the responsibility of entrepreneurship. A number of important aspects should be discussed with an appropriate professional, such as:

* the most suitable type of business organization,
* contingent liabilities,
* government requirements,
* required business records,
* the sales level requirement,
* initial and working capital requirements,
* stock turnover,
* the ratio of each item of expense to sales, and
* insurance requirements.

To cover all these areas of concern, the following discussion details mathematical calculations, standards, and legal requirements, all of which may appear to have complex relationships. Are all these details necessary?

74

Not all prospective store owners have the time or the inclination to absorb all these details of preparation. Some prefer professional advisors to keep a close watch over the operation, particularly at the beginning. This approach may be costly, but feasible. In honesty, other successful business-people start with little knowledge of such intricacies, but their lack of preparedness does not impede their success. Whatever their combinations of personal attributes and incidents were, they bring about success. So there is no absolute principle. What is certain is that, "Good detail makes good retail." And good detail should cover all the aspects of preparation. So for those who are dedicated and who have the perseverence to study the demands, let them be forewarned—and most properly prepared—by going through this chapter with care.

The cost of obtaining sound business information and direction can be the most judicious business investment. The proper guidance can minimize costly early mistakes and enhance your opportunities for success. Most subjects for consultation fall in the realm of either (1) the attorney or (2) the accountant.

MANAGERIAL REQUIREMENT

The Attorney

Choosing an attorney who is knowledgeable in the field of retailing is of vital importance. Do not, for instance, choose a criminal or divorce lawyer to give you guidance in retailing situations.

Perhaps the first topic to discuss with the attorney is which type of business organization suits your venture. The selection of a business form depends on such factors as your self-motivation, knowledge, financial situation, desire and/or capacity to coexist with a business partner, and so on. Basically you have three forms of organizations from which to choose:

1. sole proprietorship,
2. partnership, or
3. corporation.

Sole Proprietorship. This type of business is owned and operated by one individual, who has title to all its assets and who is subject to the claims of all creditors. The owner may personally claim all the profits but is also personally responsible for all the business' risks and debts. Since the proprietor is the *only* owner in this case, a sole proprietorship ceases to exist (legally) upon the death of the owner. So he or she must provide for death, injury, or illness.

TABLE 6-1. Pros and Cons of a Sole Proprietorship

Advantages	*Disadvantages*
1. Simplicity of organization.	1. Owner's possible lack of ability and experience.
2. Owner's prerogative to make all decisions.	2. Limited opportunity for employees.
3. Owner's enjoyment of all profits.	3. Difficulty in raising capital.
4. Minimum legal fees.	4. Limited life of firm.
5. Ease of discontinuance.	5. Unlimited liability.

1. Date of formation.
2. Name and addresses of people involved.
3. Statement of proposed business.
4. Name and location.
5. Amount invested by each partner.
6. Sharing ratio for partners.
7. Partners right for withdrawal of funds.
8. Provisions of accounting records.
9. Specified duties of each partner.
10. Provision for dissolution and sharing of net assets.
11. Provision for protection of surviving partners and remaining heirs.

Partnership

A partnership is a voluntary association of two or more persons who operate a business for profit as co-owners. The rights, responsibilities, and duties of partners should be stated in the articles of partnership (Figure 6-1), so as to enhance a close working arrangement and to eliminate the possibility of disagreements.

TABLE 6-2. Pros and Cons of a Partnership

Advantages	Disadvantages
1. Ease of organization.	1. Unlimited liability.
2. Combined talents, skills, and judgment.	2. Limited life.
3. Larger capital available.	3. Divided authority.
4. Definite legal status of firm.	4. Danger of disagreement.
5. More borrowing power.	

Corporation

A corporation is an artificial being in the eyes of the law. *Webster's New World Dictionary* defines it as, "a group of people who get a charter granting them as a body certain of the legal powers, rights, privileges, and liabilities of an individual, distinct from those of the individuals making up the group: a corporation can buy, sell, and inherit property." A corporation is recognized as a legal person and as a business entity. As such, it owns the assets and is liable for the debts it contracts.

TABLE 6-3. Pros and Cons of a Corporation

Advantages	Disadvantages
1. Limited liability to stockholders.	1. Government regulations.
2. Perpetual life.	2. Expense of organization.
3. Ease of transferring ownership.	3. Various corporation taxes.
4. Applicability to all sizes of firms.	4. Activities restricted by its charter.
5. Greater ability to raise capital.	
6. Certain tax advantages.	

Legal Advice Needed. *Business problems spring from a number of sources, many of which warrant legal advice.* Some of these sources are:

* real estate leases and purchases,
* collection of delinquent accounts,
* consumer protection and credit management,
* insurance coverage and liabilities,
* contracts and agreements, and
* once a business is started, federal, state, and local laws and regulations.

Although you do not have to be an attorney, you should be familiar with the laws that affect the day-to-day operation of your business. In the case of major issues, seeking legal advice is the only prudent thing to do.

The Accountant

Well maintained accounting records contribute to business success; poor records can cause business dislocations. So get the help of a competent accountant, one who is knowledgeable in retailing. Further, look for an accountant who is a C.P.A. (certified public accountant), because this professional credential is necessary for the acceptance of financial statements by banks, credit agencies, and other financial institutions.

The first thing an accountant does is set up an accounting system that is best suited to your particular type of business. After that, he or she should periodically audit your records, prepare the necessary financial reports, and take responsibility for preparing the various types of tax returns required by federal, state, and local governments.

Perhaps the most important service, however, is the preparation of two financial statements that enable you, as the owner/manager, to check on the progress of your business: (1) the balance sheet and (2) income (or profit and loss) statement. Full financial disclosure requires both these documents, because the balance sheet reflects the business' financial position at a specific date, while the income statement shows the earnings over a specified period.

Balance Sheet. A balance sheet shows the itemized assets, liabilities, and net worth of a business as of a specific date. As its name implies, the balance sheet must balance according to the following formula:

Assets = Liabilities + Net worth (capital)

1. *Assets:* Anything the business owns that has a money value is an asset. The assets of a small business commonly include cash, notes receivable, accounts receivable, inventories, land, buildings, furniture and fixtures, equipment, and other investments. They are classified as either current or fixed.

a. *Current assets:* These are cash and other assets that are expected to be converted into cash during the normal operation of the business (generally within a year). They include notes receivable, accounts receivable, inventories, and marketable securities.

b. *Fixed assets:* These are assets that are acquired for long-term use in the business, such as land, buildings, furniture and fixtures, equipment, and the like.

2. *Liabilities:* These include all debts that are assumed by the business. Among the more common liabilities are notes payable, accounts payable, and accrued liabilities, such as allowances for unpaid taxes and for wages earned. Liabilities are also classified as current or fixed.

    a. *Current liabilities:* These are debts that are due for payment within a year, such as accounts payable and short-term notes payable.

    b. *Fixed liabilities:* These are debts that are not due for payment within a year, such as a mortgage.

3. *Net worth (capital):* The difference between the totals of all assets and all liabilities is the net worth. If a business has more assets than liabilities, then it has a positive net worth. It is worth something. If liabilities outweigh assets, then the business has a negative net worth.

The *purpose* of a balance sheet is to display the liquidity of a firm. In other words, it speaks to the question, Can this business pay all its debts and still maintain enough working capital to operate on a daily basis without resorting to outside sources for more money?

Yet the balance sheet itself does not answer this question. To do so, you must resort to ratios, which help you determine your business' overall efficiency. The ratios that you calculate from the figures contained in your balance sheet can be compared to standard ratios for your industry. (These standard ratios are published annually by Dun and Bradstreet, Inc. and Robert Morris Associates, and they are put out semiannually by the Accounting Corporation of America.) Lending institutions scrutinize a business' balance sheet, in connection with the ratios it yields, to determine whether the firm is credit-worthy enough to merit a loan or other form of credit.

Measure of Liquidity

For illustrative purposes, the balance sheet in Table 6-4 will act as a source of data for all our ratio computaions.

The Current Ratio. This ratio is one of the best known measures of financial strength. Its purpose is to determine whether a business has enough current assets to meet current debts. The current ratio is computed by dividing Total current assets by Total current liabilities. Using these totals from Table 6-4, you determine current ratio as follows:

$$\text{Current ratio} = \frac{\text{Current assets}}{\text{Current liabilities}}$$

$$= \frac{\$114{,}300}{\$47{,}500} = 2.40 \text{ (or 2.4 to 1)}$$

A general rule of thumb for a current ratio is 2 to 1. But whether a specific ratio is satisfactory depends on the nature of the business and on the characteristics of its current assets and liabilities. Perhaps the surest gauge of a "good" ratio is a comparison against an industry standard.

TABLE 6-4. Illustrative Balance Sheet

XXX STORE
Balance Sheet
_____ , 19XX

Assets

Current assets:
Cash:

Cash in bank	$ 5,000	
Petty cash	500	$ 5,500
Accounts receivable	$60,000	
Less allowance for doubtful accounts	1,200	58,800
Merchandise inventories		50,000
Total current assets			$114,300

Fixed assets:

Land	$20,000	
Buildings	50,000	
Delivery equipment	6,000	
Furniture and fixtures	15,000	$ 91,000
Less allowance for depreciation		3,000
		88,000
Leasehold improvements, less amortization		5,000
Total fixed assets			93,000
Total assets			$207,300

Liabilities and Capital

Current liabilities:

Accounts payable	$30,000	
Notes payable, due within one year	15,000	
Payroll taxes and witheld taxes	1,000	
Sales taxes	1,500	
Total current liabilities		$47,500

Long-term liabilities:

Notes payable, due after one year		40,000
Total liabilities			$87,500

Capital:

Proprietor's capital, beginning of period		$109,800
Net profit for the period	$35,000	
Less proprietor's drawings	25,000	
Increase in capital		10,000
Capital, end of period			119,800
Total liabilities and capital			$207,300

The Acid-Test Ratio. This ratio, sometimes called the "quick ratio," is another excellent measure of liquidity. It is computed as follows:

$$\text{Acid test ratio} = \frac{\text{Cash + Marketable securities (if any) + Receivables}}{\text{Current liabilities}}$$

$$= \frac{\$64,300}{\$47,500} = 1.35 \text{ (or 1.4 to 1)}$$

The acid-test ratio is a much more exacting measure than the current ratio. By not including the inventories, it concentrates on liquid assets, which can be readily turned into cash and whose values are most certain. It also eliminates the possibility of using an inventory that may not be current and that consequently does not reflect a true value. A quick ratio of about 1 to 1 is considered satisfactory by fashion retail standards.

The Proprietorship Ratio. The proprietorship ratio reflects the relationship between the owner's investment in the firm (Capital, end of period) and the Total assets used in the business. It is computed by dividing Capital by Total assets:

$$\text{Proprietorship Ratio} = \frac{\text{Owner's investment (Capital, end of period)}}{\text{Total assets}}$$

$$= \frac{\$119,800}{\$207,300} = 0.5779 \text{ (or 0.58)}$$

For the XXX Store, then, the proprietorship ratio is 57.79 percent of the total investment. The equivalent ratio (0.58) is safely above the conservative minimum of 50 percent.

Working Capital. Working capital is the difference between the Total current assets and the Total current liabilities, expressed in dollars. Hence it is a gauge of how well a business can meet its obligations. On the XXX balance sheet, Total current assets are $114,300, and Total current liabilities are $47,500. Working capital is computed as follows:

$$\text{Working capital} = \text{Current assets} - \text{Current liabilities}$$

$$= \$114,300 - \$47,500$$

$$= \$66,800$$

Profit and Loss (Income) Statement

A profit and loss (or income) statement details the financial operations of a business within a specified period. It summarizes sales (income), expenses (the cost of the operation), and finally the profit or loss for the period. Hence its name: profit or loss (P & L) statement.

How much of a period should the statement cover? Or in other words, how often should this statement be made up? Your accountant should make up such a statement every month to keep you apprised of operational activities. You should also call for a year-end statement to analyze the business for a period of one year, as well as to provide information for a comparison with other businesses of comparable size. With a year-end statement, you have the opportunity to make an in-depth analysis of all activities in the past year and, if necessary, to make adjustments for the one coming. The profit and loss statement is an excellent tool for correcting past errors and for improving on successful methods.

The profit and loss statement is also of great interest to potential investors and creditors. While the balance sheet shows the basic soundness of a company by reflecting its financial position at a given date, the profit and loss statement shows the record of its activities over a period of time. Its historical data serves as a valuable guide in anticipating how a company may do in the future.

The historical data supplied by the profit and loss statement is analyzed, particularly in the retail business, to forecast the future trends of a business. It is therefore of the utmost importance that your accountant use standard procedures in preparing your financial statements, so that they are based on a uniform format within the industry.

Components. As shown in Table 6-5, a profit and loss statement has five major components:

1. Net sales = Gross sales (income from customers) – (Sales tax + Sales discounts + Returns and allowances)
2. Cost of goods sold = Inventory + Purchases — ending inventory
3. Gross profit (or Gross margin) = Net sales — Cost of goods sold
4. Operating expenses = Total of all expenses needed to operate the business from day to day (as itemized in Table 6-5)
5. Net profit (or Net income) = Gross profit — Operating expenses

By studying these components, you attain a more accurate in-depth analysis of the functions of the business. You can then make decisions in an intelligent manner, which may affect the continued growth of the enterprise. For example, if the gross profit (margin) is not large enough to cover all the operating expenses, the business cannot make a profit.

Ratios. An income statement is better analyzed when the numerical figures are changed to percentages or ratios, as shown in the right-most column of Table 6-5. Your store's present ratios may be compared with those of similar firms, with industry averages, or with the store's own past ratios, to evaluate its performance. (A period of 3 to 5 years gives a good comparative indication of its progress, if the firm has been in business that long).

Using net sales as a basic denominator, you have a universal basis of comparison of all other figures in the statement. For example, the Cost of goods sold, valued at $144,350, is not in itself enough for a comparative study. But when it is reduced to a percentage of 57.7 percent, it may be easily compared with past statements or with firms in a similar business:

$$\frac{\text{Cost of goods sold}}{\text{Net sales}} = \frac{\$144,350}{\$250,400} = 57.7\%$$

Importance of the P&L Statement. When the five major components of this statement are analyzed, they point to strengths and weaknesses, as well as to possible changes to ensure continued success. Comparing the ratios for your business to averaged or standard ratios for your industry tells you where your business stands. Table 6-6 lists general operating expense ratios that are industry-approved and that therefore may be used for such com-

TABLE 6-5. Illustrative Profit or Loss Statement

XXX STORE
Income Statement
For the Year Ended December 31, 19XX

Gross sales			$255,000	
Returns and allowances		$1,800		
Sales discounts		2,800	4,600	
Net sales			250,400	(100%)
Cost of goods sold:				
Inventory, December 31, 19XX (beginning of year)			50,000	
Purchases		$150,000		
Purchase returns & allowances	$2,000			
Purchase discounts	3,750	5,750		
Net purchases		144,250		
Transportation		4,100	148,350	
Cost of goods available for sale			198,350	
Inventory, December 31, 19XX (end of year)			54,000	
Cost of goods sold			144,350	(57.7%)
Gross profit on sales			106,050	(42.3%)
Operating expenses:				
Store rent	(F)		16,000	(6.4%)
Advertising	(V)		6,260	(2.5)
Delivery	(V)		3,200	(1.3)
Transportation out	(V)		3,500	(1.4)
Sales' commissions	(V)		20,032	(8.0)
Miscellaneous selling expenses	(V)		4,000	(1.6)
Office expense	(V)		3,000	(1.2)
Property taxes	(F)		3,000	(1.2)
Bad debt expense	(V)		1,500	(0.6)
Office salaries	(F)		7,000	(2.8)
Unemployment insurance	(V)		1,000	(0.4)
Insurance	(F)		900	(0.35)
Total expenses			69,392	(27.7%)
Net operating income			36,658	(14.6%)
Other revenue:				
Rent of land		2,200		
Interest earned		800	3,000	
Other expense:				
Interest expense		1,200	1,800	
Net income before income tax			34,858	
Income tax			6,260	
Net income (net profit, exclusive of owner's salary)			$28,598	(11.4%)

F = Fixed expense

V = Variable expense

TABLE 6-6. Industry-Approved Operating Expense Ratios, Assuming Gross Sales of $250,000

Net sales	100%
Cost of sales	58.0–62.0%
Gross profit	38.0–44.0%
Expenses:	
Wages (including owner's)	18.0–20.0%
Rent	5.0– 9.0%
Utilities and telephone	1.5– 1.7%
Advertising and promotion	2.5– 3.0%
Insurance	0.8– 1.0%
Professional services	1.0– 1.5%
Licenses and taxes	0.7– 1.0%
Supplies	1.0– 1.2%
Depreciation	0.7– 1.0%
Travel	0.6– 0.9%
Miscellaneous	0.5– 0.7%
Total expenses	32.5–41.0%
Net income (before taxes)	3.0– 5.5%

These figures are based on data prepared by the National Retail Merchants Association (NRMA), Dun and Bradstreet, Inc., NCA, and Robert Morris Associates.

parisons. Figure 6-2 is a form on which you can enter the necessary figures for your own business, calculate the corresponding percentages, and then compare them with industry averages in the right-most column. This form, used in connection with the ratios in Table 6-6, gives you an easy-to-read comparison of your business to industry standards. For example, total wages in this table should absorb only 18 to 20 percent of net sales. If the wages in your retail operation take up a greater share, then you know that wages constitute an unusual expense for you.

Breakeven Point

The breakeven point of a business is reached when sales equals fixed plus variable expenses. At this point there is neither a profit or a loss. Note that each expense in Table 6-5 is marked as either variable or fixed. So a profit and loss statement contains all the information necessary to determine a business' breakeven point. But what exactly is the difference between fixed and variable expenses?

Fixed Expenses. These are expenses that do not vary with the volume of the business, such as rent, insurance, property taxes, and depreciation. Fixed expenses are those over which there is no immediate control.

Variable Expenses. These expenses vary in direct proportion to the business volume, and they can therefore be controlled on a short-term basis: sales commissions, advertising, travel expenses, delivery expenses, and the like.

Calculating Breakeven. Using the figures in Table 6-5, you can use the following procedure to determine a breakeven point (as shown in Figure 6-3, which

FIGURE 6-2. Expense Comparison Form

	Your figures		Averages Figures
	Dollars	% of Sales	
Net sales		100%	100%
Cost of goods sold			
Gross profit or margin			
Operating Expenses:			
Total expenses			
Net profit			
Rate of Stockturn			

Use this form to make your own comparisons with typical operating experiences of other retailers in your line of business.

Place your sales figures on the Net sales line in the dollars column. Then place the dollar amount of each of your expenses in the dollars column. Convert the dollar amounts into percentages by dividing the Net sales figure into each of the item amounts. Place these percentages in the % of sales column.

This chart enables you to compare your ratios with the ratios of the average store.

FIGURE 6-3.   85

The Need for Professional
Advice

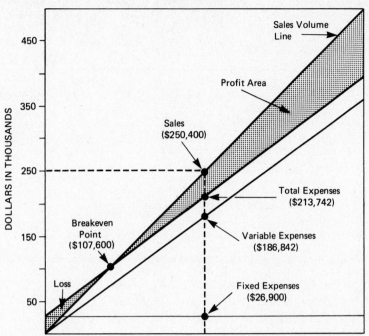

shows the relationships of fixed, variable, and total expenses to sales at all volumes of sales.

1. Draw a perfect square and bisect the angle from the lower left-hand side to the upper right-hand side. This line is the sales volume line.
2. Scale the vertical axis in even units from zero to a potential sales volume. (In this example, the potential volume is $500,000.)
3. Draw a dotted line from the sales volume ($250,400) horizontally to where it reaches the sales volume line. From that point, draw a vertical dotted line to the bottom of the chart.
4. On the vertical dotted line, plot the points for fixed, variable, and total expenses against the vertical axis scale.
5. Draw the lines for fixed, variable, and total expenses from the left axis to the plotting points on the vertical dotted line. The variable expenses connect at point zero on the vertical axis. Fixed expenses and total expenses connect at the point of fixed expenses ($26,900) on the vertical axis.

The breakeven chart is a visualization of what sales volume is needed to "break even." What volume do you need to cover all costs? It also shows the potential profits that can be derived from any planned expansion of sales, and, conversely, the losses that may occur with a decrease in sales. It is a helpful tool in plotting the growth of a business. By knowing the break-even point, you can anticipate problems before they arise.

The breakeven point may also be determined mathematically as follows:

sales = Fixed + Total variable expenses (Variables + Cost of goods sold)

sales = $26,900 + $186,842 (74.6% of Net sales)

Therefore: Fixed expenses = 25.4% of Net sales

$$\frac{\text{Fixed expenses } (\$26{,}900)}{0.25} = \$107{,}600 \text{ (Breakeven Point)}$$

(For purposes of mathematical rounding, the fixed expenses of $26,900 was divided by 0.25 instead of 0.254).

The knowledge that is required of a prospective entrepreneur is comprehensive. Rarely can a small business entrepreneur be conversant with every phase of a small ready-to-wear specialty store. For this reason, experience plays an important role in a successful venture.

The competitive nature of the fashion retail business demands self-discipline, motivation, and persistence. It is a challenge to your initiative, intelligence, and self-esteem.

It has been often said that no one fails in business by knowing too much about one's business. So prospective entrepreneurs should either learn all there is to know about their businesses or be surrounded with professional advisors who can help them down the road to success. Business law and accounting are two areas with which business owners should become familiar. Retail merchants cannot always be lawyers or accountants. But anyone who is going into business should learn as much as possible in both areas to be prepared for the upcoming problems.

1. Use the balance sheet shown in Table 6-7 to determine the factors that contributed to the success of this store, which has completed its first successful year of operation.
   a. Analyze the following business ratios:
      (1) current ratio,
      (2) quick ratio,
      (3) proprietorship ratio, and
      (4) working capital.
   b. Comment on the measure of liquidity shown by this firm, and submit your answer to your instructor for future analysis and discussion.

2. Analyze the profit and loss statement (shown in Table 6-8, and determine the percentages of the five major components).
   a. Compare the percentages with the recognized averages as given in Chapter 1.
   b. Analyze the operating expenses, and offer suggestions for improving profits in the profit and loss statement.
   c. Discuss methods of improving the overall operation, and suggest any changes that might be made for the coming year.
   d. Prepare a chart depicting the breakeven point, and mathematically determine the breakeven point necessary to cover all costs.
   e. Submit the worksheet forms to your instructor giving your impression of the efficiency of the operation for the period just ended. Relate your research to your own store.

TABLE 6-7. Balance Sheet for Assignment 1

XYZ FASHION STORE
Balance Sheet
Period Ending December 31, 19XX

				XYZ Ratios	*Industry Ratios*
Assets:					
Current assets:					
Cash	$10,000				
Accounts receivable	20,000				
Inventories	22,500				
Total current assets		$52,500			
Fixed assets:					
Furniture and fixtures	$20,000				
Building	28,000				
Land	10,000				
Total fixed assets		58,000			
Total assets		$110,500			
Liabilities & Owner's Equity (net worth)					
Current liabilities:					
Notes payable	$10,000				
Accounts payable	15,000				
Accrued liabilities	3,000				
Taxes payable	2,000				
Total current liabilities		30,000			
Net worth		$80,500			
Total liabilities and net worth		$110,500			

TABLE 6-8. P&L Statement for Assignment 2

XYZ FASHION STORE
Profit and Loss Statement
Period Ending December 31, 19XX

			Percentage	Average Percentage
Net sales		$125,000	100%	100%
Cost of goods sold		70,000		
Gross margin		$55,000		
Operating expenses:				
Salespersons' salaries	$12,000			
Commissions	4,000			
Advertising	4,000			
Rent	8,750			
Telephone	2,500			
Insurance	1,250			
Travel	1,875			
Utilities	1,000			
Owner's salary	15,000			
Total expenses		$50,375		
Net profit (before taxes)		$4,625		

OPERATING A STORE (MERCHANDISING) PART II

Setting Policies

A straight line, it is said, is the fastest way to get somewhere. By the same logic, entrepreneurs plan long- and short-term goals, as well as the strategies to attain them. With clarity of purpose and designated strategies, they plan for the following important objectives and/or goals:

* customer-identifiable image,
* employee understanding of how business is to be conducted,
* management of time and effort by entrepreneur,
* the best chance for success, and
* merchandising policies to insure proper direction.

These elements relate to the entire spectrum of retailing: merchandise, employees, operation, customers, and the retailers themselves.

Planning and policy go hand in hand. As part of planning, management's responsibility is to anticipate probable merchandising events and to implement courses of action that best respond to them. Yet an unfortunate truism is that the majority of small entrepreneurs do not take the time to formulate long-range plans and goals since they are pressured by immediate problems and lack of experience. Growth in small operations is therefore usually a happening, rather than the result of careful planning.

Nonetheless, your chances of success are greatly enhanced by setting definitive policies. Profit and viability are the products of setting policies, adhering to them, and attaining goals through carefully worked-out strategies. They are also the result of flexible policies that may be changed to fit new circumstances, such as stiffening competition, altered government laws,

and possibly shifts in the economy.

The following are reasonable and specific objectives for a small store:

* to successfully penetrate a trading area,
* to attain a planned volume,
* to develop a particular store image,
* to appeal to a designated customer group,
* to communicate in a manner that is consistent with the store image,
* to achieve a strong community position, and
* to obtain maximum profit on investment.

Such objectives can best be reached by setting store policies.

Merchandising Policies

Pricing

* Price lines (specific points)
* Price ranges (top to bottom)
* Price zones (most important price lines within price ranges)
* Markup
* Markdown

Timing

* Stock peak date (time of widest assortment and depth)
* Fashion position (fashion leader or follower)

Exclusivity

* Share resources or seek limited or complete control of certain manufacturers

Sales promotion

* Format
* Message content
* Layaway plan
* Credit facilities
* Delivery facilities
* Customer returns
* Special orders
* Nonstore selling

Financial

* Paying debts promptly
* Reinvestment of profits
* Borrowing for expansion

FIGURE 7-1

Policy guideline

```
┌─────────────────────┐
│       STORE         │
│     OBJECTIVES      │
├─────────────────────┤
│      POLICIES       │
├─────────────────────┤
│      MARKETING      │
│        PLAN         │
│   IMPLEMENTATION    │
├─────────────────────┤
│     ATTAINMENT      │
│        AND          │
│    ACHIEVEMENT      │
└─────────────────────┘
```

PRINCIPLES AND PRACTICES

As a matter of sound business principle, enlightened organizations structure marketing activities so that goals and policies are the foundation of marketing practices, as shown in Figure 7-1. Yet many small store owners—because of numerous pressures, limited time, lack of organization and professional help—often "fly blind." They continually react to situations rather than work from planned objectives. Due to their limited capitalization and many duties, an accepted practice among wise owners is to adopt and to adapt the successful practices of sophisticated concerns, scaled down to acceptable proportions for the use in small store operations.

ASSIGNMENT

1. Visit a department store and a specialty store.
   a. List all the services and conveniences available to customers (see Figure 7-2).
   b. List those that are lacking and should be available.
   c. List the facilities for customer credit.

2. Write a detailed explanation (Figure 7-3) of how customer segmentation relates to store policies and how you intend to respond to this relationship.

FIGURE 7-2

Analysis of Store Policies, Part I

a. Services and conveniences available to customers

_____

_____

_____

_____

_____

_____

_____

_____

b. Services and conveniences that are lacking and should be available

_____

_____

_____

_____

_____

_____

_____

_____

c. Facilities for customer credit

_____

_____

_____

_____

_____

_____

_____

_____

FIGURE 7-3

Analysis of Store Policies, Part II

Relationship of customer segmentation to store policies:

_____

_____

_____

_____

_____

_____

_____

_____

_____

_____

_____

_____

_____

_____

_____

_____

_____

_____

_____

_____

_____

_____

Planning and Control of Merchandise

Profit is not an accidental occurrence. It results from careful planning, a large part of which includes techniques to determine merchandise requirements by type, in dollars, and in units. Large-scale retail operators employ sophisticated planning systems, including electronic data processing, because layers of personnel are involved in decision-making and in the need for deep capital investment. In fact, operations of any size can buy computer time and have printouts of their merchandising activities.

Yet small store owners, who function in the dual role of manager/buyers, have neither the time nor the need for complicated planning and control methods. It is well within their ability to maintain orderly and meaningful records by hand, with relatively limited effort, and to develop sufficient information for effective planning and control. The purpose of this chapter is to discuss and to exemplify techniques by which small store owners can maintain a balance between sales and inventory within the constraints of a limited budget.

MANAGERIAL REQUIREMENT

In an operation of limited scope, merchandise must be confined to a well selected narrow assortment of styles, price lines, colors, and sizes. Yet it must still be consistent with probable consumer demand. In other words, the focus of the merchandising goal is to minimize investment and to maximize the rate of sale.

Merchandising by Classification

The first merchandising decision is what type of merchandise to stock. As a practical matter, prospective owners, in all probability, make that decision when they first visualize their stores. To open a ladies' specialty shop, for example, you might consider a range of merchandise types, such as:

* dresses,
* suits,
* coats,
* sweaters,
* tops,
* skirts, and the like.

In retail terms these are *merchandise classifications:* that is, a group of merchandise reasonably interchangeable from the customer's point of view. In a large operation, a classification can encompass a broad assortment and considerable depth. But even with its extensive space, capital, and traffic, such a large operation as, say, a department store still unitizes classifications into *subclassifications:* narrowed segments of expected consumer wants.

Return on Investment. By concentrating on the most consumer-desired types of merchandise, retailers speed up the process of buying and selling goods. Given an adequate markup, the store's return on investment increases in pace with the frequency of this input-output process. Besides the financial benefits of keeping up a quick pace, store owners also have an ongoing flow of new merchandise in stock.

Example: A store has an investment of $30,000 in inventory, which translates into $50,000 at retail value. The sales are $100,000 (two stock turns), and the net profit is $4,000. The return on investment is therefore 13.3 percent: ($4,000 ÷ $30,000).

In another, similar store, sales can be maintained at $100,000 with an inventory whose retail value is $40,000 and which represents an investment of $24,000. The stock turn is therefore 2.5 ($100,000 ÷ $40,000), and the return in merchandise investment is 16.7 percent ($4,000 ÷ 24,000).

The same dollar profit is achieved in both examples, but the percentage of return on investment is greater with the faster stockturn. So by stocking goods with great precision and by speeding up the stockturn, you increase your ratio of average inventory to sales (Net sales:/Average inventory) — and thus the return on your investment. A high ratio is indicative of a healthy fashion stock.

Subclassifications. A prime requisite of small store operation is the determination of subclassifications, specific segments within a classification.

For example, within the *classification* of *sweaters*, you might perceive the *subclassifications* of:

* cashmere long-sleeve cardigan,
* lambs wool crewneck long-sleeve slip-on, and
* cashmere V-neck long-sleeve slip-on.

Because this technique anticipates consumer buying behavior with precision, you can avoid the duplication of merchandise, reduce markdowns, and achieve maximum selling with a minimum investment.

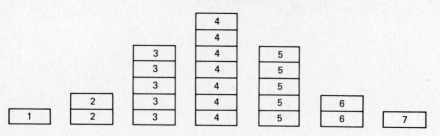

How many classifications, subclassifications, colors, sizes, and other aspects of stock building do you need? The particular answer in any situation depends on sales potential, store size, available capital, and other related retailing demands. In general, however, Figure 8-1 exemplifies the typical initial thinking as to how a stock can be balanced in breadth (assortment) and depth. The classifications are 1 through 7. Each box within a classification represents a subclassification. At the "ends" of your classification range (1 or 2, 6 or 7), the breadth and depth are limited. You have only one or no subclassifications. Toward the heart of your classifications, you have increasingly more subclassifications, for greater assortment and availability. You don't stock everything in the same quantities.

Dollar Planning

The next step is to formulate a budget that allocates a certain number of dollars to each classification and then to each subclassification. As noted in Chapter 6, goods are priced by the retail method of inventory, that is, by keeping track of all stock in terms of retail-value dollars. This method has a number of advantages over the cost method:

1. When inventory is valued at retail prices, it is easier to count (that is, to take inventory).

2. The retail method automatically gives a market value for inventory.

3. It requires a perpetual retail inventory—a value of what is in stock at all times (with adjustments for errors or shortages).

4. It affords a system of goals: You can compare the percentage of merchandising activities to the easily obtainable base of sales, such as markdowns to sales.

Six-Month Merchandising Plan. Using the retail method, the standard device for controlling purchases is the *open-to-buy* (OTB) budget. This is a dollar budget for the purchase of merchandise for delivery within a given period. You derive the open-to-buy figure from the six-month (or dollar) plan. Six-month (as opposed to twelve-month) terms are used because two such plans make up one fiscal year: February through July, and August through January. Each plan has six units, one for each month.

For effective dollar planning and control you need:

1. a sound estimate of sales, that is, an estimate of customer demand for the month;

2. a beginning-of-the-month (B.O.M.) inventory, which is your estimated inventory need for the month based on the planned sales;

3. the maintenance of a planned inventory level, which is controlled by making your purchases based on merchandising events.

On a more pragmatic basis, as shown in Figure 8-2, you have to pin
down several numbers in order to put the dollar plan into operation. To
assess the dollars you require, you must determine:

1. planned sales,
2. planned closing stock for the month, and
3. planned markdowns.

Although the six-month plan seems complicated, in reality it is very logical
and needs only practice for you to become familiar with it. So let's take a
practice example.

Example: Your business is opening on August 1. So you estimate sales
for the *month*, the inventory that should be available at the end of that
month (the opening stock for September 1), and the markdowns for
August. In dollar terms, they are:

Planned sales for August	$25,000
Planned stock for end of month (EOM)	20,000
Planned markdowns	200
Planned purchases (or open-to-buy)	$45,200

The $45,200 is the open-to-buy budget for August, for a new store opening.

That is how you would stock for a new store opening. In a going
operation, you have to adjust the planned purchase (or OTB) figure to the
merchandising activities of the previous month or to what is happening
during the current month.

Example: The figures for August 1 in an ongoing operation are:

Planned sales for August	$25,000
Planned EOM stock	20,000
Planned markdowns	200
Total requirements	$45,200
Less planned inventory as of August 1	18,000
Planned retail purchases	27,200
Less (or minus) stock variation	4,000
Total unadjusted OTB	23,200
Less unfilled orders for delivery this month	1,100
Planned purchases (or open-to-buy)	$22,100

The calculations for an ongoing operation take into account the stock
left over from the preceding month (July), stock variations during August,
and orders placed in the preceding month that have to be filled in the
current month (August). All these factors influence how much you should
purchase for the August B.O.M. stock. The *stock variation* in particular,
which is the difference between the planned and the actual August B.O.M.
stock, in this example was caused by the merchandising activities of the
actual sales, purchases, and markdowns of the previous month (July).

Figure 8-2 is a form that contains information used by most large-scale

FIGURE 8-2

Six-Month Merchandising Plan

SPRING 19–	FEB.	MAR.	APR.	MAY	JUNE	JULY	SEASON TOTAL
FALL 19–	AUG.	SEP.	OCT.	NOV.	DEC.	JAN.	
SALES $							
Last Year							
Plan							
Percent of Increase							
Revised							
Actual							
RETAIL STOCK (B.O.M.) $							
Last Year							
Plan							
Revised							
Actual							
MARKDOWNS $							
Last Year							
Plan (dollars)							
Plan (percent)							
Revised							
Actual							
RETAIL PURCHASES							
Last Year							
Plan							
Revised							
Actual							
PERCENT OF INITIAL MARKON							
Last Year							
Plan							
Revised							
Actual							
ENDING STOCK July 31 Jan. 31							
Last Year							
Plan							
Revised							
Actual							

retailers. In the absence of this form, you can figure a simplified dollar

plan by using this modified formula:

$$\underset{\text{sales}}{\text{Planned}} + \underset{\text{E.O.M. stock}}{\text{Planned}} + \underset{\text{markdowns}}{\text{Planned}} - \underset{\text{B.O.M. stock}}{\text{Actual}} + \underset{\text{orders}}{\text{Unfilled}} = \underset{\text{to-buy}}{\text{Open-}}$$

Using the figures in our example:

$$(\$25,000 + \$20,000 + \$200) - (\$22,000 + \$1,100) = \$22,100$$

We arrived at the same open-to-buy amount in the computation for an ongoing operation. (Total of actual B.O.M. stock and unfilled orders is often referred to as *commitments to date.*) Yet note that the amount of the Actual B.O.M. stock, $22,000, is $4,000 larger than the amount in the original computation, which was $18,000. The difference is the stock variation, which is included in the actual B.O.M. stock. Why? The answer is that, if an August open-to-buy is prepared on August 1, the actual B.O.M. is a known figure.

In an ongoing operation, the OTB must be used on an ongoing basis. Although we have been speaking in terms of months, the OTB can be figured at any time during a month, as well as for any classification of merchandise. With that figure, you control what you purchase to maintain a balance between inventory and sales. At any time of the month, you can check the inventory/sales equilibrium by taking into account:

1. the current rate of sales,
2. the inventory on hand,
3. merchandise commitments, and
4. markdowns taken.

If your stock on hand and your commitments to buy are too heavy, as compared with current sales, then you are *overbought*. So you know you have to restrain further commitments.

Allocating the OTB Among Classifications. Besides your general inventory, you can control each classification of your merchandise in the same manner. Having established a total dollar figure to be spent on merchandise in general, you simply parcel out that amount to various classifications and then to subclassifications, dealing on this level in units and in dollars.

Example: The total OTB for the month of August is $25,000, parceled out as follows:

Sweaters	$10,000
Skirts	5,000
Jackets	4,000
Blouses	6,000

Each of these classification allotments must, in turn, be distributed among its subclassifications by units and dollars by price points. Let's single out sweaters ($10,000) as an example:

Retail	Units on Hand	Units on Order	Total Commit-ment	OTB in Units	OTB in Dollars
$50	0	0	0	130	$6,500
40	0	0	0	50	$2,000
30	0	0	0	50	$1,500
					$10,000

Assuming that this OTB breakdown is for an ongoing operation, the absence of any existing inventory might indicate that the owner is offering a new line of merchandise. If, on the other hand, the owner had some units either on hand or on order, the owner would likely have allocated less of the overall OTB to the sweater classification, in light of what was already in stock or coming in.

In this example, sweaters were bought in three types. If you need greater refinement, a separate subclassification detailing could be:

Cashmere Sweaters

	Retail Price	Units On Hand	Units On Order	Total Commit-ment	OTB	Total Units	$
Long-sleeve cardigan	$60	0	0		11		$660
V-neck long-sleeve slip-on	$50	0	0		11		$550
Short-sleeve slip-on	$40	0	0		14		$560
Short-sleeve cardigan	$50	0	0		15		$750
							$2,520

Further breakdowns could be made for colors, sizes, silhouette, or any other fashion demand.

In way of summary, therefore, you achieve the greatest planning efficiency by taking these steps:

1. Estimate sales for the period of need (one month or two, depending on the time of year, the store's location, and the type of merchandise carried).

2. Estimate the stock you need to keep up with the estimated sales, as well as to have the merchandise level you want at the end of the period.

3. Control your purchases, according to the open-to-buy plan.

4. Allocate the open-to-buy to classifications and to subclassifications (by units and dollars for each price level).

5. Plan colors, sizes, silhouettes, and other stock variations according to their estimated needs, if you see a need for this type of breakdown.

Adhere to these steps, and you should be able to balance your stock with a minimum of peripheral or sluggish selling styles.

When the store is in operation, you should follow some method to achieve a balance not only between dollar sales and inventory, but also between sales and *units*. More specifically, you should know how many units of each subclassification are being sold. Generally, store owners keep track of units through some sort of addition system, called "unit control," which in truth is not a "control" system. Actually, it is a way to compile information about expressed consumer preferences and to establish the selling rate of each style carried. You are thus armed with information to make your upcoming buying decisions.

Three options are available for a small store operation:

1. The *visual system* operates with no records. A visual observation system has nothing inherently wrong with it for a small store application, as long as the manager/buyer is close to the scene. You must be constantly on the selling floor and able to determine how much of what is needed, merely by looking at the stock. In most small-scale operations, the owners are conversant with all phases of requirements since they are constantly "eyeballing" the sales. However, the visual system is not recommended because the owner's illness, absence, or memory loss can become costly mistakes.

2. You can also keep a *running tally* at the cash register by making a tick mark or other notation whenever a sale is made. Select the best-selling styles and record their sales for, say, a day or a week. Then make up a sales tally. An alternative method is to use sales tickets for a later tally, but this approach can be time-consuming and annoying to customers.

3. The most accurate and detailed technique is the *perpetual inventory system*, which makes available:

1. an inventory of every piece of merchandise in stock,
2. the selling rate of every style,
3. the sort of information necessary to make analysis of: the best selling price levels, colors, sizes, garment details, manufacturers, classifications, or whatever factors make for a buying advantage.

Here's how the system works. Make one card for each style you purchase. Record all the details of the purchase, and then put the card into a file by merchandise classification. The information on the card should be as follows:

* manufacturer's name,
* manufacturer's style number,
* classification of merchandise,
* cost,
* retail price,
* number of pieces ordered,
* colors, and
* sizes.

When you receive the merchandise, make a notation on the card. Similarly, when the goods move in any way—through sales, returns to manufacturer, or returns to stock (customer refund)—also note the movement. Theoretically, each card has a book inventory of every piece of merchandise in stock.

Figure 8-3 is an example of a style activity card, which contains the

FIGURE 8-3.

104

Planning and Control
of Merchandise

Manufacturer: Jones & Co.	Style #: 711	Classification L/S CC	Cost $49⁷⁵	Retail Markdown $85⁰⁰		Daily Sales				
Description: L/S Cashmere Cardigan				Week	8/1	8/8	8/15	8/22	8/29	
Sizes	34	36	38	40						
Color					M	/				
Black	//	///⬤	///⬤	/⬤	T	/⬤				
White	//	////	////	//	W					
Ecru	//	////	////	//	Th					
					F					
					S					
Date Ordered: 6/15		Quantity Ordered: 48		Quantity Received: 48		Net Sales: 2 Received: 48 On hand: 46				

record figures needed for the perpetual inventory system. The card can be any size and contain any desired information. The notations to show receipt and movement can vary. In the figure, a vertical line indicates the receipt of merchandise. A circle around the proper vertical line indicates a sale, and a red circle means a return to stock (customer refund).

To record the selling of merchandise, you have two alternatives: one is using sales slips with all the information noted; the other is to use price tags attached to merchandise. The price tag method is called "stub control."

Stub control information, which is taken from the order duplicates the merchandise information placed with the manufacturers, is put on hang-tags. Each order must therefore be "retailed" and completed for hangtag information, which consists of:

1. the retail value of each style,
2. the season letter (the codified time of receipt of merchandise),
3. the merchandise classification (codified),
4. the manufacturer's name (codified), and
5. the size.

These price tags should have at least two parts, one that stays on the garment after it is sold, and one that is retained for activity card recording. (See Figure 8-4). So after a sales transaction is completed, one part of the price tag, the stub, is put into a box for an end-of-day posting.

The hangtag in Figure 8-4 does not resemble those seen in large stores. In modern retailing, large stores use electronic data systems, which require hangtags, or price tickets, to conform to computer-handling requirements.

Summary

A unit control system can vary with the size of store, with the kind of information needed, with how the information is recorded, and with the forms needed to record the information. Texts on merchandising and retailing contain more detailed information about dollar planning (six-month merchandising plans), about the quantitative aspect of merchandising, and about merchandising by classification, including the unit control system,

FIGURE 8-4.

105

Planning and Control
of Merchandise

A style activity card

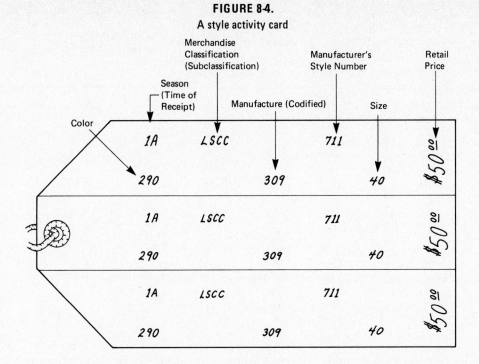

the qualitative aspect, and other retailing methods or systems. This discussion has been confined to the essentials, as tailored to small store considerations.

PRINCIPLES

A systematic approach assures the best use of resources, which is clearly to the advantage of a small business operator. You can use the systems according to the described methods, as discussed, or you might modify them to accommodate the availability of assistants, your own ability to keep records, or any condition that makes you comfortable. The main point is that, whatever planning and control methods you use, they should be complete and realistic enough for decision-making.

You need all the information you can get, especially when first starting out. All plans are estimates, based on experience plus anticipation. When opening a store, you lack the experience factor, and all your decisions must be founded on estimations. The most important plan elements—planned sales and planned stock—must be reasonably accurate to avoid: the dislocation of capital, a poor customer view of what the store represents, or a stock that is out of trend—*the cardinal sin of fashion merchandising!*

If your planning and control prove effective, you will have a good turnover rate, which can be a yardstick of merchandising efficiency. Turnover is the average number of times the inventory "turns over" in a period. A four-time stock turnover, for instance, makes better use of capital than a two-time turnover.

When planning a stock level for a particular time, such as August 1, merchandisers use a related calculation: the stock/sales ratio (as discussed in Chapter 2).

Example: You estimate for August, and the inventory requirement is $100,000. The stock/sales ratio would therefore be 2: ($100,000 ÷ $50,000).

This ratio is established on the basis of stock turnover. In this instance, the stock turnover for a six-month period is set at 3. So as an average for each month, the stock/sales ratio is 2. In practice, the ratio can be different for each month, depending on the relationship of the stock need to the anticipated sales for a period. If the stock/sales ratio is averaged correctly, it will result in the planned stock turnover.

Regardless of size, a retail stock must be planned so that its composition is balanced with sales. The elements of stock planning are:

1. estimated rate of sale,
2. estimated inventory level,
3. classification and subclassification budgets,
4. stock turnover (stock/sales ratio),
5. open-to-buy control,
6. unit control, and
7. markdown provision.

Regardless of method, you should have enough information to know whether:

1. merchandise is in fashion trend;
2. it is in the proper assortment and depth; and
3. sales velocity will yield a satisfactory return on investment.

Today is May 15, and you plan your store opening for August 1. You intend to be in the market the second and third weeks of June to purchase merchandise. You have planned the following:

Sales for the year	$300,000
Sales for the first 6 months	$150,000
Markdowns (10% of sales)	$30,000
Stock turnover for the year	6 times

On the basis of these figures:

1. Plan an open-to-buy for your buying trip (plan to spend 80 percent of the requirements of August and September). Keep in mind that, although your opening stock needs the best coverage you can get, you wish to maintain a "liquid" position, as well as to have open-to-buy for later market fashion developments and for customer-expressed choices. (The maintenance of a liquid position is the practice of prudent fashion buyers.) See Figure 8-5.

2. When you figure the open-to-buy, allocate a budget for *each classification*. First use total dollars for each classification, then divide the allocations into units and dollars for each subclassification. (Have separate plans for each.) See Figure 8-6. Forms for both requirements follow.

3. Submit your plans to your advisor (instructor).

FIGURE 8-5

Six-Month Merchandising Plan

FALL 19		AUG.	SEPT.	OCT.	NOV.	DEC.	JAN.	SEASON TOTAL
SALES $	Last Year							
	Plan							
	Percent of Increase							
	Revised							
	Actual							
RETAIL STOCK (BOM) $	Last							
	Plan							
	Revised							
	Actual							
MARK-DOWNS $	Last Year							
	Plan (dollars)							
	Plan (percent)							
	Revised							
	Actual							
RETAIL PURCHASE	Last Year							
	Plan							
	Revised							
	Actual							

Note: End of month stock is the beginning inventory of the month that follows.

FIGURE 8-6a

Planned Subclassification Stock
(Units and Dollars)

Classification _____ Total $ Allotted = _____

Price Range	Units on Hand	On Order	Total Units Commitment	Open to Buy In Units	Total Units	$

Classification _____ Total $ Allotted = _____

Price Range	Units on Hand	On Order	Total Units Commitment	Open to Buy in Units	Total Units	$

Total _____
Allotted $_____

FIGURE 8-6b

Planned Subclassification Stock
(Units and Dollars)

Classification _____ Total $ Allotted = _____

Price Range	Units on Hand	On Order	Total Units Commitment	Open to Buy in Units	Total Units	$

Classification _____ Total $ Allotted _____

Price Range	Units on Hand	On Order	Total Units Commitment	Open to Buy in Units	Total Units	$

Total _____
Allotted $ _____

FIGURE 8-6c

Planned Subclassification Stock
(Units and Dollars)

Classification _____ Total $ Allotted = _____

Price Range	Units on Hand	On Order	Total Units Commitment	Open to Buy in Units	Total Units	$

Classification _____ Total $ Allotted _____

Price Range	Units on Hand	On Order	Total Units Commitment	Open to Buy in Units	Total Units	$

Total _____
Allotted $ _____

FIGURE 8-6d

Planned Subclassification Stock
(Units and Dollars)

Classification _____ Total $ Allotted = _____

Price Range	Units on Hand	On Order	Total Units Commitment	Open to Buy in Units	Total Units	$

Classification _____ Total $ Allotted _____

Price Range	Units on Hand	On Order	Total Units Commitment	Open to Buy in Units	Total Units	$

Total _____
Allotted $ _____

FIGURE 8-6e

Planned Subclassification Stock
(Units and Dollars)

Classification _____ Total $ Allotted _____

Price Range	Units on Hand	On Order	Total Units Commitment	Open to Buy in Units	Total Units	$

Classification _____ Total $ Allotted _____

Price Range	Units on Hand	On Order	Total Units Commitment	Open to Buy in Units	Total Units	$

Total _____
Allotted $ _____

FIGURE 8-6f

Planned Subclassification Stock
(Units and Dollars)

Classification _____ Total $ Allotted _____

Price Range	Units on Hand	On Order	Total Units Commitment	Open to Buy in Units	Total Units	$

Classification _____ Total $ Allotted _____

Price Range	Units on Hand	On Order	Total Units Commitment	Open to Buy in Units	Total Units	$

Total Allotted $ _____

Merchandising Research CHAPTER 9

From the small store owner's point of view, merchandising research can be INTRODUCTION defined as:

1. the gathering of data about planning, buying, and selling apparel;
2. interpreting that information; and
3. investing in merchandise so as to reduce your risk and to maximize your profit.

Fashion merchandising research techniques are unique because fashion is unique. Hardly any other type of merchandise has the same degree of sensitivity to consumer wants and changes of attitude. In fact, its definition reflects its capricious nature: "fashion apparel is that which is *accepted* by a substantial group of people at a given time and place."

Fashion Merchandising Problems

Fashion merchandising requires adequate preparation through constant research, as well as carefully planned stock. Some of the reasons are:

1. *the inherent psychological obsolescence* — Americans discard apparel when the fashion idea is worn out;
2. *the low intrinsic value relationship* — a $500 dress at retail can contain only three yards of $5-a-yard fabric;
3. *seasonality* — five seasons a year require five retail "shows";
4. *high markdowns* — "old" or slow-moving styles must be sold to make room for the new (older is cheaper);

5. *the fast stock turnover requirement* — the five seasons a year and the constancy of new style development demand stock replacement (as discussed in Chapter 8); and

6. *emotional value* — consumer motivation and emotion demand dramatic promotion.

In this environment, an entrepreneur needs to be highly sensitive to:

* market fashion trends
* activities of competition
* consumer wants, consumer motivation: what people are likely to want . . . at what prices . . . at what time . . . in what quantities.

In fashion merchandising, therefore, research is a fundamental demand for success. Your decisions are not always consistent with actuality, but research effort can help minimize mistakes. A limited scale operation, with finite resources and powerful competition, must make investment decisions on logically developed conclusions.

In Chapter 8, the discussion centered on how to plan a retail stock in terms of dollars and units. In this chapter, we are concerned with merchandise specifics — fashions that are supposed to be in future consumer demand. The research techniques that follow are used in planning a stock for a store opening as well as for maintaining a balanced inventory.

We have made several references to a "balanced stock" — that is, to an assortment and depth of styles appropriate to consumer demand. Even though some texts refer to a "model" stock, such a condition never exists in reality. As a merchant, you must realize that, despite careful planning, you are going to make some buying mistakes. Careful research is the means to stock the right merchandise, at the right time, in the right quantities, at the right prices — with the fewest mistakes. Many sources of information are readily available to you for estimating fashion trends and consumer demands.

MERCHANDISING REQUIREMENT

1. sales records,
2. a resident buying office,
3. competitive stores,
4. magazines and trade publications,
5. resources,
6. fashion services,
7. newspapers,
8. your awareness of current lifestyle,
9. the textile market, and
10. regional markets.

Sales Records

In planning a stock for a store opening, obviously you have no sales records. You have no experience that reveals customer preferences of merchandise types, price levels, manufacturers, colors, sizes, and other merchandise elements that can form the basis for future buying decisions. Yet you can obtain such information from two sources: friendly, noncompeting merchant(s) and a resident buying office. Noncompeting merchants are a commonly used source in a business that depends on preseason judgments of what is right for the season ahead, a subject that is often highly subjective. Everyone in the business exchanges information since no one is secure and knowledgeable enough before the fact — prior to customer-expressed choices at the cash registers. The resident buying office, on the other hand, is a service paid to obtain this information.

Resident Buying Office

A resident buying office is an organization located in a major market for the purpose of representing stores that have their own complement of buyers. These representatives perform three major functions:

1. They research the market.
2. They buy for stores with buyer permission and store buyer direction.
3. They help stores promote goods.

Different types of offices serve different types of retail organizations. For detailed information about offices, texts are available that classify office types and that explain the services they render. For our purpose, two types are suitable:

1. *A small store office:* This office, which caters to small stores, charges a yearly fee, paid monthly.
2. *The merchandise broker or commission office:* This office charges nothing, but it receives remunerations from cooperating manufacturers in the form of a commission based on a percentage of orders placed for their clients. Of the many commission offices, Apparel Alliance lists hundreds of store clients.

When store buyers use a resident buying office during a market visit, they typically discuss the following points with an office representative (the appropriate buyer):

1. the client's store — its size, segmented customer group, location, volume, and related factors;
2. the general market outlook;
3. fashion trends (styles, colors, and the like);
4. recommended manufacturers (and specific merchandise);
5. recommended stock peak dates (when assortment and depth is geared for high traffic);
6. market deliveries;
7. the merchandise recommended for promotion;
8. how and when to promote merchandise;
9. the recommended stock composition (balanced stock); and
10. the open-to-buy relationship to current required commitment.

An office offers many other services, including free ad mats, which are required by stores for local newspaper advertising. Having full-time market

representatives is a required communication linkage in a business that is
characterized by frequent product changes.

Competitive Stores

A thorough examination of local store stocks is one of the most revealing
ways to determine:

1. the importance of price level,
2. the specific styles in the greatest consumer demand,
3. the most effective displays,
4. the important manufacturers, and
5. the required merchandise mix — the percentages of colors, sizes, prices, and so on.

Visit other stores, local and "foreign," and consider your ongoing
visits as a pre-opening necessity and as a continued merchandising demand.
During these research excursions, visit all the fashion departments and
study the merchandise to discern any trends that can be or should be considered for immediate or future inclusion in your stock. While you are on
such trips, another technique is to speak with store salespeople. Through
friendly conversation, you can gather a wealth of information about current
and recurring consumer wants — most valuable data.

Magazines and Trade Publications

Fashion Magazines. These magazines are a communication conduit between
the market and the consumer. Each has a segmented audience (age, income,
and so on), and each has considerable influence in introducing, popularizing,
and motivating consumers to accept fashion ideas. As a fashion retailer,
you should be conversant with fashions selected by magazines, and so you
would subscribe to and note the viewpoints of such magazines as: *Vogue*,
Harper's Bazaar, *Glamour*, and *Mademoiselle*.

Trade Publications. These periodicals perform research and publish information for professionals in the fashion industry. They cover business conditions, as well as national and international information that includes fashion
trends. Hardly any merchandise classification is not covered. At a minimum,
a fashion merchandiser should subscribe to *Women's Wear Daily* and *Retail
Week*. Before opening a store, the prospective merchant should make a
habit of reading the daily issue of *Women's Wear* (published weekdays) and
the weekly issue of *Retail Week* for fashion trends and market development
information.

Resources

Manufacturers are most anxious to impart fashion information, for the
obvious reasons that their lines express their ideas of fashion importance and
their intent to sell them. Yet they can and do relate what other stores are
doing, and so they have retail trend information to give you. In a business
in which all merchants are to some degree insecure, "follow the leader" is
a pervasive practice. For example, Carson, Pirie Scott would surely like to

know what Marshall Field is going to do and vice versa. As a newcomer to fashion, you should seek out manufacturers and their sales representatives for their knowledge, many of whom can be culled out as honest and objective. When you are buying an opening stock for a new store, manufacturers more often than not will "feel" for you in your newness, and they will be anxious to steer you in the right direction — to make you a steady customer.

Fashion Services

Fashion services, such as I.M. International and Tobe, sell information to retailers. Fashion services digest the fashion market — national and international — and then project their estimations of fashion trends. But for a store opening, when you must consider costs, the expense of such a service may be a burden. So this valuable means of fashion direction could be deferred to a later date, when you establish sales, inventories, and the costs of doing business and when you can project expenses in line with probable margin results.

Newspapers

Newspapers are a daily account of the activities of people. Their store advertisements constitute a "filtered" collection of styles that have become the "winners" of fashion market collections. By studying what is currently featured by stores that have fashion eminence, you can get a sense of current fashion trends. True, particular styles may not have a current bearing on your future purchases, but they point to the *direction* of fashion.

Keeping abreast of this direction has become more difficult recently, because fashion acceptance, as an evolutionary process, has greatly speeded up for two reasons: (1) the speed of modern communication and (2) the market's ability to "knock off" practically any style. "Knocking off" is the copying of a high-priced style, usually at a lower price. This is an all-pervasive practice of the fashion market, a way of life.

So fashion merchandisers study newspapers religiously to see what the competition is doing, as well as to compare their thinking with other stores in and beyond their trading areas. For example, merchandisers who subscribe to *The New York Times*, *The Chicago Tribune*, *The Miami Herald*, and *The Los Angeles Times* can compare their current fashion thinking on a regional basis, in addition to obtaining information from stores located in "advance season" areas. As a case in point, Miami stores sell warm weather fashions long before stores in the Midwest and Northeast. So the Miami store advertisements furnish information about what professional buyers selected as the "cream" of the market. The northern merchandiser, after reading the Miami paper, can check the manufacturers of the featured merchandise for selling results. In this manner, you can determine customer preferences in some classifications before placing your new season commitments.

Regardless of a store's size, a merchandiser should become addicted to reading newspapers. As part of the plan for a store opening, the future fashion merchandiser should "digest" current advertisements and even go as far as examining newspaper back issues (in a library or newspaper morgue).

Awareness of Current Lifestyle

Because you can consider fashion (the acceptance of ideas or artifacts) as the current culture, you should not only be alert to how people conduct their lives, but you should also be able to relate their common activities and attitudes to consumer behavior. For example, with greater leisure time and an increased number of women in the work force, certain types of merchandise have become wardrobe requirements, such as jogging outfits, tennis and golf apparel, and three-piece suits for women.

In a sense, a merchandiser must be a practical expert on consumer motivation—on what impels the purchase and use of apparel. You can buttress this awareness by observing what people wear at events that range from ball games to the opera. Other forms of research include observing fashions worn by screen actors, TV performers, and other groups of personalities in the media who have varying degrees of influence on potential consumers.

The term "lifestyle" may be a cliché, but clothing does reflect, in a large measure, who we are and who we would like to be. Your awareness of people's opinions, attitudes, and beliefs is a demand of fashion merchandising. Certainly this requirement plays a part in influencing your decision, as a prospective store owner, to open a store and cater to consumer wants that relate to lifestyle.

Textile Market

Since the materials of fashion are developed years ahead of finished apparel, the textile area is a primary source of information about future fashion trends. Fashion directors and other retail professionals "work" this market before predicting fashion direction. Clearly, this research technique requires time, which a small-scale retailer can use to better advantage. But this information is available in the form of bulletins that a retail buying organization (RBO) fashion director sends to client stores. These bulletins constitute another reason for engaging the services of a firm that specializes in market representation (RBO).

Regional Markets

During the past ten years, merchandise marts have been erected at a surprising rate in strategically located cities. The growing importance of these newly created centers, as well as of those established earlier, is evidenced by the thousands of visiting buyers, by the impressive number of manufacturers, including those with brand name identification, who maintain permanent showrooms, and by the widespread participation of territorial representatives in seasonally held apparel shows. New York, for example, is the mass-produced fashion merchandise capital of the world, and buyers should and do flock to it for many reasons. A regional market outside of New York has advantages for a small store owner, some of which are:

1. The nearness of the market saves money and time.
2. The wide range of merchandise offers the opportunity to compare values.
3. It is an opportunity for merchants to exchange views.
4. It offers one-stop shopping.
5. It has the convenience of evening openings (in most).
6. Frequent seminars by professional fashion organizations keep merchants informed of all developments in all major fashion markets of the world.

A regional mart allows a merchant to:

1. see up to 10,000 lines in one complex (such as in Dallas);
2. become educated in fashion trends with relative ease,
3. exchange merchandising information with peers in the same locale (trading area); and
4. make commitments with assurance that the merchandise is in trend.

A future merchant, by all means, should visit the nearest regional mart, obtain an overview, and relate the availability of merchandise and services to accommodate future needs.

Research Summary

The observational research requirements for a balanced stock essentially consist of personal curiosity, your ability to relate to people, and your capacity to listen carefully. The proof of selling results is a matter of records: the sales results of stores and manufacturers. There is no mystery or state of perfection about building a balanced stock.

Ongoing Operations Need Ongoing Research

The need to research fashion availability and consumer preferences is constant, a part of which is routinized.

Merchant/buyers' knowledge of customers and of their wants and needs should be continually evaluated and reevaluated. Buyers must be people-watchers. Their primary research focuses on market size, on the statistics of the population (demographics), and on their opinions, attitudes, and beliefs (psychographics). They should also be aware of any changes in those values that led to the selection of the particular site or trading area.

They should analyze sales records, when available, for possible indicators of what fashion route they should follow. In researching for a store opening, they might use the sales records of noncompetitors and manufacturers for the same purpose.

Their daily research procedures should include reading newspapers, trade publications, and resident office bulletins, as well as seeing traveling salespeople. They should read fashion magazines. They should watch TV programs and motion pictures with an eye for the apparel worn by the performers.

If salespeople are hired, they should be instructed to listen to customers and to speak up when something was wanted but not in stock, particularly when a sale is lost because of a stock omission.

In conclusion, market research has to come as close as possible to building a stock that responds to the "whats" of merchandising (product, price, time, and quantity).

Essentially you have two reasons for making a market trip:

1. To fill your need at the beginning of a season: How often you go in this case depends on how many seasons your store observes.
2. To replace merchandise: How often you go for this purpose depends on your rate of sale.

Season	Better & High Priced	Moderate Priced	Popular Priced
Fall	April/May	June	July
Holiday	September	September/October 15	October
Resort & cruise	September 15/October	—	—
Spring	October 15/November	October 15/November	November*
Summer	January	January/February	March/April*
Transition	May	May/June	—

*These markets start showing in these periods, but they continue style development throughout the season.

Aside from these reasons, the number of market trips depends on:

1. your store's volume,
2. the merchandise required and the speed of style development, and
3. your distance from the market.

Some big store fashion buyers can be in a market as often as once a week. Table 9-1, for example, is a calendar of fashion buyer visits to the New York market. At the other extreme, some small store owners can visit a market as infrequently as two or three times a year, with considerable dependence on local trade shows and road salespeople. If a regional market is within easy reach, a small store owner might make a buying trip every two weeks. The timing of purchases depends also to a great degree on the lead time required by manufacturers to produce merchandise and to deliver it.

The beginning of season need and merchandise replacement are the two essential purposes for a market trip. The latter depends upon a rate of sale. The former relies on how many of the six fashion seasons a store observes.

ASSIGNMENT

Based on the type of store you intend to establish:

1. Select from the media (newspapers, fashion magazines, trade publications) featured merchandise that you believe represents fashion trends you would stock currently. A minimum of one tear sheet should exemplify each merchandise classification, so that your analysis covers the entire range of calssifications you would stock.
2. Label each tear sheet that supports your decision, as shown in Figure 9-2.
3. Any selected classification that cannot be exemplified by a picture should be exhibited by a rough sketch.
4. The second analysis requires an explanation of why classifications were selected, and how long you estimate they will remain in consumer preference. (See Figures 9-3a through 9-3e.)
5. Submit completed forms to your advisor (instructor).

FIGURE 9-2

Fashion Trend Analysis

Date: _____

	Classification	Exemplified by Item #	Medium	Publication Date

1. _____

_____

2. _____

_____

3. _____

_____

4. _____

_____

5. _____

_____

6. _____

_____

7. _____

_____

8. _____

_____

9. _____

_____

10. _____

_____

11. _____

_____

12. _____

_____

FIGURE 9-3a

Selected Fashion Trend Explanation
(Reason for selection and estimated period of popularity)

Classification (subclassification) _____

_____

_____

_____

_____

_____

_____

_____

_____

Classification (subclassification) _____

_____

_____

_____

_____

_____

_____

_____

_____

Classification (subclassification) _____

_____

_____

_____

_____

_____

_____

FIGURE 9-3b

Selected Fashion Trend Explanation
(Reason for selection and estimated period of popularity)

Classification (subclassification) _____

_____

_____

_____

_____

_____

_____

_____

Classification (subclassification) _____

_____

_____

_____

_____

_____

_____

_____

Classification (subclassification) _____

_____

_____

_____

_____

_____

_____

_____

FIGURE 9-3c

Selected Fashion Trend Explanation
(Reason for selection and estimated period of popularity)

Classification (subclassification) _____

_____

_____

_____

_____

_____

_____

_____

_____

Classification (subclassification) _____

_____

_____

_____

_____

_____

_____

_____

_____

_____

_____

Classification (subclassification) _____

_____

_____

_____

_____

_____

_____

_____

_____

FIGURE 9-3d

Selected Fashion Trend Explanation
(Reason for selection and estimated period of popularity)

Classification (subclassification) _____

_____

_____

_____

_____

_____

_____

_____

_____

Classification (subclassification) _____

_____

_____

_____

_____

_____

_____

_____

_____

Classification (subclassification) _____

_____

_____

_____

_____

_____

_____

_____

_____

FIGURE 9-3e

Selected Fashion Trend Explanation
(Reason for selection and estimated period of popularity)

Classification (subclassification) _____

_____

_____

_____

_____

_____

_____

_____

Classification (subclassification) _____

_____

_____

_____

_____

_____

_____

_____

_____

Classification (subclassification) _____

_____

_____

_____

_____

_____

_____

Techniques of CHAPTER 10
Merchandise Procurement

Due to its intimate relationship with customer patronage motives, store character, and profit, one of the most important activities of retailing is purchasing merchandise. The merchandiser's job consists of searching out and selecting the most appropriate resources, relating their importance to the store, choosing their most suitable styles, negotiating for best possible purchase terms, and creating resource relationships for mutual profitability. Since in Chapter 9 we discussed how often a small store owner visits a market, in this chapter we will treat the "where" and "how" of merchandise procurement.

Merchandise can be purchased by visiting a market or by in-store methods. The total scope of merchandise procurement methods is:

1. visiting the New York market (the largest),
2. visiting a regional market,
3. working with travelling sales representatives,
4. telephone or mail, and
5. using a resident buying office.

Merchandise Plan Importance

You should complete all your buying plans before making merchandise commitments. So prior to visiting a market or placing orders, formulate the following information:

1. the merchandise plan,
2. the established open-to-buy figures (dollars and units),

3. an allocation of a budget for each classification and/or subclassification, and

4. an open-to-buy in units within each classification at specific price points.

Discretionary plans might include your estimated requirements of colors, sizes, and fabrics. Note, though, that the pattern of customer size preference is fairly consistent; variations depend on current silhouette characteristics, so when a style feature is of ample specifications, a size 10 can fit a size 12 figure.

Purchase plans are not rigid. They can be changed in terms of subclassifications, colors, fabrics, and price lines, depending on new fashion trends and current market conditions. Yet you should exercise restraint in the area of the dollar budget, the open-to-buy. Unless you have compelling reasons, *keep your merchandise purchases within the planned dollar commitment.*

Whether you are buying for a new store or for an ongoing operation, the guidelines for selecting *new* resources are the same. In the fashion market the number of manufacturers far exceed any retailer's need. So you must have criteria for the selection of vendors that offer conditions of greatest advantage—short- and long-term. The following are manufacturer practices and/or standards that you as a retailer should investigate before selecting the most suitable ones for your operation:

Merchandise

1. Suitability of type
2. Distinctiveness for clientele
3. Timing
4. Brand name importance (if store desired)
5. Specifications

Competitive strategies (manufacturer's)

6. Clearance policies
7. Distribution policy
8. Price maintenance attitude

Promotion Availability

9. Cooperative advertising
10. National advertising
11. Dealer aids

Sale Terms

12. Transportation cost
13. Anticipation
14. Quantity requirements
15. Price

The technique of procuring merchandise is essentially the same for both new stores and stores in operation. The difference is that a new store has no past experience to help in evaluating the sources of merchandise. Let's take the two situations one at a time.

**MERCHANDISING
REQUIREMENT**

From the outset, a merchant without experience should never purchase merchandise in the store before its opening—that is, before getting out to the market for a broader perspective. Although manufacturers' representatives can eventually become important allies, a neophyte retailer has no basis for weighing what these representatives say in presenting their lines. The newcomer to fashion is hardly in a position to evaluate the importance of particular lines of merchandise before seeing the larger picture—total market merchandise availability. You have to "shop around" before buying.

As a corollary strategy to formulating unit and dollar plans, you should learn what is accepted in the trading area of the store. To ascertain which resources are of importance to competitive retailers, shop both the department and the specialty stores. With this preparation, you find out "how much" you need in dollars and units, as well as "where to obtain what."

Since your first market trip is a kind of orientation, visit the New York market—the mecca of fashion marketing. By visiting various resources and by meeting their principals to establish relationships, you start to grasp the tempo, the operations, and the nature of the fashion business—a unique sector of American industry.

The Buying Office. Besides the advantages of a resident buying office discussed in Chapter 9, an RBO gives you "eyes, ears, and legs" in the market. You have the trend information available as part of a composite fashion market picture. After in-depth discussions with the appropriate RBO representatives (dress, coat and suit, raincoat, and sportswear "buyers"), as well as with the office fashion director, you are ready to shop the market.

Shopping the New York Market. As a first step, concentrate on the general fashion trends. Spend the first two days as an observer. Regardless of merchandise's appeal, make no commitments. Accompanied by the resident representative (the RBO "buyer"), obtain information about recommended resources, such as the background of individual manufacturers' relations with stores, their delivery records, their reorder performance, their dependability, and their market importance.

Beginning with the third day, shop resources with a mind for which ones you might select for order placement. To make the best choice, shop resources by classification. For example, shop junior dress resources of particular price ranges, then pant makers, skirt manufacturers, and so on. In this manner, you can compare the best prices, styles, quality, and finally which merchandise is most appropriate for your store's clientele. As a technique for merchandise evaluation, buyers use self-developed code numbers for styles. For example, a check could denote "good style," a double check "very good," and a triple check "excellent." With this sort of system, they determine the probability of style importance for:

1. regular stock inclusion,
2. advertising possibility,
3. fashion prestige, and
4. testing for customer acceptance ("prophetic" styles for possible future trends).

Most storekeepers, even those of large stores, make temporary "commitments" on manufacturer order forms, which they *take with them for later review* to insure that the commitments are *within the original mer-*

chandise plan by dollars and units. You can do so also. Particularly as a first-step safeguard, after having "spent" the budget on paper, review all the orders with the resident representatives to ensure:

1. trend coverage,
2. proper resources,
3. competitive prices,
4. timely deliveries, and
5. compliance with merchandise plan.

Once you are assured that the intended commitments are in line with the merchandise plans, you can detail your orders on store forms, either in the hotel during the market trip or upon your return to the store. You really should send all your orders to the resident representative for placement with manufacturers since the office has an established relationship with the resource, which you probably do not have yet.

The Order Form. Although a commitment placed with a manufacturer is a contract that binds both parties, manufacturers sometimes violate delivery dates. So to ensure proper and prompt delivery and to stay abreast of which part of commitments will not be honored, give copies of your orders to the RBO representatives, who are in a position to follow up unfilled orders when you request them to do so.

As a contract, an order should detail the following information:

1. the date of order,
2. your proper address,
3. shipping instructions (carrier and FOB terms),
4. order terms (trade and cash discounts),
5. a specific order completion date,
6. the details of colors, sizes, and quantities,
7. the price per style,
8. the total cost,
9. insurance, and
10. any special arrangements.

Also keep a copy of the order in a file, awaiting delivery of the merchandise. Upon delivery, you need this copy to check the merchandise received against the order as written, to verify proper shipments as to styles, colors, sizes, and quoted prices. The order copy may also be used to maintain the book inventory, to maintain unit control records, and to prepare retail price tickets.

Regional Markets. Since the development of modern ready-to-wear clothing, New York has maintained the position of "fashion capital of the world" for mass-produced apparel. Yet as part of the post-World War II boom phenomenon, merchandise mart construction has also flourished. As we have already noted, these relatively new centers enjoy immense popularity among buyers, manufacturers, and territorial representatives. Among the mart's advantages are:

1. convenience of location,
2. reduced travelling cost,

3. wide range of merchandise for buyer comparison,
4. adequate parking and hotel facilities,
5. the opportunity for buyers to exchange views in in-house restaurants,
6. one-stop shopping, and
7. the buying convenience of some night and weekend openings.

The most numerous participants of regional markets are small stores because they save time, money, and effort at these marts. In addition, owners don't have to take on extra help in the store during their absence, and, at the marts, they can exchange merchandising and financial information with their peers.

To illustrate the importance of the regional mart:

* Chicago's Apparel Center includes 1,300,000 square feet of permanent showroom space and a 140,000 square feet in its Expo Center, with over 4,000 featured lines.
* Dallas houses 1,600 showrooms and more than 10,000 fashion lines.
* Los Angeles contains 2,000 showrooms, covers more than 2,500,000 square feet, and shows as many lines as Dallas, with annual sales that exceed $2 billion—about 15 percent of the nation's total apparel business.

Obviously, regional marts can serve the small store owner's needs. Yet you should realize that when local retailers swarm to one general source of merchandise, the stores in a local trading area tend to acquire a look-alike image. So a complete dependency on a regional mart may have a negative effect on the retailer's plan to be "different." Another disadvantage is that, since manufacturers' decision makers make New York their headquarters, advantageous terms are difficult to obtain from their representatives or agents. Still another disadvantage is that in some areas manufacturer delivery control is beyond the marts, since it is controlled by personnel in firm headquarters.

Shopping a mart is much the same as shopping the New York market, with one difference. You don't have the services of a resident office in a regional market.* So you don't have the security of a merchandising confidant, who is an asset of considerable value when you depend so much on a delayed "approval" of your decisions—that is, on customer acceptance.

Small Store Considerations. When a large retail operation procures merchandise, it has a chance at three advantages:

1. a better price than a small store might get,
2. preferential delivery, and
3. merchandise exclusivity.

Despite national laws, for practical purposes, a powerful retailer enjoys advantages not available to small retailers. A small store with limited buying power is often penalized because the average manufacturer has a greater interest in serving the powerful, who influence other stores within a trading area. As a complementary reason, small orders represent a great delivery cost to manufacturers, who prefer to concentrate on larger orders.

So small store owners must be creative in the selection of their re-

*There is RBO service in some major markets, such as Los Angeles.

sources. A retail truism is that, with some exceptions such as designer names or nationally branded merchandise, customers buy merchandise classifications. On the other hand, a specialty store's strengths are personal service and merchandise uniqueness. So it behooves the smaller retailer to play into specialty store strengths, rather than into those of big stores. Brands can have important meaning, but many successful entrepreneurs prosper with few or no brand name styles.

A constant small store problem consists of late or incomplete deliveries. This problem should be recognized and handled in a routinized manner. Recognizing that, on occasion, some nationally distributed manufacturers either do not complete small store orders or do not ship them at all, you must follow a method of merchandise control so that you do not tie up capital unnecessarily. When you make a commitment, set aside a budget that cannot be duplicated. Then energetically follow up your orders. But once you deem an order as too late — beyond the cancellation date — cancel the order, and use the set-aside budget for similar merchandise with a more cooperative manufacturer.

A Store in Operation

When procuring merchandise for a store in operation, you have the advantage of experience. A store in operation has records, which show:

1. the merchandise's rate of sale,
2. the best price lines, colors, fabrics, sizes, and the like,
3. the manufacturer's cooperation (original and reorder delivery dates),
4. the merchandise returned,
5. the timing of consumer buying patterns, and
6. the manufacturer's contribution to profit.

These records give you a foundation for planning and for buying with a certain degree of confidence based on past experience.

Styling Out. As trends develop during a season, you have to "style out." In this method, you compare accepted styles within a category to determine specifically what attracts consumers. The best-selling classifications or subclassifications then receive reorder concentration based on their importance, and those of minor importance are sold off or marked down. In this manner, you increase your selling rate because the stock contains a greater percentage of merchandise that is the most wanted or desired.

Classifying Resources. Another good business practice is to classify your resources according to their importance in effecting favorable store image and in contributing to profit:

Key or *preferred* resources are suppliers who are used in far greater proportion than other manufacturers. They contribute volume, profit, and a favorable store image. They are important also because they influence customer patronage and give your store a fashion point of view. Every well-developed fashion operation is founded on the inclusion of key or preferred resources.

Not every resource has what it takes to become a key resource. When evaluating manufacturers for possible use as key (or prime) resources, consider their:

1. financial security,
2. production capacity,
3. distribution policy,
4. reliability and dependability, and
5. fashion leadership.

Stock resources have moderate store success and are stocked on a fairly consistent basis. They are well regarded, but their importance is somewhat lower than a key resource.

Item or *fringe resources* are suppliers who specialize in a selected fashion item or who concentrate their production on an opportunistic basis — knocking off one of the market's current best reorder styles.

Secondary resources are suppliers who are used from time to time, when their styles are sufficiently important and competitive. Although they are not prime resources, they deserve to be shopped because they often feature styles for fast delivery when current sales demand a short delivery term.

Shopping resources are suppliers whom a store does not use currently but who are worthy of shopping in case they develop potential "winning" styles.

The manufacturing sector of the fashion industry has over 15,000 competing firms that offer to sell merchandise to stores. Even with a small store owner's limited personal knowledge and statistical records, finding out where manufacturers are located and what they make presents no problem. Trade publications, building directories, newspapers, regional mart information kits, hangtags on merchandise, and travelling sales representatives are all sources of information that list manufacturers for potential use. The critical issue of merchandise procurement is the selection of the proper number and kind of makers who contribute the best retail value to your store — who deliver timely fashions in demand by your store's selected customer group.

PRINCIPLES OR PRACTICES

Resource Usage

As a rule of thumb, purchases of small quantities from numerous manufacturers is usually considered as "scattered buying," which can cause customer confusion and low-profit stock. Having something of everything for everybody is not a small store's mission. Rather, merchandise concentration can result in adequate stock depth, the continuity of quality, and consumers' recognition of your store's fashion expertise. The specialty store's concept is the specialization of merchandise type and price lines for a selected audience. Again, a small store should play up its own basic strength.

Vendor Analysis

With well kept unit control records, you should be able to examine the performance of every resource on a planned periodic basis. Poor performers should be eliminated and replaced. But if a resource is stocked for the purpose of prestige or for another specific purpose, you can apply a different rating system.

You should apply a qualitative resource analysis against every style performance. Individual style performance investigation can reveal a store's ability to sell particular types of merchandise. With knowledge of the best-selling styles, you can be more selective in your choice of new merchandise, and you can deal more advantageously even with key resources.

Group Purchases

Although large-scale retail operations have the inherent ability to make volume purchases, the small store may join with other stores to enjoy the same advantage. For example, a store can participate in group purchases initiated by its resident buying office. Or it can make an alliance with other stores of similar size and characteristics that are not competitors for the purpose of pooling their purchase power.

Market Fashion Information

Seasonally held fashion shows, which are presented during market weeks, are sources of fashion trend information and resource merchandise availability. These fashion shows are presented by manufacturers, fashion magazines, and resident buying offices. They are attended by most retailers as a source of fashion news. Fashion shows are an excellent means of viewing new season trends since the merchandise represents the extrapolation of styles most likely to succeed based on the analysis of fashion experts.

Market Visits

As discussed in Chapter 9 how often a store owner visits a major market is related to store size, volume, location, and policy. Yet small store merchants can visit regional markets with frequency because of their typical convenience. On the average, small store owners should be in the market at least five to six times a year to cover the total range of market trip purposes of:

1. new season coverage,
2. stock fill-ins,
3. new market developments,
4. special purchases,
5. reusage of money (from the cancellation of overdue orders),
6. group purchase arrangements.

Special Buying Arrangements

In the fashion market, which is subject to so much change and so many variables, manufacturers often have to dispose of their finished goods. When they have to do so, retailers have opportunities to purchase merchandise well below its original wholesale cost. Obviously, large stores are in the best of circumstances to take advantage of such offerings. Yet small stores have similar opportunities to make this type of deal. So if you are offered merchandise that looks like a good deal, exercise extreme caution. Excess goods are the result of someone's miscalculation — a resource mistake. Buying such a bargain could be a second mistake — yours.

The best promotional purchase is the repurchase of successful merchandise from a key resource. A purchase under these conditions can be a true bargain. The assurance is that a key resource can be depended on to respect a mutually profitable relationship, and consumers recognize the value of current best-selling styles at a new lowered price.

Summary

The time-honored merchandising hypothesis is that merchandise well purchased is merchandise half-sold. As a retail truism, a retailer must stock merchandise only after searching, evaluating, selecting, negotiating, and reviewing the offerings of a wide variety of potential vendors.

1. Visit a local specialty store and a department store. Analyze six classifications of merchandise in each store, and list under each classification the manufacturers who are "key" resources and why? Use the sheet in Figure 10-1.

2. Make a list of five nationally known manufacturers in the stores you have visited that you might not consider for your store and why? Use the sheet in Figure 10-2.

3. Assuming that you are in the planning process of opening a store, list four major merchandise classifications. Based on this in-store project, list two resources you would select for each classification as probable key resources. Why? Use the sheet in Figure 10-3.

ASSIGNMENT

FIGURE 10-1
Classification Analysis

SPECIALTY STORE   DEPARTMENT STORE

Classification   *Classification*

1. _____   1. _____

_____   _____

_____   _____

_____   _____

Key resource and why   Key resource and why

2. _____   2. _____

_____   _____

_____   _____

_____   _____

Key resource and why   Key resource and why

3. _____   3. _____

_____   _____

_____   _____

_____   _____

Key resource and why   Key resource and why

4. _____   4. _____

_____   _____

_____   _____

_____   _____

Key resource and why   Key resource and why

5. _____   5. _____

_____   _____

_____   _____

_____   _____

Key resource and why   Key resource and why

6. _____   6. _____

_____   _____

_____   _____

_____   _____

FIGURE 10-2

Classification Analysis

SPECIALTY STORE	DEPARTMENT STORE
Nationally known resources	*Nationally known resources*

1. _____

_____

_____

_____

Not considered and why

2. _____

_____

_____

_____

Not considered and why

3. _____

_____

_____

_____

Not considered and why

4. _____

_____

_____

_____

Not considered and why

5. _____

_____

_____

_____

Not considered and why

1. _____

_____

_____

_____

Not considered and why

2. _____

_____

_____

_____

Not considered and why

3. _____

_____

_____

_____

Not considered and why

4. _____

_____

_____

_____

Not considered and why

5. _____

_____

_____

_____

Not considered and why

FIGURE 10-3

Classification Analysis

Major Classifications

1. _____

2. _____

3. _____

4. _____

Probable Key Resources

1. _____

Why?

_____

_____

_____

_____

_____

2. _____

Why?

_____

_____

_____

_____

_____

Sales Promotion CHAPTER 11

Sales promotion is the third "P" of merchandising. It follows planning and purchasing, and it exerts considerable influence in creating the main "P" of retailing — profit.

The term "sales promotion" is loosely used, often as synonymously with the term "advertising." Actually, it includes *any* means that influences the purchase of a product or an idea. With such a definition, sales promotion encompasses a wide range of activities. Partially on account of its scope, it requires a plan for selecting and implementing ways to turn customers into buyers, with the longer-term goal of influencing continued store patronage by old customers while attracting new ones.

Sales promotion activities are classified into two types:

1. *Nonpersonal activities* are so numerous that they must be confined to those that prove effective as part of a coordinated promotional mix within the constraints of your budget.
2. *Personal selling* consists of "an oral communication with a prospective customer for the purpose of making a sale of merchandise." It is one of the most effective sales promotion tactics of small store merchandising.

Since this is not a book on personal selling techniques, this chapter concentrates largely on nonpersonal sales promotion methods.

Sales Promotion Activities

Nonpersonal activities that are available to small store operation include:

1. exterior displays (discussed previously),

140

2. interior displays (discussed previously),
3. newspaper advertisements,
4. fashion shows,
5. direct mailing pieces (including catalogs),
6. radio,
7. publicity,
8. telephone, and
9. "personalized" advertisements (such as artfully conceived shopping bags, wrapping paper, and flyers).

As a prospective store owner with an eye on cost as well as your plan for promotional effectiveness, you should analyze and select sales promotion components on the basis of how each promotional element can contribute to:

1. the acceleration of sales, and
2. customer patronage motives.

Prior to the store's opening, your sales promotion plan should be in place and ready to go. Its goals should be:

1. to announce the store's opening, and
2. maintain a program of communications with current and future customers (after the store opening).

The average sales promotion budget of a small store is based on a rounded 3 percent of sales, excluding the cost of sales personnel.

MANAGERIAL AND MERCHANDISING REQUIREMENTS

Store Opening

To attract customers to a new store opening, you must settle on two plans:

1. how to reach the segmented group, and
2. how to stimulate enough interest in that group for them to visit the store.

The many alternative sales promotion activities involve standard procedures, but they also require professional support.

Direct Mail. Commonly used by larger retailers, this approach can also be part of a small store's promotional program. *Direct mail* is advertising sent through the mail. It generally takes the form of the advertising that most firms use when they start into business. Yet the message of a direct mailing piece can take one of a variety of forms: a reproduction of a scheduled newspaper advertisement, an invitation to attend a "private" showing, or any message that serves the ultimate purpose of stimulating the desired response — a store visit.

Although the audience size of a specialty shop varies, a list to cover any group size can be purchased ready-made from a mailing list firm. Most such lists, however, do not necessarily target prospects with a "rifle" approach, so they may include people who have no interest in a given product or store. Nonetheless, the cost of a "buckshot" mailing could be regarded as a sound investment.

Subsequent to a store opening, consider direct mail as an important periodic communication to highlight such events as seasonal fashion presentations or close-outs (that is, store-wide reductions of merchandise).

You can also prepare a modest seasonal catalog at a relatively nominal cost. But one that is comparable to those mailed by department stores is costly, beyond the budgeted percentage of most small operations. To do a catalog, you must have a long-term merchandise commitment to assure timely delivery and a plan for replacement of the goods sold. You also incur expenses for artwork, modeling fees, and mailing. If your store is a member of a resident buying office, it has the opportunity to participate in office-prepared catalogs for its clientele. In this way, your cost is held to a minimum, within the budget of most stores, and the store logo can be inserted to make the catalog appear store-prepared. Merchandise is selected by the resident buying office (usually in conjunction with a steering committee of member store buyers), and some reorder arrangement is made for participating stores.

Publicity. Also a characteristic of a large store's activities, publicity is in a sense not a part of sales promotion, particularly because it cannot be necessarily controlled for inclusion in a program. It is an unsigned and unpaid commentary in public information media. In another sense, it is news that a medium publishes because of probable reader interest. A small store in a metropolitan area could hardly expect a submitted publicity release to be published. But a store opening in a locale of limited population could be a news event worthy of publication. So, regardless of location, explore the availability of local media as sources of "free advertising." To ensure the greatest possibility of publication, make sure the release contains information that is newsworthy to the readers of the selected publications. To do so, the press release is best done by an advertising person. In a small town, a visit to a news editor might turn the "trick."

Radio. In competition with a more recent technological development, television, radio has become a popular medium for advertising. Radio messages can reach local audiences at minimal cost with relatively easily prepared messages. The broadcasting of a store opening, depending on message frequency, can be surprisingly low in cost in many sections of the country. It is certainly worthy of your consideration as part of the opening campaign, and later as a continued promotion medium.

Program Maintenance

For a small store's growth, you must increase specialized group patronage. In the course of doing business, satisfied customers will spread the good word about your small store through customer testimonials — a much desired merchandising result. So, regardless of your promotional strategies and tactics, their ultimate goal is simply to convince consumers that your store is a "better mousetrap."

What is the best mix of promotional activities? The composition of media and their programmed costs depend on the variables that you encounter during operation. The regularity of advertisements, media effectiveness, promotional themes (fashion or price), and other sales promotion elements are all a matter of your experience and of what you expect in way of the trading area's environment. As a general evaluation of what constitutes good advertising, Figure 11-1 contains a checklist from the Small Business Administration booklet, *Small Store Planning for Growth*.

FIGURE 11-1. Checklist for Promotional Advertising

*Merchandise	Does the ad offer merchandise having wide appeal, special features, price appeal, and timeliness?
Medium	Is a newspaper the best medium for the ad, or would another — direct mail, radio, television, or other — be more appropriate?
Location	Is the ad situated in the best spot (in both section and page location)?
Size	Is the ad large enough to do the job expected of it? Does it omit important details, or is it overcrowded with nonessential information?
*Headline	Does the headline express the major single idea about the merchandise advertised? The headline should usually be an informative statement and not simply a label. For example, "Sturdy shoes for active boys, specially priced at $6.95," is certainly better than "Boys' Shoes, $6.95".
Illustration	Does the illustration (if one is used) express the idea the headline conveys?
*Merchandise information	Does the copy give the basic facts about the goods, or does it leave out information that would be important to the reader? ("The more you tell, the more you sell.")
Layout	Does the arrangement of the parts of the ad and the use of white space make the ad easy to read? Does it stimulate the reader to look at all the contents of the ad?
Human interest	Does the ad — through illustration, headline, and copy — appeal to customers' wants and wishes?
*"You" attitude	Is the ad written and presented from the customer's point of view (with the customer's interests clearly in mind), or from the store's?
*Believeability	To the objective, nonpartisan reader, does the ad ring true, or does it perhaps sound exaggerated or somewhat phony?
Type face	Does the ad use a distinctive typeface — different from those of competitors?
*Spur to action	Does the ad stimulate prompt action through devices such as use of a coupon, statement of limited quantities, announcement of a specific time period for the promotion or impending event?
*Sponsor identification	Does the ad use a specially prepared signature cut that is always associated with the store and that identifies it at a glance? Also, does it always include the following institutional details: Store location, hours open, telephone number, location of advertised goods, and whether phone and mail orders are accepted?

*The seven items starred are of chief importance to the smaller store.

The fundamental purpose of sales promotion is to reach the most important merchandising objective: to keep the selling rate equal to or better than planned sales. To achieve this end, consumers must be impressed with your store's ability to cause a state of betterment.

Personal Selling

By now you know how critical small store personal service is to the success of a small store — that its importance cannot be overstressed. As a practical matter, you also know that most products that you can offer for sale are not meaningfully different from those of your competition. A "fashion," after all, is only the consumer's acceptance of a combination of style elements: silhouette, color, fabric, and details. In the sense that either your merchandise or its counterpart is available only in a given store, style exclusivity is a fallacy.

Consumers search mainly to satisfy their needs. They seek a state of betterment through the acquisition of apparel — largely a psychological need. As a retailer you must recognize that your customers' emotional needs are best satisfied when you are knowledgeable, willing, and able to understand their quest. You must also exercise patience and fill their needs to their benefit. If you approach personal selling this way, your customers will have a good experience and favorable memory of your store. Buying satisfaction is the foundation of long-term consumer loyalty. In essence, a small store operator has the unique opportunity to create a most pleasant selling environment by creative selling, by causing discontentment in customers with their present wardrobe, and by stimulating them to achieve satisfaction by buying a new one. As a principle, product quality contributes to successful retailing without question. But the great advantage of a small store customer relationship is that the typically limited traffic permits you to offer consumers the opportunity to enjoy a buying experience.

Special Promotional Events

Although most customers favor stores carrying regular assortments at maintained price levels, they also respond to special events. At these periodic events, you can offer merchandise at special prices, thereby extending bargains to old customers and widening your customer base. To round out a comprehensive program to widen the customer group, even beyond the trading zone, you might try:

1. private sales for regular customers;
2. lay-away plans (out-of-season purchases with payment later);
3. trunk showings (previews on the selling floor of the coming season's fashions prepared with a salesperson's samples); or
4. fashion shows held in a local auditorium, possibly to aid a civic or charitable purpose.

Sales Promotion Considerations

Sales promotion is a major part of the retail effort. Continually attaining your planned sales rests to a great degree on the effectiveness of your promotional activity, personal and nonpersonal. Your efforts should be honest, consistent, and characteristic of the operation. Particular promotional ploys lean heavily on objectives, costs, and promotional results.

How do you know whether your promotional activities make any difference in sales? To evaluate that promotional factor—the difference between your normal selling rate and the added selling that results from promotion—just maintain an advertising diary. Place your advertisements in chronological order, detailing:

1. the sales generated by reason of advertisements,

2. the stock prepared for advertisements,

3. the weather on sale days, and

4. any comments that can be used when planning future sales promotion activities.

ASSIGNMENT

You have estimated sales as $150,000 for the first six months of operation.

1. Prepare a sales promotion budget for:
   a. The store opening (allocate a budget for each activity), and
   b. the six-month period of operations (allocate a budget for each activity, that is, the Promotion Calendar in Figure 11-2).

2. Explain the reasons for the selection of each activity, the total budget, and the sum allocated for each activity. Use the Analysis of Promotional Calendar in Figure 11-3.

3. Write a publicity release to be submitted to a local newspaper. Use the Publicity Release sheet in Figure 11-4.

4. Submit the formal analysis to your advisor (instructor) for comments.

FIGURE 11-2

Promotion Calendar

From _____ To _____

Medium   *Size*   *Purpose*   *Cost*

Store Opening

_____

_____

_____

_____

_____

_____

_____

_____

_____

_____

Maintained Program

_____

_____

_____

_____

_____

_____

_____

_____

_____

_____

_____

Total Cost $ _____

FIGURE 11-3

Analysis Promotion Calendar

From _____ To _____

Activity	Explanation	Cost

A. _____

_____

_____

B. _____

_____

_____

C. _____

_____

_____

D. _____

_____

_____

E. _____

_____

_____

F. _____

_____

_____

G. _____

_____

_____

H. _____

_____

_____

FIGURE 11-4

XYZ Store Publicity Release

Date _____

From _____

To _____

_____

_____

_____

_____

_____

_____

_____

_____

_____

_____

_____

_____

_____

_____

_____

_____

_____

_____

_____

_____

_____

_____

_____

_____

_____

Evaluation of the Merchandising Effort

CHAPTER 12

Retail evaluation is the analysis of performance, whose main purposes are to:

1. assess strengths and weaknesses,
2. eliminate or lessen mistakes, and
3. establish premises for new directions.

For our purpose, this evaluation is handled in two units:

1. merchandising, and
2. total retailing activities.

This chapter is concerned with merchandising efficiency. Chapter 13 will concentrate on all activities of management as they affect net profit.

The evaluation of a small store operation is a unique process because it is a kind of self-examination; as the owner/manager, you represent both staff and management. But despite your dual role as buyer/controller, you can work in terms of figures that give objectivity to your self-measurement standards regarding:

1. planning,
2. buying, and
3. selling.

Your evaluation system, programmed before the store's opening, should incorporate all you know from preceding chapters about:

1. the stock/sales ratio (stock turnover),
2. dollar inventory control (six-month plan),
3. merchandising by classification,
4. a unit control system, and
5. discretionary plans for color, size, and fabric.

These standards methods are designed and maintained to minimize your investment and to maximize your profit, goals that are achieved when merchandising results are equal to or better than planned sales. One proviso is that net profit, of course, takes into account *all* costs of doing business. So even though your planned sales are attained, expenses *other* than merchandising could reduce your net profit. In this chapter, then, "profit" will mean the difference between net sales and the total cost of goods sold, that is, gross margin. With this definition, we can concentrate on the effect of merchandising efficiency on your gross margin.

Merchandising efficiency is measured by three standards, that is, the results of:

**MERCHANDISING
REQUIREMENT**

1. sales,
2. inventory, and
3. gross margin.

Sales and Markdowns

Sales. A fundamental requirement of profit is sales. Yet even though greater sales seem to equate with greater profit, this assumption is not necessarily correct. Nationally known retail organizations have been forced out of business while doing volume in the multimillions of dollars! Sales figures are "raw," and they need refinement or analysis. As a barometer of merchandising efficiency, sales must be qualified and put into context, to see whether the results are truly profit-producing. You need to qualify quantitative sales figures.

Even an increase in sales can be a deceptive factor. If the economy is inflating at a rate of, say, 15 percent and your sales increase is only 5 percent, the additional sales volume cannot keep pace with inflation. In fact, the increase would represent a 10-percent loss — an ironic economic reality. Sales increases attained by other retailers in the same trading area have a similar effect on your sales increases. When trade and government figures report retail gains of 10 percent, for example, your store's increase of 5 percent becomes a below-par record.

One of the key elements of sales analysis is the number of units sold, a good indicator of selling trends. When, for example, the sales record shows a 15-percent gain over estimated dollar sales and a 10-percent loss in units, merchandise is certainly being purchased at higher price levels with fewer customer transactions. If your plan is *not* to sell goods at higher price levels at the expense of fewer sales transactions, you should carefully analyze why you are ringing fewer sales. Perhaps you are concentrating stock above the customer-wanted price points. If so, you might be discouraging customers and causing a permanent loss of business.

Markdowns. As a buyer, your concern is to meet or to better sales estimates — daily, monthly, and for every planned period of operation. But when sales figures are below those estimated, your inventory is in an overbought condition; your stock is out of balance to sales, which is a merchandising "dislocation." This excessive merchandise means that you have to accelerate the selling rate. The most obvious way to do so is to mark down goods (that is, to lower the selling price) and thereby influence customers to recognize the improved value of the goods.

A *markdown* is a reduction from the original or previous price. Properly used, markdowns are an effective way to dispose of merchandise that is unsalable at its present price. They help you keep stocks liquid, assist in the promotion of sales, and aid in keeping pace with or bettering competition. They can also aid you in taking a more precise fix on consumer wants, if you record the reasons for markdowns.

Although markdowns cut into profit, no retailer operates without them. For example, some merchandise in stock might consist of overages of colors, sizes, and sales that call for repricing to lower levels to effect stock disposal (promotional selling). Infallibility, in fact, is not part of merchandising. Buyers are expected to — and do — make mistakes. In reality, if markdowns do not occur, you have reason to suspect that the records are being manipulated. Actually, taking markdowns is a means of adjusting stock to certain external conditions, such as:

1. the level of customer acceptance,
2. competition,
3. new market conditions, and
4. the time of the year.

When should a store take markdowns? The answer is a matter of store policy. Some stores prefer "washing" at the end of the season, when current season remainders are marked down to clear the stock and make room for the new. Other stores prefer to adjust prices of slow-moving styles as quickly as they are recognized, so that liquidation speeds up the stock turnover rate and keeps the inventory fresh and new.

How deep should the reduction be? The extent of the markdown is related to the *time* of the reduction. Is it late or early in the season, for example? It must also be deep enough to make merchandise attractive to customers of possibly a lower income or of a price-conscious group. As a retail principle, one of the reasons for markdowns is to widen the base of your potential customers.

"Babying" a style out of stock with a shallow reduction is not an effective policy. The proven theory is that your first reduction should be the best one. In this way, you revalue goods to a level that makes for immediate sales acceleration.

Inventory

There are three yardsticks of inventory results that measure merchandising performance:

1. stock turnover,
2. old goods versus new goods, and
3. stock shortage.

Stock Turnover. Turnover measures the velocity with which merchandise passes through the store into the hands of customers. It is the number of times in a given period that a retailer sells stock and replaces it with fresh merchandise. A good turnover—or a desired rate of merchandise flow into and out of a store—is the result of good merchandising management. It is a valuable yardstick to measure merchandising performance and capital usage. (As noted in Chapter 8, a fast "turn" can reduce your capital requirements by reflecting an inventory of fashion currency.)

Calculating Turnover. As noted in Chapter 8, stockturn can be figured as part of a merchandise plan on an estimated basis, or it can be calculated on actual results. You can figure it out for *any* period of time. To arrive at the number of stockturns obtained in a given period, just divide the net sales of the period by the average inventory for that period:

$$\text{Turnover rate} = \frac{\text{Net sales}}{\text{Average inventory}}$$

You can use either cost or retail figures, but, as noted, most retailers use the retail inventory system. You can also take inventories from book figures without taking a physical count. To figure an average inventory, add the inventory at the beginning of each month of the period to the inventory at the end of the last month of the period. Then divide that total by the number of inventories. If the period consists of a year, the average would be a total of thirteen inventories divided by thirteen. For an average of six months, seven inventories are used.

Example: Table 12-1 contains the monthly sales figures and book inventories for a typical retail operation. Net sales total $850,000, and total inventories are $1,470,000. To calculate average inventory, divide by 13: $1,470,000 ÷ 13 = $113, 077. To calculate stock turnover use the formula:

$$\text{Turnover rate} = \frac{\text{Net sales}}{\text{Average inventory}}$$

$$= \frac{\$850,000}{\$113,077}$$

$$= 7.517 \ (7.5)$$

The Stock Turnover/Sales Ratio Relationship. As discussed in Chapter 2, the stock/sales ratio provides the stock level you need in terms of dollars and expressed in relationship to sales. This ratio is easily arrived at. Just divide the stock at the beginning of the month by the sales of that month.

Actually, the stock/sales relationship and stockturn are closely related and measure the same merchandising plans or results. For example, a stockturn of 6 times a year is the same as a stock/sales average of 2 for each month (12 ÷ 6 = 2). Naturally, each month's stock/sales ratio varies. Although the turnover calculation is more complicated, both plans are easily computed, and either can be used or both. They serve the same purpose. The difference is that, while turnover is an average over a period of time, the stock/sales ratio is taken at a specific time—the beginning of the month. Perhaps another distinction between the two is how they are used: Stock turnover is of concern to management, whereas the stock/sales ratio is used by a buyer to plan the beginning of the month inventories.

TABLE 12-1. Sample Data for Calculating Stock Turnover Rate

	Sales	Book Inventory
January	$50,000	$80,000
February	35,000	65,000
March	60,000	80,000
April	80,000	140,000
May	90,000	130,000
June	80,000	125,000
July	60,000	110,000
August	75,000	135,000
September	80,000	155,000
October	50,000	75,000
November	95,000	175,000
December	95,000	120,000
December 31		80,000
	$850,000	$1,470,000

Stockturn Value. In a fashion operation particularly, a constant flow of new merchandise is a sales stimulant; it creates consumer enthusiasm and a willingness to buy. In a small operation especially, where customer traffic can be limited, customers tend to seek fashion ideas at other stores, unless they see stock changes of adequate frequency. In most instances, therefore, high-turnover stocks are high-profit stocks, and those with low turnover are likely to be high-markdown stocks. There is a close relationship between turnover and the real dollar value of inventory. A fast turnover stock has the additional advantages of:

1. the greatest use of capital,
2. the reduction of shopworn goods that need markdown,
3. the most efficient use of store space, and
4. the reduction of insurance costs (less stock is maintained).

High Turnover Rate. A stock turnover that is too rapid results in an incomplete stock condition, that is, you might find yourself lacking in adequate sizes, colors, or style assortment. As a merchandiser, your responsibility is to maintain a stock turnover (or stock/sales ratio) that is consistent with consumer demand. When your turnover rate is too rapid, you have three ways to slow it down:

1. Increase your plan sales figure and maintain the original stock/sales ratio.
2. Increase the stock/sales ratio.
3. Increase the degree of stock concentration on the higher levels of the price range.

Correcting Substandard Turnover. A slow turnover is often caused by some merchandise that does not sell well. If you do not provide new merchandise, the value of your stock can deteriorate if other merchandise also becomes slow-moving. Standing pat is a negative merchandising ploy—whatever your reason. If something is new in fashion and if it will probably meet with customer acceptance, you must bring it into stock—regardless of an overbought condition, despite the contingency of a slower turn, or irrespective of an out-of-proportion stock/sales relationship.

One of the best ways to improve turnover is to analyze your classifications and compare them with those of other stores. Also review your classification records of the past year. As a merchandising principle, try to establish a selling rate for each classification. Early purchases and the careful monitoring of sales and stock records can help you make sound merchandise decisions to improve a slow turnover rate.

As a practical purchasing method, maybe you can cut down the stock/sales ratio by buying for a shorter period. For example, instead of using a 2× stock/sales ratio (6 stock turns a year), maybe you could stock merchandise for, say, a 6- or 7-week selling period. You can do so, of course, if the market lead time requirement for delivery permits more frequent purchases and timely stock.

Old Goods Versus New Goods. Overbuying, shopworn goods, broken sizes and colors, promotional purchase remainders, and unsatisfactory consumer response are all major reasons for the accumulation of "old" goods — merchandise that does not have price ticket value. If the proportion of old goods is high as compared to new goods, you have a merchandising problem. You have no alternative but to take markdowns and "whip" the stock into shape. The ratio of old stock to new stock is an important standard for measuring your inventory's value and effectiveness.

Stock Shortage. Stock shortage is the difference between book inventory and the dollar value of a physical count. Somewhere along the line, you've lost stock. Such shortages are bound to occur. In fact, only in extremely rare instances does a store operate without some stock loss. But your job is to hold these shortages down by recognizing the reasons why they occur and by taking safeguards to prevent them. Part of your merchandising effort is therefore to minimize this loss of stock, which reduces gross margin — a critical yardstick of your merchandising performance.

One of the more obvious reasons for an apparent shortage is an inaccurate count. So physical counts should be taken with the greatest degree of accuracy. Basically, shortages are due to:

Clerical Errors:

* Failure to record markdowns properly.
* Incorrect retailing of invoices.
* Errors in recording returns to vendors.

Errors in Selling:

* Errors in packing sold goods — such as a charge for one, give two.
* Sales at incorrect prices.
* Customers given credit for wrong prices (when price tickets are not on the garments returned).

Theft:

* Shoplifting.
* Internal theft by employees.

Poor Inventory Taking:

* Errors in counting goods.
* Poor arrangement of stock preparatory to stock counting.

Poor Housekeeping:

* A lack of respect for merchandise invites theft.

* Mishandled merchandise can end up "lost."

As a merchandiser, you should realize that respect for merchandise fosters its close supervision, as well as an awareness of its condition, of its movement, and of its value.

Profit (Gross Margin)

There is only one reason for being in business—to make a profit. To make a profit, you must keep the dollar sales volume in excess of your cost of doing business. So the profit from the sale of merchandise must be sufficient to cover the cost of merchandise, to provide funds to pay for expenses, and to leave a net profit. Three elements go into the net profit that you need:

1. initial markup,
2. maintained markup, and
3. gross margin.

Initial Markup. This is the first markon, the difference between the invoice cost and the original retail or selling price. Invoice cost is the quoted wholesale price, the cost before any trade or cash discounts are taken.

Maintained Markup. Because the retail price of merchandise is subject to change, we must distinguish between original markup and maintained markup. Whereas the original markup is the proposed markup, the *maintained markup* is calculated with the actual figures—*after* taking into account all markdowns, employee discounts, and shortages. Net sales you can only estimate. And the gross cost of goods, which is the actual aggregate dollar amount of merchandise cost of all goods sold within a period, is only an estimate at the beginning of that period. So unlike initial markup, you cannot calculate a maintained markup *exactly* in advance, because the net sales and the gross cost of goods are merchandising results—things that have to actually happen.

The formula for figuring maintained markup is:

Maintained markup = Actual selling price - Cost of goods sold

Merchandising fashion goods is among the most difficult aspects of retailing management because consumer demand is so discontinuous. What is commonly accepted today may be out-of-date tomorrow. How much merchandise should be stocked? What kind? And when? The decisions to respond to these complex questions are predicated on a merchandiser's experience and studied anticipation.

As much as merchandising is an art, its value is judged coldly by the results of sales, inventory conditions, and the level of profit as compared to investment. To ascertain how well a merchant has planned, bought, and sold goods with greatest effectiveness, certain standards have been established to measure performance. The most widely used standards are those gathered by the Financial Executives Division of the National Retail Merchants Association,* published yearly as the MOR (merchandising

PRINCIPLES

*100 West 31 Street, New York, N.Y. 10001

and operating results). Each edition contains the preceding year's merchandising performance figures for department and specialty stores that are members of the association. These figures are averaged and compiled by "Department, Demand Center or Subclassification," and they include the following:

* merchandise description,
* number of store respondents,
* cumulative markon,
* markdowns,
* stock shortage,
* gross margin,
* cash discounts,
* stockturns, and
* stock age.

All figures are expressed as percentages, and rated "median" or "superior."

Evaluating merchandising performance is a continuous retailing process, which includes such daily concerns as: How much business was done last year on this day? How much is done this day? And finally how much profit was made last year as compared to this year?

1. Visit a department store and a specialty store:
   a. Select three styles from the stock of a fashion department in each store (for a total of six styles) that you believe are probable markdown candidates.
   b. Note their current prices and the prices you believe will "move" the merchandise.
   c. Support your estimations with reasons. Use Figures 12-1a and 12-1b.

2. Based on a plan to do $200,000 in a six-month period, August through January, with a yearly 4X stock turnover rate:
   a. Estimate monthly sales volume using the monthly sales percentages of:

August	16%
September	19%
October	12%
November	18%
December	25%
January	10%
	100%

   b. Estimate the opening inventory of each, based on a stock/sales ratio in line with the projected stock turnover. [Use the same stock/sales ratio for each month (an average)]. Use Figure 12-2.

3. Submit the completed reports to your advisor (instructor) for relevancy of your findings to the operation of the store you intend to open.

ASSIGNMENT

FIGURE 12-1a

Stock Analysis for Markdowns

Store _____ Date _____

Item (Describe)   *Present Price*   *Suggested Price*

1. _____

Comments: _____

_____

_____

_____

_____

_____

_____

2. _____

Comments: _____

_____

_____

_____

_____

_____

_____

_____

3. _____

Comments: _____

_____

_____

_____

_____

_____

_____

FIGURE 12-1b

Stock Analysis for Markdowns

Store _____ Date _____

Item (Describe)   Present Price   Suggested Price

1. _____

Comments: _____

_____

_____

_____

_____

_____

_____

_____

2. _____

Comments: _____

_____

_____

_____

_____

_____

_____

_____

3. _____

Comments: _____

_____

_____

_____

_____

_____

_____

_____

FIGURE 12-2

Sales/Inventory Relationship

	August	September	October	November	December	January

Sales

Inventory BOM

Stock/Sales
   Ratio

EVALUATING A STORE'S PERFORMANCE

PART III

Evaluation of the Retail Performance

The Profit and Loss Statement

Like a human organism, a retail operation's health can be assessed by measuring the performance of its vital "organs." The most basic measuring device of a business is the profit and loss (or "operating") statement, which is a summary of results over a period of operation. With its account of sales and of the cost of doing business, the statement provides the basis for a logical self-appraisal and a diagnosis of any malfunctioning areas of the retail "body."

The bottom line of the statement is net profit—the most important goal of a business enterprise—which reflects the owner's merchandising and administrative abilities. A satisfactory net profit depends on an adequate markup and a level of operational costs that is consistent with its contribution.

Figure 13-1 shows the relevance to net profit of sales, of the cost of

FIGURE 13-1.

Revenues, cost of goods sold, and expenses

| REVENUES (SALES) |
| LESS COST OF GOODS SOLD |
| GROSS MARGIN |
| LESS EXPENSES |
| NET PROFIT |

goods sold, and of expenses. This configuration shows the narrowing effect of each element on net profit, as well as the need to control profit through the analysis and correction of profit "leaks." So, like a medical examination, the profit and loss analysis concentrates on the three "organs" singled out in this figure:

1. revenues,
2. cost of goods sold, and
3. expenses.

Besides its diagnostic uses, the profit and loss statement also serves other purposes:

* It is a document for tax calculations.
* It is a source of information for you to assess the performance of the store and thus your return on investment
* It supplies you with information to determine new objectives or strategies.
* It is a proven record to qualify for business loans.

Pro Forma Statements

In the pre-planning stage, you should prepare, with the help of an accountant, a pro forma profit and loss statement. The pro forma document contains probable levels of performance that, if reached, will yield a satisfactory return on capital. By comparing the figures of actual results after a year of operation with the planned profit and loss statement, you can conclude whether:

1. the rewards are consistent with your expectations and efforts;
2. your retail decisions are in line with reality; and
3. the customer segment, the merchandise carried, and the manner in which business is conducted are all working together effectively.

If the planned and actual statements show positive conditions after a full year of operation, you might also consider the options of:

1. enlarging the store,
2. widening the customer base,
3. establishing a branch operation, or
4. enhancing the retail mix to gain a step on competition.

The Profit and Loss Statement

**MANAGERIAL
REQUIREMENTS**

The basic merchandising elements of this statement are contained in Table 13-1. Note that the gross cost of merchandise sold plus cash discounts and alteration expenses equals the total cost of merchandise sold. Gross margin is the bottom line of merchandising activities. Maintained markup, which we discussed in the last chapter, is only the intermediary profit.

There are two methods of analyzing a profit and loss statement:

1. the skeletal approach, or
2. the in-depth method.

Gross sales
- Customer returns and allowances   _____
= Net sales   _____

Cost of goods sold
  Inventory at the beginning (at cost)
+ Purchases (at cost)   _____

- Returns and allowances (at cost)   _____
  Net purchase

+ Cost of transportation   _____
  Total merchandise handled

- Inventory at end of period (at cost)   _____
= Gross cost of merchandise sold

- Cash discounts   _____
  Net cost of goods sold

+ Alteration and workroom costs   _____
  Total cost of merchandise sold   _____

= Gross margin (Net sales - Total merchandise costs) _____

Skeletal Approach

Table 13-2 presents a pro forma statement, constructed with industry standards and reasonably probable estimates. Table 13-3 contains the actual figures for the same operation after a year in business. Using the skeletal (or overview) approach, you would not concern yourself with the detailed itemizations in either of these statements. Instead you would draw out only the total amount of each major element in the tables. For example, you would not review the items labeled Inventory, beginning of year or Net purchases. Instead you would go immediately to the total Cost of goods sold, which is $144,350 in the pro forma statement and $187,202 in the end or year statement. Confronted with the two statements, then, you would make up an abbreviated or capsule report for yourself, as shown in Table 13-4.

This table shows—at a glance—that the actual sales are well above those planned, but that the cost of goods sold turned out also to be much higher than anticipated. Further, the gross percentage is lower than expected, and the net profit came out less than projected. Taking just this broad view, you can detect trends in current performance and become alert to business patterns in general, without making an in-depth analysis. These figures would alert you to the fact that, although sales are satisfactory, the cost of doing business is relatively higher than you anticipated, and that an in-depth analysis of all cost factors are needed to determine how to improve profit results.

In this approach, you must study the figures of each line in a complete statement—a mandatory practice at the end of the fiscal period.

The In-Depth Method

Net Sales. Gross sales, the *total* sales of a given period, must be adjusted by deducting customer returns and allowances. Comparing the actual sales of Table 13-3 with the planned sales of Table 13-2, you see a positive rela-

TABLE 13-2. Pro Forma (Planned) Profit and Loss Statement

			L.Y.
Gross Sales:			$255,000
Sales returns and allowances		$1,800 (.70)	
Sales discounts		2,800 (1.09)	4,600
Net sales			$250,400 (100%)
Cost of Goods Sold:			
Inventory, beginning of year		$ 50,000	
Purchases	$150,000		
Purchase R&A $2,000 (1.3)			
Purchase discounts 3,750 (2.5)	5,750		
Net purchases	144,250		
Transportation-in.	4,100 (2.7)	148,350	
Cost of goods available for sale		198,350	
Inventory end of year		54,000	
Cost of goods sold			144,350 (57.7)
Gross margin			$106,050 (42.3)
Operating Expenses:			
Direct (Variable) Expenses			
Advertising	$ 6,260 (2.5)		
Delivery	3,200 (1.3)		
Transportation-out	3,500 (1.4)		
Selling expenses (salespersons)	20,032 (8.0)		
Miscellaneous selling expenses	4,000 (1.6)		
Office expenses	3,000 (1.2)		
Bad debt expenses	1,500 (.6)		
Unemployment insurance	1,000 (.4)		
Total direct expenses	$42,492 (16.9)		
Indirect (Fixed) Expenses			
Store rent	16,000 (6.4)		
Property taxes	3,000 (1.2)		
Office salaries	7,000 (2.8)		
Insurance	900 (.35)		
Total indirect expenses	$26,900 (10.8)		
Total operating expenses			$69,392 (27.7)
Net operating income			$36,658 (14.6)

TABLE 13-3. Profit and Loss Statement (End of Year)

Gross Sales:			$310,000
Sales returns and allowances		4650 (1.54)	
Sales discounts		3410 (1.09)	8,060
Net sales			301,940 (100%)
Cost of Goods Sold:			
Inventory, beginning of year			$ 70,000
Purchases	$200,000		
Purchase R&A	4,000 (2.0)		
Purchase discounts	5,000 (2.5)	9,000	
Net purchases		191,000	
Transportation-in		7,000 (3.5)	$198,000
Cost of goods available for sale			268,000
Inventory end of year			80,798
Cost of goods sold			187,202 (62%)
Gross margin			$114,738 (38%)
Operating Expenses:			
Direct (Variable) Expenses			
Advertising		12,077 (4.0)	
Delivery		6,038 (2.0)	
Transportation-out		4,227 (1.4)	
Selling expenses (salesperson)		24,155 (8.0)	
Miscellaneous selling expenses		6,038 (2.0)	
Office expenses		4,529 (1.5)	
Bad debt expenses		3,019 (1.0)	
Unemployment insurance		3,019 (1.0)	
Total direct expenses		$63,102 (20.9)	
Indirect (Fixed) Expenses			
Store rent		16,000 (5.3)	
Property taxes		3,000 (1.0)	
Office salaries		7,000 (2.3)	
Insurance		900 (.29)	
Total indirect expenses		26,900 (8.9)	
Total operating expenses			$90,002 (29.8%)
Net operating income			$24,736 (8.2%)

TABLE 13-4. Abbreviated Profit and Loss Statement Comparison

Pro Forma Income Statement		%	End of Year Income Statement		%
Net sales	$250,400	100	Net sales	$301,940	100
Cost of goods sold	144,350	57.7	Cost of goods sold	187,202	62
Gross margin	106,050	42.3	Gross margin	114,738	38
Operating expenses	69,392	27.7	Operating expenses	90,002	29.8
Net profit	36,658	14.6	Net profit	24,736	8.2

tionship, a better-than-anticipated record. Yet note that the percentage of returns and allowance, as well as the sales discounts, were almost double the planned figures. The high amount for returns, a reduction from gross sales, calls for analysis of several possibilities: Perhaps your personnel is not carefully examining merchandise when they receive it from manufacturers. Maybe merchandise in stock is not being handled properly. Perhaps sales personnel are high-pressuring customers, or they might be selling on approval (take two, return one). The figures warrant your analysis of the merchandise flow from the time it is received from manufacturers to when it is bought and placed in the hands of customers.

Cost of Goods Sold. The actual cost of goods sold for that year in business is $187,202, itemized as shown in Table 13-5. Since this cost turned out higher than expected, you should be concerned about reducing it as much as possible. In general, you have to study the cost of merchandise line for line to determine one or a combination of the following ways to increase profit:

1. buying goods that allows for adequate markup,
2. increasing discounts (anticipation), or
3. reducing transportation costs.

Although the wholesale *prices of goods* at the beginning of a season are not negotiable, you can reduce the cost of merchandise by belonging to a resident buying office group purchase. You can cut costs also by working with some manufacturers who offer timely values (during or after the height of the selling season) and lowered costs, which give you the opportunity to sell goods at a higher-than-usual markup.

In the two tables, *purchase discounts* are shown as a reduction of purchase costs, whereas the formula in Chapter 12 shows it as a reduction of the gross cost of merchandise sold. Either way of handling it is correct since the net effect is the same. Yet larger stores use the method described in Chapter 12 so that statistical comparisons with other stores are then based on a uniform accounting method. Small stores usually employ the method shown in the tables.

So different purchase terms can lower the cost of merchandise and therefore enhance profit. As examples, in Table 13-2, discounts (and returns

TABLE 13-5. Cost of Goods Sold

Inventory, beginning of year		$70,000
Purchases at cost	$200,000	
Minus		
Discounts and returns to Mfrs.	9,000	
Equals		
Net purchases	$191,000	
Plus		
Transportation-in	7,000	$198,000
Equals		
Cost of goods available for sale		$268,000
Minus		
Inventory at end of year		80,798
Equals		
Cost of goods sold		$187,202

Alteration/work costs were not incurred.

to manufacturers) are $9,000 and transportation-in is $7,000, both variable costs. By paying the manufacturer invoices before their due dates, you increase your discounts and lower the cost of goods. Prepayment of bills, known as anticipation, can be taken with the manufacturer's permission at the current rate of cost of money.

To further reduce cost, cut the *expense of transportation* by having cooperative manufacturers ship goods FOB store (although, in truth, this advantage is more obtainable by big stores). As a more practical cost-cutting procedure, be aware of how goods are shipped to you: with insurance, in bulk, with a certain type of carrier, and so on. The cost factors for these methods vary greatly, and they should be studied to select the most economical way. The cost of transportation in, $7,000, could be $6,000—a $1,000 addition to profit—if you explore all the transportation options and find a way to reduce the cost of the present method.

Gross Margin. Gross margin, the profit from the sale of merchandise, is only an intermediate step to net profit. To have a net profit, you must sell goods with enough of a markup to cover *all* the expense of operating your business and still have a remainder.

The actual gross margin in Table 13-3 was 38 percent, or $114,738. If the planned gross margin percentage of 42.3 percent had been met, the profit (margin) would have been $127,720, for an additional $12,982. In addition to monitoring and seeking ways to obtain favorable purchase terms, you should also concentrate on the purchase of goods that offer an opportunity for ample initial markup, and you should reject, whenever possible, merchandise that requires a low markup. Along these lines, remember that some traditional retail price levels carry higher markups than others.

> *Example:* An item that costs $4.75 and retails for $8.95 has a markup percentage of 47 percent, whereas an article that costs $21.75 and retails for $35 has a markup of 38 percent. Obviously, you have two alternatives: Either pay less than $21.75 for a $35 item, or eliminate the price level.

Initial markup and maintained markup percentages are so vital to gross margin that you should always consider them before placing your commitments for merchandise. Since gross margin must be sufficiently high to cover your operational costs, it is, as the initial level of profit, a barometer of the performance of the major activity of retailing.

Operating Expenses. These expenses include all the costs of running a store, and their total is deducted from the gross margin to arrive at net profit. Expenses can be identified as expenditures for efforts that are intended primarily to sell goods. Of greatest significance is that expenses represent a necessary and sizable cost of doing business. So they must be recognized, planned as a reduction to profit, and incurred on an equitable basis.

There are two basic classes of expense:

1. natural, and
2. functional.

Natural expenses are based on the nature of the service realized from the outlay, rather than on the function of the business for which the outlay is made. The Controllers Congress of the National Retail Merchants Association identifies seventeen standard natural divisions of expenses:

1. payroll,
2. property rental,
3. advertising (media costs),
4. taxes,
5. imputed interest,
6. supplies,
7. services purchased,
8. unclassified,
9. traveling,
10. communication,
11. pensions,
12. insurance,
13. depreciation,
14. professional services,
15. decorations,
16. losses from bad debts, and
17. equipment rentals.

Though ambiguous, a *functional expense* is best explained as one that does not fit into natural expenses precisely and that must be identified by the function for which it was incurred, such as for administration or publicity.

Generally speaking—and most important to a small store's operation —expenses should be categorized as direct and indirect. *Direct expenses* are considered variable or controllable, such as advertising. As a principle, controllable expenses are directly related to volume: the greater the sales, the higher the direct dollar expenses. *Indirect* or *noncontrollable* expenses remain the same regardless of the volume of business, such as rent, insurance, and property tax.

Analysis and Comparison of Operating Expenses. Recognizing that expenses are reductions of profit, you should classify them into direct and indirect groups. By isolating the direct expenses, which are variable, you may be able to reduce or to eliminate them. After the profit and loss statement is completed, follow these steps to ensure a complete analysis:

1. Review all your expenses over a period of time to see their progression and to identify reasons for any increases.
2. Compare each expense with those of other retailers of comparable size and nature.
3. Compare the actual and planned figures.
4. Compare expense percentages with industry averages (such as the MRMA figures).

Example: In Tables 13-2 and 13-3, total actual direct expenses expenses exceeded the planned figure by approximately $20,000, a difference of 4 percent. This extremely high increase should alert you to the need for taking immediate corrective steps. As a matter of good managerial practice, you must determine the particular reasons for the out-of-proportion expenses as soon as possible.

The actual cost of advertising shows 4 percent as against a planned figure of 2.5 percent, for a dollar difference of $5,529. This increase leads to several questions. Could the sales increase for the period have been accomplished with the planned advertising budget? Did the increase in sales warrant the increase in advertising cost—that is, greater profit . . . more store traffic . . . improved store image?

Actual delivery expenses were $6,038, as opposed to a projected $3,200. Analysis might lead you to conclude that daily deliveries are too costly or that the method and/or carrier should be changed.

Actual transportation-out and selling expenses are consistent with planned figures and require no analysis. Although actual selling expenses were $24,155 ($4,123 over plan), its percentage against net sales remained the same as the planned figure, because the base of the percentage, net sales, increased. So the selling expenses of both the planned and actual statements work out to 8 percent.

The indirect expenses show no difference in dollars, but the percentage of actual expense to net sales is less than planned, due to the increase in sales, a positive factor.

Total actual expenses were 29.8 percent as compared with the planned figure of 27.7 percent, which decreased the planned net profit percentage from 14 to 8.2 percent. If the planned net profit percentage was met, the net profit would be $36,658 instead of $33,736.

Analysis of the operation of the first year indicates that the store's performance was generally satisfactory. The one possibility is that of increasing profit through the tighter control of expenses.

Applying Corrective Steps to Expense Control. Although classifying, distributing, and analysing expenses are essential steps in their control, the last step is taking corrective action to reduce, to control, or to eliminate them. After your store has been in operation for a while and you have been able to compare actual costs with your planned figures, discuss the operating results with an accountant. After that discussion, which will probably focus on standards and probabilities for the future, seek advice from specialists. For example, a traffic manager of a larger firm can identify methods and carriers which, if used, might result in considerable savings for you. A bank official could be the source of information on how to obtain short-term loans to take advantage of cash discounts, the net effect of which might increase your profit. Every such corrective step that reduces an expense, without changing the character of your store, improves the net profit.

PRINCIPLES

The basic device for summarizing the performance of a retail store is the profit and loss statement, which summarizes the relationship between revenues, costs, and expenses. You must understand the components of this statement, as well as their interrelationships, because they reflect your store's performance level. Their analysis can tell you what steps to take in specific areas that need corrective action.

An analysis of sales should include why and how they were obtained, with an eye for increasing them. An additional qualitative factor is the difference between gross sales and net sales, most importantly when the reductions are significant.

Costs include:

1. the cost of merchandise,
2. the cost of buying,
3. the cost of freight-in, and
4. the cost of receiving and checking incoming merchandise.

Each of these elements must be given careful attention to ensure profitable merchandising performance.

Expense control is the all-important aspect of retailing management. Direct expenses can be corrected more quickly because they are variable and controllable. Indirect expenses are fixed but can be adjusted on a long-term basis.

In the final analysis, a profit and loss statement is the "cardiogram" of retailing, a recording of retail performance. When the "heartbeat" is not normal, you must take steps to make the operation healthy.

ASSIGNMENT

Tables 13-6 and 13-7 contain the information for the profit and loss statement (statement of earnings) for your first year of operation. Sales are obviously far in excess of your plans. Yet, as a now-seasoned entrepreneur, you are going to take two approaches to analyze the store's performance.

1. Prepare a capsule (or skeletal) profit and loss statement indicating the results in dollars and percentages. See Figure 13-2, item 1.

2. Analyze the income statement for possible areas of improvement. Select five expenses that you feel are disproportionate. (See Figure 13-2, item 2.)
   a. Establish the possible reason for these high costs.
   b. Explain the corrective steps that might be taken to insure their elimination, reduction, or control.

3. Prepare a pro forma profit and loss statement for the ensuing year.

TABLE 13-6. Statement of Selling, General, and Administrative Expenses

Particulars	
Salary Expenses:	
Direct store salaries	$ 38,931.22
% of direct store salaries to net sales	10.33%
General manager	3,268.61
Personnel manager	1,758.20
Total salary expenses	$ 43,958.03
Rent	35,280.92
Depreciation of furniture and equipment	6,437.22
Warehouse expense	6,183.26
Utilities	8,269.69
Payroll taxes	3,757.93
Store supplies	3,606.72
Amortization of leasehold improvements	3,576.96
Repairs and maintenance	2,455.00
Advertising	2,505.93
Insurance	2,228.71
Charge card expense	1,916.08
Data processing service	1,898.99
Telephone and telegraph	920.55
Window trim	1,400.37
Automobile and truck expenses	
Maintenance and expense	1,273.09
Depreciation	888.69
Help-wanted advertising	1,107.68
Professional services	1,091.50
Personal property taxes	1,000.16
Travel	817.59
Buying expense	591.89
Hospitalization insurance	370.10
Protective service	326.94
Postage	292.04
Dues and subscriptions	262.50
Medical expense plan	254.30
*Cash short	254.20
Bank charges	—
Collection expense	49.17
Sundry other expenses	249.20
Total selling, general, and administrative expenses	$133,225.41
% of net sales	35.35%

*Cash short—cashier errors.

Particulars	
Net Sales	$376,867.85
Cost of Goods Sold:	
Inventory, beginning of year	$ 69,812.55
Purchases	250,222.44
Freight-in	1,784.37
Purchase Discounts	(20,203.19)
Total	$301,616.17
Inventory, end of year	72,538.20
Cost of goods sold	$229,077.97
% of net sales	60.79%
Gross profit	$147,789.88
% of net sales	39.21%
Selling, General, and Administrative Expenses:	133,225.41
% of Net Sales	35.35%
Net Earnings or (Loss) before Officer's Salaries and Other Income and Expense	$14,564.47
% of Net Sales	3.86%

FIGURE 13-2

Analysis of the Profit and Loss Statement

	Dollars	*Percentage*
1. Net Sales		
Cost of Goods Sold		
Gross Profit		
Operating Expenses		
Net Profit		

2. *Disproportionate expenses:*

1. _____

2. _____

3. _____

4. _____

5. _____

3. *Reasons for high costs:*

1. _____

2. _____

3. _____

4. _____

5. _____

Corrective steps:

_____

_____

_____

_____

_____

_____

_____

_____

Conclusions

A small store is a miniature of a large retail marketing structure, with all the responsibilities centered on the owner—*you*. When considering entrepreneurship, therefore, you must respond to a number of major considerations and questions:

1. *Financing:* Can you obtain enough capital to open and operate a store?

2. *Location cost:* Can you acquire a location within a budget based on projected sales and profit potential?

3. *Physical plant:* Is the selected store in good repair? Is it surrounded by appropriate retail stores? Can it be made attractive to potential customers? Is it functional in size? Will it be able to provide adequate parking space?

4. *Merchandising:* Can you plan, buy, sell, and control merchandise assortment and depth in a way that satisfies a segmented group of customers?

5. *Administration:* Can you handle accounting records, insurance, and taxes?

Although the concerns of a small store owner are many, thousands of independent merchants handle them successfully every day. With certainty, it is a great feeling to be your own boss—not having to report to anyone. But with that "freedom" must go great dedication.

The test that follows is from the *Small Business Reporter*, a Bank of America publication, which states:

> If you can honestly say "yes" to all, or almost all of the following questions, then — and only then — can you begin to think about starting your own business.

Business Know-How Quiz

Yes   *No*

___ ___ I know that going into business for myself will involve the whole family.

___ ___ My wife thinks it's a good idea. She's willing to help.

___ ___ I like to make my own decisions and try my own ideas.

___ ___ I enjoy being challenged and thrive on competition.

___ ___ I want to improve my stature in the community.

___ ___ I want to improve my financial position; build an estate for my family.

___ ___ I know that my standard of living will be lowered for a while —until the business begins to show a profit. It may take several months, maybe even a year or two, to make a profit.

___ ___ There's less than a 50-50 chance that I'll still be in business two years from now. I may spend the rest of my life barely making a go of it.

___ ___ Only about 10 percent of the businesses started are really successful—50 percent fail; 40 percent are marginal operations.

___ ___ I might fail.

Management

___ ___ I realize that about 90 percent of business failures are caused by inexperience and poor management.

___ ___ I have several years or more experience in this business.

___ ___ I know the good things people do to improve a business. I know the mistakes that drive business away.

___ ___ I know the suppliers and the assistance they provide.

___ ___ I know the trade association people. I know what they expect of me and what to expect of them.

___ ___ I have a head for figures.

___ ___ I have experience in keeping inventory records, sales records and reports, withholding taxes for the federal government and making out state employee records and reports.

___ ___ I know I'll always be able to meet my payroll.

___ ___ I can shoulder the full responsibility of running a business.

___ ___ I know how to juggle all the little details without cracking under the strain.

___ ___ I know how to manage my business.

___ ___ I've always protected myself, my family, and my possessions with insurance and sensible safeguards.

___ ___ I know that employees are the vital link between the business and its customers.

___ ___ I've had experience in selecting, training, and supervising employees.

___ ___ I know how to develop an assistant—a "backup" man—to run the business when I'm not there.

___ ___ I know how to forecast sales and expenses and how to use this information to help make my business more successful.

Merchandising

___ ___ I know how to find the right location for my business.

___ ___ I've had experience in arranging attractive and convenient merchandise displays.

___ ___ I can make my place of business attractive—and stay within the budget.

___ ___ I've had experience organizing the help and establishing ways of doing things.

___ ___ I know what, how much, and when and where to buy.

___ ___ I know how to price my goods and services competitively.

___ ___ I know how to pay for merchandise, meet expenses and still make a profit.

___ ___ I know how to control my inventory to coincide with peak and slack periods of the business.

___ ___ I know how to advertise sensibly.

___ ___ I know how to encourage customers to buy by making them feel welcome.

___ ___ I take part in community activities.

___ ___ I'm a good neighbor; I go out of my way sometimes to do little extra things that build good will.

___ ___ I've always created a clean, attractive and pleasant atmosphere for customers and employees wherever I've worked.

___ ___ I've had experience in handling merchandise efficiently.

___ ___ I know the types of credit to offer that are appropriate to the business and the customer.

___ ___ I know how to collect past due accounts without losing the customer.

Finances

___ ___ I have some money saved that I've been putting away for my own business.

___ ___ I have enough money to go into the business I want and I can get more from other sources—my friends and family and from my bank.

___ ___ I know that the money must be paid back out of profits, after taxes and before I take any money for myself.

___ ___ I realize that my savings will be the "risk capital" for my business.

___ ___ I know that it's possible for me to lose my savings—as well as the money I borrow from others.

___ ___ I know that even if my business fails I will have to pay back all I owe.

—— —— I know my community wants, needs, and can support this business.

—— —— My community has enough people with enough inclination to spend money for the goods or services I plan to supply.

—— —— I've studied my competition. I know who my competitors are, and where they are.

—— —— I know what people think of my competition and how good they are.

—— —— I know how I can be better than my competitors.

—— —— I want to have the best business in town.

Relationships

—— —— I have friends to lean on.

—— —— My friends can help me because they are capable of impartial thinking and judgment when they know it will help me.

—— —— My banker will help me, give me counseling and advice.

—— —— My attorney will help me. He's interested in my problems.

—— —— My accountant will keep me informed of my affairs and business progress.

—— —— My insurance man will help me select the best protection for my business.

—— —— My suppliers provide a whole range of services to help me in the conduct of my business.

Personal Inventory

—— —— I know myself.

—— —— I know what's required of me.

—— —— I have evaluated my personality; it lends itself favorably to my business.

—— —— I am frank about discussing my financial condition. I have nothing to hide.

—— —— I am honest and ethical and have a good record with the people I have done business with.

—— —— I always get things done on time and plan ahead.

—— —— I have will power, lots of self-discipline.

—— —— I am stable. I've never jumped from job to job.

—— —— I like to work. My own business requires me to work hard — 12 to 16 hours each day. The work is never really done. There's always more.

—— —— I have the energy to do all the necessary lifting, hauling, standing, walking, talking and smiling that the day-to-day operation of my business will require.

—— —— I realize that I can't be all things to all people at all times — but that this will be expected of me in my own business. I can withstand the strain that this will create for me.

—— —— I really like people; I'm friendly and outgoing by nature and I have a sincere, willing-to-serve attitude.

____ ____ I understand people. I am the kind of person who can put myself in the other guy's shoes.

____ ____ I don't know everything. There are still things to learn—new ideas I should consider.

____ ____ I am adaptable. I am not so routine-bound or rigid in my ideas that I can't change if my business required a change.

____ ____ I make sound judgments. I know I will have to make decisions every day in my own business.

____ ____ I can take advice from others.

____ ____ Common sense is one of my strong points.

____ ____ I haven't reached my final decision.

____ ____ I haven't signed anything yet. I haven't put up any non-returnable cash deposits, made any lease arrangements or merchandise commitments.

____ ____ I've considered all of the alternatives to entering business for myself.

____ ____ I know the advantages of a sole proprietorship, of a partnership, of incorporating my business.

____ ____ I've investigated the possibility of a franchise operation. I'm aware of the advantages of franchising—buying someone elses' know-how and proven operating techniques.

____ ____ I'm aware of the advantages of working for someone else and not going into business for myself.

DO YOU MEASURE UP?

These questions should make you think about yourself, about what you need to know to go into your own business. Depending on the type of business that interests you, some questions will have more weight than others. This variability makes it impossible to say, "If you score more than 75 right, you're ready for your own business." It just isn't that easy.

The really important outcome of the test is that you are thinking about yourself and how you measure up. You care about whether you and your business will be successful, and you are preparing yourself for your own business.

PRINCIPLES

As an independent businessperson, you can operate a store with a greater efficiency than a large retail operation. This comparison is justified on the basis of the relative returns on capital. As an entrepreneur, you do not have to contend with the difficulty of communicating with people at different levels of the retail hierarchy. Your decisions are self-researched, and you don't face the costly errors of commission or omission by some people who have limited interest in their jobs.

As a wearer of many "hats," a mini-businessperson must be a very flexible manager and worker—a jack-of-all-trades. But that is not to say that you must be an expert in all areas of business management. Policies, controls, and management standards can be established with the help of specialists—an accountant, lawyer, insurance person, and others. Your main objectives are first to obtain specific sound advice of what it takes to open and operate a store, and then to apply that knowledge with hard work and business acumen.

Read the appendix for additional details on how to open and operate a small store.

    And please accept our very best wishes for success — if you are ready!

ASSIGNMENT

Bibliography

Baumbeck, Clifford M., et al., *How to Organize and Operate a Small Business.* Englewood Cliffs, N.J.: Prentice-Hall, Inc., 1973.

Bolen, William H., *Contemporary Retailing.* Englewood Cliffs, N.J.: Prentice-Hall, Inc., 1978.

Broom, H. N. and Justin G., *Small Business Management.* Cincinnati, Ohio: Southwestern Publishing Co., 1979.

Burton, Philip Ward, *Retail Advertising for the Small Store.* Englewood Cliffs, N.J.: Prentice-Hall, Inc., 1959.

The Buyer's Manual: A Merchandising Handbook. New York: National Retail Merchants Association, 1905, new edition, 1978.

Corbman, Bernard P., *Mathematics of Retail Merchandising.* New York: The Ronald Press Company, 1952.

Diehl, Mary Ellen, *How to Produce a Fashion Show.* New York: Fairchild Publications, 1976.

Frantz, Forrest H., *Successful Small Business Management.* Englewood Cliffs, N.J.: Prentice-Hall, Inc., 1978.

Gist, Ronald R., *Basic Retailing Text and Cases.* New York: John Wiley & Sons, Inc., 1971.

Gore, Bud, *How to Sell the Whole Store as Fashion.* New York: National Retail Merchants Association, 1970.

Kneider, Albert P., *Mathematics of Merchandising.* Englewood Cliffs: Prentice-Hall, Inc., 1974.

Larson, Carl M., Robert E. Wiegand, and John S. Wright, *Basic Retailing.* Englewood Cliffs, N.J.: Prentice-Hall, Inc., 1976.

Marcus, Stanley, *Minding the Store.* Boston: Little, Brown and Company, 1974.

Markin, Rom J., Jr., *Retailing Management — A Systems Approach.* New York: The MacMillan Company, 1971.

MacFarlane, William N., *Principles of Small Store Management.* New York: McGraw-Hill Book Company, 1977.

National Retail Merchants Association, *Department Merchandising and Operating Results of Department and Specialty Stores.* New York: The Association, published annually.

Packard, Sidney and Miriam Guerreiro, *The Buying Game: Fashion Buying and Merchandising.* New York: Fairchild Publications, 1979.

Packard, Sidney and Abraham Raine, *Consumer Behavior and Fashion Marketing.* Dubuque, Iowa: Wm. C. Brown Co., 1979.

Packard, Sidney, Arthur Winters, and Nathan Axelrod, *Fashion Buying and Merchandising.* New York: Fairchild Publications, 1976.

Rackman, David J., *Retail Strategy and Structure.* Englewood Cliffs, N.J.: Prentice-Hall, Inc., 1975.

National Retail Merchants Association, *Readings in Modern Retailing.* New York: The Association, 1969.

Shaffer, Harold and Herbert Greenwald, *Independent Retailing.* Englewood Cliffs, N.J.: Prentice-Hall, Inc., published in cooperation with the National Retail Merchants Association, 1976.

Shipp, David D. Jr., *Retail Merchandising: Principles and Applications.* Boston: Houghton Mifflin Co., 1976.

Small Business Administration, *Advertising — Retail Stores.* Washington, D.C.: 1963.

Small Business Administration, *Advertising for Profit and Prestige.* Washington, D.C., 1963.

Steinhoff, Dan, *Small Business Management Fundamentals.* New York: McGraw-Hill Book Company, 1974.

Steinmetz, Lawrence L. et al., *Managing the Small Business.* Homewood, Ill.: Richard D. Irwin, Inc., 1968.

Stone, Bob, *Successful Direct Marketing Methods.* Chicago, Ill.: Crain Books, 1974.

Taylor, Charles G., *Merchandise Assortment Planning.* New York: National Retail Merchants Association, 1970.

Will, Ted R. and Ronald W. Hasty, *Retailing.* San Francisco, Cal.: Canfield Press, 1977.

Wingate, John W., Elmer O. Shaller, and Robert Bell, *Problems in Retail Merchandising.* Englewood Cliffs, N.J.: Prentice-Hall, Inc., 1974.

Winters, Arthur A. and Stanley Goodman, *Fashion Advertising and Promotion.* New York: Fairchild Publications, 1978.

Wolff, Janet, *What Makes Women Buy.* New York: McGraw-Hill Book Company, Inc., 1958.

Small Business Administration "For-Sale" Publications

These "for-sale" booklets may be ordered from the Superintendent of Documents, Government Printing Office, Washington, D.C. 20402. Payment may be made by check, money order, or document coupons. Do not send postage stamps or cash. These booklets are not sold by the Small Business Administration. Latest listings and prices are available on SBA Publications List 115–B, which may be obtained from your nearest SBA field office.

The booklets in this series provide discussions of special management problems in small companies.

SMALL BUSINESS MANAGEMENT SERIES

	Catalog No.	Pages
An Employee Suggestion System for Small Companies Explains the basic principles for starting and operating a suggestion system. It also warns of various pitfalls and gives examples of suggestions submitted by employees.	SBA 1.12:1	18
Human Relations in Small Business Discusses human relations as the subject involves finding and selecting employees, developing them, and motivating them.	SBA 1.12:3	68
Improving Material Handling in Small Business A discussion of the basics of the material handling function, the method of laying out workplaces, and other factors to setting up an efficient system.	SBA 1.12:4	42
Handbook of Small Business Finance Written for the small businessman who wants to improve	SBA 1.12:15	80

his financial-management skills. Indicates the major
areas of financial management and describes a few of
the many techniques that can help the small businessman.

New Product Introduction for Small Business Owners   SBA 1.12:17   69
Provides basic information which will help the owners
of small businesses to understand better what is involved
in placing a new or improved product on the market.

Ratio Analysis for Small Business   SBA 1.12:20   65
Ratio analysis is the process of determining the relationships between certain financial or operating data of a
business to provide a basis for managerial control. The
purpose of the booklet is to help the owner/manager in
detecting favorable or unfavorable trends in his business.

Practical Business Use of Government Statistics   SBA 1.12:22   Available
Illustrates some practical uses of federal government   Fall
statistics, discusses what can be done with them, and   1975
describes major reference sources.

Guides for Profit Planning   SBA 1.12:25   52
Guides for computing and using the break-even point, the
level of gross profit, and the rate of return on investment.
Designed for readers who have no specialized training in
accounting and economics.

Personnel Management Guides for Small Business   SBA 1.12:26   79
An introduction to the various aspects of personnel management as they apply to small firms.

Profitable Community Relations for Small Business   SBA 1.12:27   36
Practical information on how to build and maintain
sound community relations by participation in community affairs.

Small Business and Government Research and Development   SBA 1.12:28   41
An introduction for owners of small research and develop-
ment firms that seek government R and D contracts. Includes a discussion of the procedures necessary to locate
and interest government markets.

Insurance and Risk Management for Small Business   SBA 1.12:30   72
A discussion of what insurance is, the necessity of obtaining professional advice on buying insurance, and the
main types of insurance a small business may need.

Management Audit for Small Retailers   SBA 1.12:31   50
Designed to meet the needs of the owner/manager of a
small retail enterprise. 149 questions guide the owner/
manager in an examination of himself and his business
operation.

Financial Recordkeeping for Small Stores   SBA 1.12:32   131
Written primarily for the small store owner or prospective
owner whose business doesn't justify hiring a full-time
bookkeeper.

Small Store Planning for Growth   SBA 1.12:33   99
A discussion of the nature of growth, the management
skills needed, and some techniques for use in promoting
growth. Included is a consideration of merchandising,
advertising and display, and checklists for increases in
transactions and gross margins.

	Catalog No.	Pages
Selecting Advertising Media — A Guide for Small Business	SBA 1.12:34	120

Intended to aid the small businessman in deciding which medium to select for making his product, service, or store known to potential customers and how to best use his advertising money.

	Catalog No.	Pages
Franchise Index/Profile	SBA 1.12:35	56

Presents an evaluation process that may be used to investigate franchise opportunities. The Index tells what to look for in a franchise. The Profile is a worksheet for listing the data.

	Catalog No.	Pages
The First Two Years: Problems of Small Firm Growth and Survival	SBA 1.20:2	233

This discussion is based on the detailed observation of 81 small retail and service firms over a 2-year period. The operations of each enterprise was systematically followed from the time of launching through the end of the second year.

Nonseries Publications

	Catalog No.	Pages
Managing for Profits	SBA 1.2:M31/11	170

Ten chapters on various aspects of small business management, for example, marketing, production, and credit.

	Catalog No.	Pages
Buying and Selling a Small Business	SBA 1.2:B98	122

Deals with the problems that confront buyers and sellers of small businesses. Discusses the buy/sell transaction, sources of information for buyer/seller decision, the buy/sell process, using financial statements in the buy/sell transaction, and analyzing the market position of the company.

	Catalog No.	Pages
Strengthening Small Business Management	SBA 1.2:M31/14	158

Twenty-one chapters on small business management. This collection reflects the experience which the author gained in a lifetime of work with the small business community.

Small Business Administration
Free Management-Assistance Publications

Single copies of Management Aids, Technical Aids, Small Marketers Aids, and Small Business Bibliographies may be ordered from the nearest SBA field office shown in Appendix A. There is no charge for this service. Since listings are periodically updated, ask for a copy of SBA Publications List 115-A, which also contains a convenient order form.

	Catalog No.	Pages
Better Communications in Small Business	SBA 1:12:7	37

Designed to help smaller manufacturers help themselves in winning cooperation by means of more skillful communications. It also seeks to explain how communications within the firm can improve operating efficiency and competitive strength.

These leaflets deal with functional problems in small manufacturing plants and concentrate on subjects of interest to administrative and operating personnel.

32. How Trade Associations Help Small Business
46. How to Analyze Your Own Business
49. Know Your Patenting Procedures
80. Choosing the Legal Structure for Your Firm
82. Reducing the Risks in Product Development
85. Analyzing Your Cost of Marketing
92. Wishing Won't Get Profitable New Products
111. Steps in Incorporating a Business
161. Proving Fidelity Losses
170. The ABC's of Borrowing
174. Is Your Cash Supply Adequate?
176. Financial Audits: A Tool for Better Management
177. Planning and Controlling Production for Efficiency
178. Effective Industrial Advertising for Small Plants
179. Breaking the Barriers to Small Business Planning
182. Expanding Sales Through Franchising
185. Matching the Applicant to the Job
186. Checklist for Developing a Training Program
188. Developing a List of Prospects
189. Should You Make or Buy Components?
191. Delegating Work and Responsibility
192. Profile Your Customers to Expand Industrial Sales
193. What Is the Best Selling Price?
194. Marketing Planning Guidelines
195. Setting Pay for Your Management Jobs
197. Pointers on Preparing an Employee Handbook
198. How to Find a Likely Successor
201. Locating or Relocating Your Business
203. Are Your Products and Channels Producing Sales?
205. Pointers on Using Temporary Help Services
206. Keep Pointed Toward Profit
208. Problems in Managing a Family-Owned Business
209. Preventing Employee Pilferage
214. The Metric System and Small Business
215. How to Prepare for a Pre-Award Survey
216. Finding a New Product for Your Company
222. Business Life Insurance

Small Marketers Aids

These leaflets provide suggestions and management guidelines for small retail, wholesale, and service firms.

187

Small Business
Administration "For-Sale"
Publications

Small Business Administration "For-Sale" Publications

Glossary

accessories: Women's fashion apparel worn with dresses, coats, suits, sportswear; includes fine and costume jewelry, neckwear, scarfs, handbags, and small leather goods, millinery, gloves, hosiery, shoes, handkerchiefs, watches, artificial flowers, ribbons.

advertising: Any paid-for form of nonpersonal presentation of goods, services, or ideas to a group to influence selling.

anticipation: Paying a bill before it is due, with benefit of extra discount.

area: Size of store; usually requires additional detailed definition. Example: Total area means gross floor space, including stock room and nonselling areas, plus sales area; selling area, only floor space devoted to selling.

assortment plan: Complete range of merchandise in a category planned to various depths of inventory to meet customer demand.

audited sales: Resulting net figures of the sales for any period—daily, weekly, monthly, semi-annually, or annually.

automatic reorders: Reordering staple merchandise on the basis of a predetermined minimum quantity; when this minimum is reached, the quantity of the initial order is again purchased.

average gross sale: Dollar amount of gross sales divided by number of sales transactions or saleschecks that produced the gross sales.

balanced stock: Balanced stock and/or assortment makes available what the customers want throughout all price zones or price ranges in proportion to that demand.

basic stocks: Items, numbers, or models that must be included in a line or classification. A basic stock is primarily an assortment of the bread-and-butter items that enjoy day-to-day customer demand. Basic stock is usually staples, but nonstaple items become basic when, for fashion or fad reasons, they enjoy temporarily increased customer demand. The best rule for basic stock is having what customers want when they want it.

beat last year's figures: The unending battle to sell more every day than was sold on the same day a year ago or at least to meet last year's figures and not fall behind.

best-seller or runner: Seasonal or year-around item or number in a line that sells fast throughout a season or a year at full markon, that merits continuous promotion in displays, advertising, suggestive selling.

better business bureau: Financed by local media and business interests for purpose of promoting accuracy and honesty in advertising and selling.

better versus inexpensive: Better dresses or shoes are where higher price merchandise is sold; inexpensive departments sell medium-priced merchandise.

book inventory: The amount of retail stock shown to be on hand by a perpetual inventory system, wherein sales, markdowns, and discounts are statistically deducted from total purchases to date.

boutique: Small shop, especially one that sells fashionable clothes and accessories for women (recently department stores have expanded "boutique" to include just about everything from men's wear to home furnishings).

brand: A word, letter, or group of words or letters composing a name or design or a combination of these which identifies the goods as services of one seller and/or distinguishes them from those of competitors. "Brand" is a more inclusive general term than "trademark."

break-even point: A mathematical calculation and/or graph that shows when the level of profit just covers the cost of doing business and when, therefore, there is no return on investment.

buying by specifications: Where store submits definite specifications to manufacturer, rather than selecting from goods already on the market. Private or controlled brands are normally purchased by an individual store or through an RBO on specifications.

buying group (buying office, resident buying office): Organization representing group of noncompeting stores, formed primarily for buying merchandise; may be independent, store-owned, or own the stores (examples: Allied Stores Corp., Associated Dry Goods Corp., and Mercantile Stores Co. own stores; Associated Merchandising Corp., Frederick Atkins, Inc. are owned by stores; Independent Retailers, Inc. charges stores a fee.).

carrier: A railroad, trucking firm, airline, express company, bus line, steamship, or river barge company that transports merchandise from vendor to store.

cash discount: Percentage of billed price; concession for paying bills within time period indicated on invoice. (Example: 8/10 means 8 percent deductible from bill, if paid within ten days of date of invoice). Cash discounts include anticipation; cash discounts are merchandising gains, included in computing gross margin.

COD (cash on delivery): Transaction whereby customer agrees to pay when goods are delivered.

cash receipts report: Form used by salespeople to list cash received from sale of merchandise at end of each day's business. The change fund is first deducted and placed in change fund bag. The balance of cash is counted, listed, and placed in the receipts bag together with the report.

central business district: Generally the original retailing center, it remains the center of business activity in most towns, but it has usually lost its predominant influence on the retailing community.

classification: All merchandise of given type or use, regardless of style, size, color, model, or price (such as men's dress shirts).

classification merchandising: Classifying merchandise in groups that are interchangeable from customer's viewpoint.

cluster of stores: That which will produce enough sales volume in a geographical area to provide a profitable operation, while bearing the costs of advertising, central warehousing, and distribution.

commitment: Unconfirmed order for merchandise that the buyer has obligated store to accept.

consignee: Shipping term applied to the ultimate receiver of goods.

consignment purchase and dating: Purchase wherein title to merchandise does not pass at time of shipment but at expiration of specified period, when buyer is privileged to return to vendor any unsold goods.

consolidated delivery: Delivery service of an independent organization, which accumulates and delivers packages from various stores.

consumer demand: Quantity of goods or service the customer is willing to buy at various prices.

consumer goods: Destined for use by the ultimate consumer without additional processing.

consumer obsolescence: Rejection of presently owned goods in favor of something newer, even though the old still has utility value.

consumer orientation: Knowing what people want, when they want it, at what price they can afford to pay for it, and in what quantities they can absorb it.

coop money, coop: Abbreviation for cooperative; money; what the vendor contributes toward helping promote his goods.

cooperative advertising: Partial payment of cost of advertising by the manufacturer to the retailer to help promote merchandise.

costume jewelry: Relatively inexpensive jewelry (versus jewelry of gold, silver, or platinum, generally set with precious stones). Sometimes referred to as "junk jewelry."

creativity: To evolve from one's own thoughts or imagination; development of a plan, an idea, a program, a product to fill a need.

customer demand: How much merchandise (how many items or how much in dollars at cost or retail prices) customers buy in a stated period of time.

customer segmentation: Selection of a group(s) of people as potential customers, to whom the strategies of marketing will be directed.

dating: "Deadline" for paying for goods; to allow reasonable grace period for resale.

departmentalizing: Organization of related merchandise and subsequent identification as a department.

direct expense: Expenses that occur as a direct result of the operation of the business.

direct mail: Use of the mails to make announcements, to sell merchandise, to sell services, or to sell the store—its divisions, its departments, its character, and its ways of doing business. Personal approach to a selective audience.

discount merchandising: Low-margin retailing, generally self-service, selling goods at less than list price.

display: Presentation of merchandise, usually with signing (there are usually window displays, interior displays, and outpost displays in stores).

dissection: Applied to a specific group of merchandise within a department for purposes of control by dollar volume.

dollar sales per square foot: Departmental results are derived by dividing each department's net sales by the average number of square feet of selling space occupied by the department. Increasing sales per square feet is an important objective.

electronic data processing: Putting programmed data through a computer.

enclosed mall: Shopping center where all stores face enclosed central mall with year-round air conditioning.

end of month (EOM) terms: Indicates time allowance for discount reckoned from end of month, during which period goods were bought.

ensembles: Goods that harmonize with other goods.

exurbia: Areas beyond the suburbs but still accessible to major city facilities into which increasing numbers of corporations and their employees' families are moving.

FTC guidelines: Rules and regulations established by the Federal Trade Commission for vendor in granting advertising and other promotional allowances to retailers whether made direct to retailers or through wholesaler or distributors.

fixturing: Layout and selection of fixtures to arrange merchandise for customer convenience; particularly important for self-selection.

forecast: To form an opinion beforehand; to make a prediction as to sales potentials or acceptance by a store's customers for the acceptance and purchase of a new product.

forward stock: Stock carried in the selling department.

FOB (free on board): Shipping term signifying vendor or shipper retains title and pays all charges to FOB point.

free-flow pattern layout: Physical arrangement of a store's fixtures that makes use of much open space while providing the shopper with many different choices in terms of direction. This type of layout is often used in a high-fashion dress shop.

free-standing location: A building that is not connected to other stores in the immediate area.

grid-pattern layout: Physical arrangement of a store where all the counters and other fixtures are at right angles to each other thereby forming a maze for the customer to move through (such as in food stores).

guidelines on advertisements: Specifications developed by vendor governing condition under which vendor will pay a share of cooperative advertising in newspapers, direct mail, or radio or TV broadcasting.

half-size: Sizing in coats, suits, and dresses for women who are not as tall as the average size.

housekeeping: presenting merchandise in neat, attractive, orderly manner; keeping stock in good condition in warehouse or forward stockrooms as well as on selling floor; physical maintenance (cleanliness) of entire store; also used to describe porter and maid service.

image (store image): Reputation of store; the feelings of customers toward store.

impulse merchandise: Articles of merchandise purchased on spur of moment by customer without predetermined consideration.

initial markon: Initial and/or first markon used when merchandise is originally offered for sale.

intimate apparel: Women's, misses', juniors' corsets, brassieres, underwear, slips, negligees, robes, lounging apparel.

interior display: A display within the store that serves to show items which may not otherwise be seen, to identify the department, to directly promote merchandise, and to present the store's personality.

inventory, physical: Determining by actual inspection the merchandise on hand in store, stock rooms, and warehouses; also recording of this information.

inventory shrinkage: Takes form of theft, internal or external fraud, record distortion, waste, sabotage, generally laxity, or careless operation.

invoice: Itemized statement showing merchandise sent to store by a supplier.

job lot: Miscellaneous group of assortment of style, sizes, colors, and so on, purchased by store as a "lot" at a reduced price.

Kimball tags: Prepunched tags attached to merchandise and containing size and style information, provided for high-speed processing and counting; used in inventory control reports recording and restocking.

knockoff: close reproduction of design of a textile or apparel product. Differences in the copy may be shadings in color (not readily apparent to public), small size, less weight; often refers to foreign "knockoffs," which sell for lower price than American originals.

keystone markup: Determining the price of an item by doubling its cost.

lay-away: Method of deferred payments in which merchandise is held by store for the customer until completely paid for.

loss leader: Merchandise advertised and sold at, near, or even below cost by store to bring customers into store.

manifest: Shipping form used by carriers for consolidation purposes, listing all pertinent information (consignor, consignee, commodity classification, number and weight of packages, and sometimes cost); used by carriers internally to list contents of a particular vehicle, listing same information; also used by stores in transfer operations from central warehouse to branches.

markdown percentage: Dollar value of net retail markdowns taken during a given period divided by the dollar value of net sales for that period.

market: Where retailers buy merchandise; a place, not people.

markup: Difference between the wholesale cost and the retail price of merchandise.

maintained markup: Net sales less gross cost of merchandise sold (gross cost of merchandise is the gross cost of merchandise sold after net markdowns, discounts to employees and customers, and stock shortages are taken into consideration).

market share: Part of the market's potential sales or actual sales that a company estimates or achieves.

maximizing space productivity: Arrangement of selling fixtures and display of merchandise to produce increased sales volume per square foot of selling space.

media: As used in advertising: periodical (newspaper, magazine, shopper publications); direct (direct mail, catalog, circular novelties, premiums); sign (outdoor or indoor poster, bulletin, sign, point-of-purchase, car-card, transit sign); sky-writing; motion pictures; program (theatre, menus, guides); broadcast (radio, television, public address, loudspeaker systems).

merchandising: The activities of planning, buying, and selling goods for the ultimate purpose of making a profit (classically it includes standardization and grading), sometimes defined as the planning to have the right merchandise at the right time, in the right place, in the right quantities, and at the right price.

merchandising policies: Guidelines established by a store's management that is followed in order that the store may win the patronage of the group(s) of customers it has chosen to serve.

merchandise marts: Buildings housing showrooms for manufacturers and importers where, under one room, store buyers and merchandise managers can inspect lines from resources in minimum time. The Merchandise Mart in Chicago is reported to be the largest in the world.

multiple sales: Encouraging customers to buy multiple rather than single items.

neighborhood shopping center ("Strip Center"): Ten to fifteen stores, including food, drug, sundry, and personal service stores; five to ten acres; needs at least 1,000 families trading area for support; usually under 100,000 square feet.

open-to-buy: Dollar value of planned purchases for a given period minus the dollar value of all orders scheduled for delivery during the same period.

order follow-up: To insure vendor shipment on time, stores develop an organized follow-up system, orders arranged by due date; on due date vendors are communicated with and RBO in markets represented may be assigned this duty.

order form: Provided for buyers by larger and medium size stores and chain stores; provides all necessary protection for buyers; generally made out in triplicate.

out of stock: Lack of merchandise in store in styles, colors, material content, or price lines customers want when they want it.

patronage motive: Reason for customer patronage of given stores.

perpetual inventory: Retail method of accounting whereby daily sales, discounts and markdowns are deducted from book inventory, which also includes purchases and merchandise returns "today" and "to date."

point-of-purchase display: A form of display which is on or near the point of sale.

price brackets: Definite price zones or levels at which greatest sales volume can be produced.

product mix: Full list of all products offered for sale by a company having dimension of both depth and breadth (breadth equals assortment, depth equals assortment of sizes, models, offered within each product line).

receipt of goods (ROG) terms: Cash discount terms that begin when merchandise reaches store (designed to benefit retailers far from resources; also permits check of goods prior to due date for discount).

receiving: Process of accepting new merchandise at store or warehouse; includes initiating paper work to get merchandise "on the books" and processing incoming transportation bills.

regional store: Branch store generally situated at considerable distance from central downtown or flagship store, operating under name of parent store. Its merchandise is frequently purchased by regional store's own merchandising staff, and it is frequently operated on autonomous basis.

resident buying office (RBO): Office in a resource city to which noncompeting stores belong; each store is exclusively served in its metromarket. The RBO is store's market representative and feeds it market information.

resources: A manufacturer, importer, wholesaler, distributor, selling agent, rack jobber from whom a store buys or accepts merchandise as owner or on selling consignment.

retail method accounting: Accounting method in which all percentages are relative to retail price instead of cost price. In cost method of accounting all percentages are relative to the cost. Example: In the retail method, an article purchased for $1 sells for $2. The margin is $1, but only 50 percent of retail price. In the cost method, an article is purchased for $1 and sells for $2. The margin is $1, but it is 100 percent of cost price.

retailing: Basically, the business of buying for resale to the ultimate customer; also known as "acting as the customer's agent."

return-on-investment (ROI): A measure of profitability for a store or any part thereof. ROI is determined by dividing the net profit by the amount of investment.

sales forecast: Estimate of probable sales for a given period.

sales plan: Department's promotional program for six-month period, subject to monthly revision to take advantage of opportunistic purchases and other unpredictable merchandising opportunities.

season letter: Code assigned to merchandise received during six-month spring or fall season that indicates age of stock.

seasonal merchandise: Merchandise purchased to meet demands of specific seasons (extreme instances: purchases for summer and winter clothing, outdoor furniture).

segmented merchandising: merchandising for and appealing to specific age groups or other groups with common interests.

shoplifting: Stealing of store's merchandise by customers — of growing concern to all types of retailers.

small store men: Familiar with operation, problems, and objectives of smaller retail stores; accustomed to performing all responsibilities and duties assigned to various executives in larger organizations.

special orders: Readiness to procure for the customer anything not stocked.

staple stock: There is always the problem of overlap, in defining basic stock versus staple stock. Essentially, the difference between basic and staple is assortments versus single items. Staple stock is made up of items that are in practically continuous demand. Basic stock is an assortment of items that are in current demand. Basic stock includes staple stock items.

stub: In merchandise control, second part of price ticket, removed by salesperson at time of sale for unit merchandise control.

trading area: Surrounding area from which most of store's trade is drawn, varies by individual store location. Each store, main or branch, needs to know to what extent and from what directions it draws customers; checking automobile licensed plates in shopping center parking lots, questioning customers who visit store, analyzing charge accounts, and so on will develop this information.

traffic: Number of persons, both prospective and actual customers, who enter store or department.

transactions per square feet: Number of transactions per square foot of selling space are obtained by dividing the number of gross transactions of sales checks of a department by the average number of square feet the department occupies for selling space.

turnover: Total number of times, within given period, that stock of goods is sold and replaced (Net sales ÷ Average inventory).

trading down: Adding a lower-priced item to the line of prestige products in the hope that those who cannot afford the original product will want to buy the new one because it carries the status of the higher-priced goods.

trading up: Adding a high-priced prestige product to the line in the hope of increasing sales of an existing lower priced product. In retailing, it is the greater concentration on higher-priced merchandise. (Trading down is the reverse.)

unit control: System of recording vital statistics of stock on hand, on order, and sold for a given period; "control" is interpretation of statistics as barometer showing change in customer buying habits; works best when barometer readings are taken frequently and seriously.

vendor: Manufacturer, wholesaler (jobber), importer, or commission merchant from whom merchandise is purchased.

visual merchandising: Presentation of merchandise to best selling advantage and for maximum traffic exposure, plus projection of customer "ready-to-buy." Not a display technique but a merchandising strategy.

workrooms: Generally refers to behind-scenes rooms for sales-supporting services such as alterations and repairs.

DEFINITIONS FOR INCOME TAX PURPOSES

gross margin: "Equals business receipts less cost of goods sold."

salaries and wages: "Consists of those salaries and wages not included as a deduction for "cost of labor" in the cost of goods sold schedule. Salaries to partners, to the taxpayer if a sole proprietor, are not included in this item."

payments to partners: "This account shows guaranteed payments made to a partner for services or the use of capital where such payments are determined without regard to income of the partnership."

interest: "This deduction is permitted for interest paid or accrued in connection with business indebtedness."

taxes: "State and local taxes paid or accrued on business property or incurred in conducting business are allowable deductions. Also included are Federal import and excise duties and taxes."

bad debts: "Bad debts may be deducted when there is reasonable certainty that they are uncollectible. A debt which is deducted as uncollectible, if subsequently collected, must be reported as income for the year in which collected."

repairs: "This includes cost of labor and supplies, and other costs necessary for incidental repairs to the property. It does not include capital expenditures which add to the property value. Improvements which appreciably prolong its life, or expenditures for restoring or replacing property."

amortization, depreciation, and depletion: "Amortization is the sum of deductions taken in lieu of depreciation for Government-certified emergency facilities for the national defense and the amounts of deferred expenses written off for research and experimental expenditures, exploration and development expenditures. Depreciation is a deduction of a reasonable allowance for the exhaustion, wear and tear, or obsolescence of property used in a trade or business, or of property held for the production of income. Depletion is deduction from income for a wasting asset such as a mineral deposit, or a stand of timber to recover its cost."

net profit (or loss) on business receipts: "On sole proprietorship returns net profit (or loss) represents the difference between business receipts and the sum of cost of goods sold and other business deductions. For partnerships, net profit (or loss) represents the difference between total receipts and sum of cost of goods sold and business deductions. The term net profit is used for both sole proprietorships and partnerships, although in concept the term is not strictly comparable for the two forms of business organization. For example, investment income is reflected in partnership profit but not in sole proprietorship net profit. A further difference is that salaries paid to the owner(s) are a business deduction for a partnership but not for a sole proprietorship."

APPENDIXES

Governmental Regulations

[The New York State regulations included in the following are similar to those of other states.]

While it is impossible to cover in one booklet all the special Federal and State regulations applicable to each individual business, there are certain general regulations which apply to practically all stores and service establishments. The following pages, however, are in no sense a work of legal reference, nor do they contain legal interpretations of the statutes and regulations described. Thus they are no substitute for legal advice when such is necessary.

This brochure covers the field of social control of individual business in the interest of protecting business enterprise as a whole and promoting and protecting the public health, safety and general welfare. There are particular rules and regulations imposed upon your business by your community in the form of local ordinances, and certain enterprises such as restaurants, taverns, tobacconists and filling stations must observe special rules to protect the public health. The following pages outline only those broad phases of regulation which are common to all business, an understanding of which is essential to successful operation. These include regulation of the forms of business organization with brief mention of business taxes, licensing, and the regulation of labor, competition and trade practices.

Forms of Business Organization

There are three main forms of business organizations, each subject to different legal requirements. These are the individual proprietorship, the partnership and the corporation. While theoretically the tax laws and other aspects of regulation are not designed to influence your choice of the form in which you do business, the fact remains that the state of the law influences choice.

Individual Proprietorships. This is the oldest and most common form of business organization, where one man owns and operates the business and hires all other help for pay. In organizing an enterprise under the individual or single proprietorship form, there are no special legal requirements to be met. Of course, you may have to obtain a license if you engage in certain trades (see the next section on licensing); but this is unrelated to the form of business organization.

However, you may wish to conduct your business under a name other than your own, such as the "Fix-It Shop." In such cases, to enable creditors and other interested parties to determine the actual ownership of any business conducted under a trade name, that name must be filed with the county clerk of each county in which the business is conducted or transacted. This is done on a special form designed to meet the requirements of Section 130 of the General Business Law of the State of New York, which can be obtained at most business stationery stores. Ask for "Certificate of Doing Business Under an Assumed Name." This certificate must be executed and duly acknowledged by the person or, if there be more than one, by all of the persons conducting the business. It should be made out in triplicate. You file the original with the county clerk, who, upon request, will certify the other two copies. You should send one of these certified copies to the bank in which the firm's account is to be maintained and retain the other copy for display on your business premises.

Under the individual proprietorship form you would be liable for Federal and State personal income taxes, just as though you were on a salary. As a self-employer your income will also be subject to Federal old age and survivor insurance (social security). In addition, this State levies an unincorporated business income tax on taxable income derived within the State. A base exemption plus a deduction for personal services or a percentage of total net income, less certain allowable deductions, however, whichever is lower, are provided. Also, a permanent tax credit, limited to businesses with small taxable income, is in effect.

Partnerships. Another common form of business organization is the partnership, which results from a contract or agreement in which two or more persons agree to combine property or labor, or both, for a common undertaking and the acquisition of a common profit. The key to the rights, duties and obligations of the partners is in the "partnership agreement," and you should, therefore, obtain the services of a lawyer in its preparation. Partnerships are of two general types: the general partnership and the limited partnership.

Persons organizing a general partnership must file a certificate of doing business as partners and file the firm's name with the county clerk of each county in which the business is conducted or transacted. You need not file the partnership agreement, but it is desirable to have this in written form, and containing specific provisions with respect to all organizational and operational phases of the proposed enterprise.

Copies of the form to be used for certification may be obtained in most business stationery stores. Ask for "Certificate of Conducting Business as Partners." This form should be filled out in triplicate. As in the case of proprietorships, the original is filed with the county clerk, one copy with the firm's bank and one or more retained by the partners. Also, as in the case of proprietorships, the trade name must be filed unless it contains the true full name of each and every partner. Partners are also liable for Federal and State personal income taxes, and, in addition, the partnership itself is liable for the State unincorporated business income tax.

Persons organizing under the limited partnership form have additional obligations. A limited partnership is a firm in which one or more of the partners are relieved from liability beyond the amount of the capital contributed by them, under provisions of special legislation. In New York State this legislation is contained in Section 91 of the Partnership Law, which requires persons organizing a limited partnership to file a "Certificate of Limited Partnership" instead of the "Certificate of Conducting Business as Partners." It is important to consult an attorney in drawing up a certificate of limited partnership. It must be notarized and the original filed with the county clerk of the county in which the principal office of such partnership is to be located. A certified copy should be filed with the bank in which the firm's account is to be kept. Immediately after filing, a copy of the certificate or an abstract thereof must be published once a week, for six successive weeks, in two of the county's newspapers designated by the county clerk. Proof of publication must be filed by the publishers in affidavit form with the county clerk. One of the newspapers chosen must be published in the city or town in which the principal place of business is intended to be located, or in the nearest town if that town has no newspaper.

Corporations. The third most common form of business organization is the corporation. Unlike proprietorships and partnerships, the corporation is wholly a creation of the State. Incorporation is a privilege rather than a right; and since the State can grant or withhold the privilege of doing business under this form, it can and does subject it to certain special conditions and regulations. The major distinguishing characteristics of a corporation, which also indicate the special privileges attaching to this form of organization, are threefold: (1) unlike proprietorships and partnerships it can have rights of its own differing from those of its members, and can survive those members and preserve those rights as well as its own identity; (2) the liability of the members is generally limited to the value of their particular investment; and (3) it can increase or decrease the number of owners without altering fundamentally the nature of the corporation or its rights and obligations.

There is a fourth "privilege" or "advantage" which the corporate form has over the proprietorship or general partnership: the stockholder is an owner without assuming the responsibilities of management, while the managers are employees on salary instead of depending wholly on the profits of the enterprise. All of these features mentioned have made the corporation the normal form for large-scale operations involving long-term commitments of large amounts of capital.

The New York State Business Corporation Law became effective September 1, 1963. Under it one or more natural persons of 18 years or over may form a corporation for any lawful purpose by filing a "Certificate of Incorporation" with the Division of Corporations of the Department of State, 162 Washington Avenue, Albany, N.Y. 12210. There are no other qualifications placed on the incorporators. The certificate of incorporation must be signed by the incorporators and one of these signatures must be acknowledged. The certificate is then sent to the Secretary of State for filing. The stockholders then elect a board of directors, each of whom shall be at least 18 years of age. Although the qualification of the board of directors may be further limited by a special certificate of incorporation or by Corporate By-Laws, there are no further qualifications in the Business Corporation Law.

Copies of the form to be used in drawing up a "Certificate of Incorporation" may be obtained from most business stationery stores, but it is advisable to obtain a lawyer to prepare the form and advise on other matters pertaining to incorporation.

Under existing law a corporation may not use a name already in use by a corporation or a name so similar to any other name so as to tend to confuse or deceive. There are other technical restrictions on names so that it is advisable to check with the Department of State, Division of Corporations, mentioned above, before preparing a certificate of incorporation for filing, to determine whether or not the proposed corporate name is available. A single search will be made without charge.

The fee for filing a certificate of incorporation of any stock corporation organized in New York State is $50. In addition to this filing fee, every new stock corporation organized under the laws of the State of New York must pay an organization tax. The rate is 1/20 of one percent upon the amount of the par value of all par value shares the corporation is authorized to issue and five cents per share on authorized stock of no par value. In no case, however, is the organization tax less than $10.

For instance, take the case of a corporation with authorized capital stock to the amount of 600 shares, of which 100 are preferred shares with a par value of $500 per share and 500 are common shares with no par value. The value of the preferred is then $50,000, and the organization tax on that part of the capital would be $25, or 1/20 of one percent of $50,000. On the remaining 500 no par value shares the tax would be five cents per share, or $25, making a total organization tax of $50.

The organization tax and filing fee are due and payable at the time the certificate of incorporation is filed. A rule of the Department of State requires payment in cash or by certified check or money order, except uncertified checks of $125 or less will be accepted from attorneys.

After the corporate existence has begun, an organization meeting of the incorporator or incorporators must be held for the purpose of adopting by-laws, electing directors to hold office until the first annual meeting of the shareholders, and the transaction of such other business as may come before the meeting.

Having incorporated, the corporation obtains its initial capital by selling "shares" in the corporation, represented by stock certificates. The stockholders own the corporation, while the corporation owns the business property and other assets. There is no statutory provision fixing a maximum or minimum limitation on the amount of authorized shares and, of course, the corporation can borrow money, either unsecured or secured, if it can find lenders.

The Business Corporation Law provides that every corporation shall keep at the office of the corporation in this State or at the office of its transfer agent in this State, a record containing the names and addresses of all shareholders, the number and class of shares held by each and the dates when they respectively became the owners of record thereof.

Taxation of Corporations. Under Article 9-A of the Tax Law, a corporation, being a privileged form of operation, pays an annual State tax for that privilege: the franchise tax on business corporations. The tax is imposed on the entire net income of the corporation which is its Federal taxable income with certain modifications. There are also certain alternative bases by which the tax must be computed as well as a tax on subsidiary capital. If the corporation maintains a regular place of business outside the State its "business income and capital" may be allocated within and without New York State under a formula. Its investment income and capital and its subsidiary capital are also allocable under a formula. Full information concerning this tax and forms for making returns may be obtained from the Corporation Tax Bureau of the Department of Taxation and Finance, State Campus, Albany, New York 12227.

In addition to paying the corporate organization and franchise taxes levied by the State, a corporation is also liable for certain Federal taxes on this form of business organization. These include the corporation income tax. There are also special Federal taxes on improper accumulation of surplus, personal holding companies, regulated investment companies, foreign corporations not engaged in business within the United States, a gift tax, excises, duties, licenses and occupational taxes. Since these are special cases, or unrelated to the form of business organization, they are not discussed here. The major Federal tax is the corporation tax. This tax is based on a formula similar to that of the Federal personal income tax. Full details and forms may be obtained upon application to your nearest office of the District Director of Internal Revenue.

Withholding of Federal Income Tax from Wages. Every employer of one or more persons is charged with the duty of withholding Federal income taxes from wage payments to his employees. It is immaterial whether the employer is an individual, a partnership, a corporation or any other entity.

As an employer, you must obtain withholding exemption certificates from your employees on forms supplied by your local District Director of Internal Revenue. On the basis of the information contained in these certificates you will withhold taxes from wage payments at prescribed rates. You may be required to make monthly deposits of funds collected from your employees during the previous month. You will also be required to file returns quarterly with the District Director of Internal Revenue. Annually you will file a reconciliation of your quarterly returns together with copies of your withholding statements furnished to your employees on forms provided by the District Director.

Penalties and excess payments may accrue from failure to make payments or to file returns properly. Therefore, you should procure a copy of Circular E — "Employer's Tax Guide," for reporting of Federal income tax withheld, social security taxes and Federal unemployment tax, from your local District Director of Internal Revenue and refer any problem to him for his opinion and instruction.

Withholding of State Income Tax from Wages. Every employer maintaining an office or transacting business in New York State must also withhold New York State personal income taxes from the wages of his employees subject to the New York State tax.

You should also obtain a copy of "State of New York Employer's Instructions for Withholding, Payment and Reporting of New York State Personal Income Tax" (Form IT-2100), and "New York State Income Tax Withholding Tables and Methods" (Form IT-2100.1) from the New York State Department of Taxation and Finance, Income Tax Bureau, State Campus, Albany, New York 12227.

Licensing

A license has been judicially defined as a permit granted by the governmental power, to a person, firm or corporation, to pursue some occupation or to carry on some business subject to regulation under the police power. Thus the lawmaking body of a given governmental unit prohibits some course of action, or some use or ownership of property, unless a license is obtained, and then attaches conditions or "regulations to the granting of such a license."

A license may or may not be accompanied by a fee and may involve some form of examination of the would-be licensee to see if he can qualify under certain standards (as a driving test for a motor vehicle operator), a set of rules to be observed in the future and the reservation of the right to revoke the license for failure to observe such rules.

In the Master Index of McKinney's Consolidated Laws of New York there are six pages of listings of licensing provisions. Even allowing for duplication, this indicates that there are hundreds of licenses issued under New York law alone, many of which are for the privilege of carrying on particular kinds of business activity.

The license is a tool of regulation to control a course of conduct or a line of business having some particularly close relationship to the public health, safety or morals. It is also a familiar method of municipal regulation and prospective businessmen should consult their local ordinances which may have been passed under State enabling laws.

Licensing by Towns. The pertinent enabling provisions of the Town Law of the State of New York with respect to the licensing of occupations are in Article 9, Ordinances and Licenses.

While towns may by ordinance regulate a number of trades through provisions of their building, plumbing and electrical codes and through regulations pertaining to fire prevention, use of streets and sidewalks and others designed to preserve the public peace and safety, they may regulate by license the following:

1. Auctioneers, employment agencies, pawnbrokers, junk dealers and dealers in second hand articles; the running of public carriages, cabs, hacks, carts, drays, express wagons, automobiles or other vehicles for the transportation of persons or property over or upon the streets of a town for hire, and soliciting either on private property or on the public highway or running therefor, or for hotels, boats, lodging houses, riding academies or garages; auctioneering, hawking and peddling, except for the peddling of meats, fish, fruit and farm produce by farmers and persons who produce such commodities.

2. The doing of a retail business in the sale of goods of any description within the limits of the town from canal boats, in the canals or from the lands by the side of such canals and within the boundary lines thereof, or from boats on a lake or river, except products of the farm and unmanufactured products of the forest.

3. Circuses, theaters, motion picture houses, shows or other exhibitions or performances, the keeping of billiard or pool rooms, bowling alleys, shooting galleries, skating rinks, amusement parks and other similar places of amusement, for money or hire; or the giving of exhibitions, performances or entertainments in any place within the town.

4. The use of any public hall or opera house; but such place shall not be licensed unless it has suitable and safe means of ingress and egress in case of panic or fire.

5. The running of restaurants, eating places, lunch counters, soft drink counters or similar places for the sale for consumption upon the premises of beverages of any class or description.

6. The use of any hall or place other than private homes for dancing whether in connection with some other use of the premises or otherwise, whether or not such dancing is open to the general public.

7. In a town of the first class, or in a town of the second class adjoining a city of more than three hundred thousand population, the doing of plumbing, heating, ventilating and electrical work; provided, however, that employees of public service corporations shall not require a license while engaged in the work of such corporations.

8. The running of hotels, inns, boarding houses, rooming houses,

lodging houses and associations or clubs furnishing services ordinarily furnished in hotels, inns, boarding houses, rooming houses and lodging houses.

9. The running, operation or conducting business of house trailer camps, tourist camps or similar establishments.

10. In any town in the counties of Erie, Monroe and Suffolk, or in a county adjoining a city having a population of one million or more, or in any town adjacent to such a county, the operation and use of any lands or premises for the excavation of sand, gravel, stone or other minerals and the stripping of top soil therefrom.

For other trades authorized to be licensed by towns, see Sec. 136 of the Town Law.

Licensing by Villages. Villages may regulate and license the running of any means of transportation on their streets or hawking or otherwise soliciting orders in the streets and public places or from house to house. They may also license distributors of bills and other advertising matter. Villages may license the following occupations, a list similar to that given above for towns: ". . . auctioneers, employment agencies, pawnbrokers, junk dealers, dealers in second hand articles, hawkers, vendors, peddlers, public cartmen, truckmen, hackmen, cabmen, expressmen, taxicab drivers, bootblacks, porters, scavengers, sweepers, theaters, moving picture houses, bowling alleys, shooting galleries, restaurants, eating places, soda fountains and places where beverages are sold at retail, skating rinks, halls, or places for dancing, circuses, menageries, public exhibitions of any kind, places of amusement, amusement parks and shows, the operation and use of any lands or premises for the excavation of sand, gravel, stone or other minerals and the stripping of top soil therefrom; may regulate and license any other occupations or businesses for the purpose of preserving and caring for the safety, health, comfort, and general welfare of the inhabitants of the village or visitors thereto." Villages may also license, regulate and prescribe the rates of vehicles for hire.

Villages are also empowered to license the sale of milk and meat and may license the storage, sale or discharge of firearms, fireworks and other explosives.

Village Law permits villages to prohibit the carrying on of any of the following trades without a license:

1. The running of public carriages, cabs, hacks, carts, drays, express wagons, automobiles or other vehicles for the transportation of persons or property over or upon the streets of a village for hire or soliciting either on private property or on the public highway, or running, therefor, or for hotels, boats, lodging houses or garages, auctioneering, hawking and peddling except the peddling of meats, fish, fruit and farm produce by farmers and persons who produce such commodities, provided, however, that no such ordinance shall prohibit hawking or peddling by an honorably discharged member of the armed forces of the United States who is crippled as a result of injuries received while in said armed forces or the holder of a license granted pursuant to the General Business Law which pertains to peddlers' licenses for honorably discharged veterans.

2. The doing of a retail business in the sale of goods of any description within the limits of the village, from canal boats, in the canals, or from the lands by the side of such canals and within the boundary lines thereof, or from boats on a lake or river, except products of the farm and unmanufactured products of the forest.

3. Circuses, theaters, or other exhibitions or performances, the keeping of billiard or pool rooms, bowling alleys, shooting galleries and other similar places of amusement for money or hire; or the giving of exhibitions, perfor-

mances or entertainments, or the use of mechanically-operated amusement devices in any place within the village.

4. The use of any public hall or opera house; but such place shall not be licensed unless it has suitable and safe means of ingress and egress in case of panic or fire.

5. The running of restaurants, eating places, lunch counters, soft drink counters, or similar places for the sale for consumption upon the premises of beverages of any class or description within the village.

City and County Licensing. Cities derive most of their licensing powers from their particular charters. Thus the City of New York has broad powers under its charter, into which you should inquire if you plan to operate in that city. In connection with the operation of an export-import business in New York City, no special license is required to act as an exporter or importer of ordinary merchandise. The "export" and "import" licenses that are occasionally mentioned are Federal Government permits for the exportation or importation of special products to or from certain countries and are not permits to conduct a general business. For detailed information, the United States Department of Commerce with Regional Offices at 26 Federal Plaza, New York City, and Federal Building, Buffalo, New York, should be consulted.

Also certain counties have special charters (e.g., Nassau and Westchester) which give them broad licensing authority. No further generalizations with respect to licensing by local jurisdictions can be sustained, as your particular municipality may have adopted licensing ordinances under the city or village home rule laws or under special charters issued to cities or counties. Therefore, you should check the general information on licensing given here with the particular ordinances of your community governing your type of business.

State Licensing and Regulations. In addition to any local licensing ordinances which may be on the books in the particular community in which your business is to be located, there are many licensing provisions of State law. One important group includes persons or establishments purveying or preparing food and drink. Thus restaurants, catering establishments, clubs and other places selling alcoholic beverages are all licensed and subject to State inspection. Restaurants are also subject to further State inspections. Rectifiers, distillers, vendors of wine and beer are licensed. Licenses or regulations control the operations of canneries, commission merchants and net return dealers and cold storage plants. This type of control is also extended to dairy products, persons in charge of milk gathering stations, and manufacturers of ice cream, milk sherbert, ice and ice sherbert and frozen custard. And both the taking of lobsters and the nets of commercial fisheries are licensed.

Those supervised by the State Education Department include physicians, including osteopaths and physiotherapists; dentists, including dental hygienists; podiatrists (chiropodists); chiropractors; engineers and land surveyors; nurses (professional and practical); optometrists; ophthalmic dispensers; pharmacists, including drug stores; architects; veterinarians; certified public accountants; certified shorthand reporters, and teachers in public schools. In addition State licenses must be obtained by the following: employment agencies, private trade schools, insurance agents, brokers and brokerage companies, licensed lenders, licensed cashers of checks, dealers in securities, funeral directors, embalmers and undertakers, social workers, firms furnishing character information, private investigators, agencies furnishing police or patrolmen, taxidermists, slaughter houses, processing plants.

Finally, there are many licensed occupations subject to particular State regulation in the public interest because of their close relationship to the public health, welfare, safety or morals. These include auctions and auctioneers, billiard and pocket billiard establishments, cattle dealers, chauffeurs, drivers' schools, handlers of explosives, fertilizers and feeding stuffs, laundries (certificate of compliance), ticket agents and resale of admission tickets, guides, junk dealers, pawnbrokers, peddlers and hawkers, kennels, persons engaging in industrial homework, real estate brokers and salesmen, theaters and shows, theater matrons, persons placing out children, barbers, hairdressers, cosmetologists, blood donors, midwives, maternity homes, manufacturers and wholesalers of narcotics, truckers of alcoholic beverages, weighmasters of coal and coke, and well drillers in Kings, Queens, Nassau and Suffolk counties. Counties are given by the State law special licensing powers with respect to electricians, as are cities, while the latter can also license motion picture houses and motion picture operators. These are in addition to the local licensing powers described above.

It should not be concluded from this rather extensive listing, which makes no claim of completeness, that any occupation can be subject to license at the will of the Legislature.

Protection of Employees

The man or woman starting a small business in New York State either has one or more employees or probably will have in the course of time. It is, therefore, important to know the major State and Federal laws and regulations designed to provide safe and healthful working conditions, a floor to wages and a ceiling on hours, prohibiting certain employments, restricting industrial homework, providing workmen's compensation, unemployment insurance, disability benefits insurance, social security, governing industrial relations and fair employment practices.

As a people we have also insisted that, as long as we have booms and depressions with periodic shortages and surpluses of manpower as well as goods and services, the burden of unemployment should form a part of the cost of doing business. We have provided for partial wage insurance for non-occupational disability, with costs generally to be shared by the worker, who becomes ill or disabled away from his job, and by his employer. Finally, through legislation regulating industrial relations and employment practices, we have attempted to stimulate peaceful settlement of disputes as a substitute for strikes, and to equate the bargaining positions of labor and management.

Occupational Safety and Health Act (OSHA)

It is the obligation of employers to furnish their employees a safe place to work, free from recognized hazards causing or likely to cause, death or serious physical harm and to follow specific health and safety standards adopted by the U.S. Department of Labor.

OSHA affects small business (even one employee) as well as large and requires employers of eight or more employees (throughout the entire previous year) to keep records of occupational injuries and illnesses; the records are three part . . . Form No. 100, the log . . . Form No. 101, the supplementary record and Form No. 102, the summary. In addition, *all* employers must display a poster setting forth the responsibilities of the employer.

These forms and posters are available from the OSHA regional office at the following address:

Federal Occupational Safety and Health Administration
U.S. Department of Labor
1515 Broadway
New York, New York 10036

OSHA representatives are authorized to inspect the premises of a business, interview employees privately and review required records.

Information and assistance is available from the New York State Department of Labor; the field offices of this State agency may be contacted at the following addresses:

New York State Department of Labor
Division of Safety and Health
2 World Trade Center
New York, New York 10047

New York State Department of Labor
Division of Safety and Health
Building 12 — State Campus
Albany, New York 12201

Wages and Hours. Employees engaged in manufacturing and most other areas of industry must be paid weekly, within seven days after the end of the work week. Blue collar and white collar employees must be paid in cash unless permission to pay wages by check is obtained from the Industrial Commissioner. Discriminations in rate of pay because of sex are forbidden, and on public works contracts wages must not be less than those prevailing in similar jobs in private industry.

The Minimum Wage Act of New York affects all employees in the State, with certain specified exceptions, and is not merely applicable to workers in certain industries or occupations as under prior laws.

In addition to these statutory minimums, minimum rates may be established through wage board procedure. However, the minimum wages recommended by the Wage Board cannot be less, in most instances, than the statutory required minimum.

Details concerning minimum wage rates are obtainable from the Division of Labor Standards, New York State Department of Labor, 2 World Trade Center, New York, N.Y. 10047.

Every employer is required to keep records of hours worked by each employee covered by an hourly minimum wage rate, the wages paid to all employees, and such other information as the Industrial Commissioner deems material and necessary. A sworn statement of these records must be furnished to the Industrial Commissioner upon demand.

Hours of labor are governed by Article 5 of the Labor Law. All employees, with certain specific exceptions, must have at least 24 consecutive hours off in each calendar week, plus an hour per day for lunch in factories or 45 minutes in mercantile establishments.

Occupations prohibited depend on the age of the minor, and are listed in Article 4 of the New York State Labor Law and in rules issued under the Federal Fair Labor Standards Act.

Even in permitted occupations, the New York Labor Law prohibits the employment of minors in any occupation where attendance upon instruction is required by the Education Law, unless an employment certificate or permit is obtained from the State Department of Education. When attendance upon instruction is not required, minors may be employed without such certificate or permit in certain specified occupations.

Workmen's Compensation. Workmen's compensation insurance must be carried by every business employer of one or more workers. The hazardous nature of employment is no longer a determining factor for coverage.

As personal injuries incurred in the course of employment and deaths resulting from such injuries are compensable under the Workmen's Compensation Law, insurance for workmen's compensation must be had before putting employees to work for the first time.

Rates for workmen's compensation insurance vary according to the nature of the employment and hazards involved.

Workmen's compensation insurance may be carried with any private insurance company authorized to transact the business of workmen's compensation insurance in the State of New York, or with the State Insurance Fund.

The State Insurance Fund is a non-profit agency of the State of New York. It writes workmen's compensation insurance for normal risks at a discount from standard rates, ranging from 25 percent to 32½ percent depending on the size of the premium.

The Fund emphasizes safety engineering, accident prevention, expeditious processing of claims and rehabilitation of the injured employee.

The main office of the State Insurance Fund is located in New York City with branch offices in Albany, Buffalo, Rochester and Syracuse. An employer may also become a self-insurer provided his application to do so is approved by the Chairman of the Workmen's Compensation Board.

As soon as the employer has taken out insurance for workmen's compensation, he must post and maintain in a conspicuous spot in his place of business a printed notice stating that he has complied with all the rules and regulations governing workmen's compensation and that he has secured the payment of compensation to his employees and their dependents as provided under the Workmen's Compensation Law. These printed notices are obtainable from the employer's insurance carrier. The Workmen's Compensation Board will be able to provide any additional information desired.

The Workmen's Compensation Board is at 2 World Trade Center, New York, N.Y. 10047. Other offices are located in Albany, Binghamton, Buffalo, Rochester, Syracuse and Hempstead.

Employers not covered under the Workmen's Compensation Law should carry their own accident and health insurance with a casualty insurance company.

Unemployment Insurance. The Federal Unemployment Tax Act provides for crediting employers with a percentage of the Federal tax for payments made under a state unemployment insurance plan and for a Federal subsidy to cover state administrative costs of such plans. All of the states have unemployment insurance laws now in effect.

Every employer entering business in the State of New York must fill out and file a form entitled, "Report to Determine Liability," obtained from the N.Y.S. Department of Labor, Unemployment Insurance Division, State Office Building Campus, Albany, N.Y. 12201. After filing this information, employers determined to be subject to the Unemployment Insurance Law are given a registration number, a wall poster, and a Handbook for

Employers, and must submit payroll reports as required. The Handbook explains the employer's responsibilities and rights under the State Unemployment Insurance Law.

Under the State Unemployment Insurance Law, an employer becomes liable as of the first day of any calendar quarter in which he pays remuneration totalling $300 or more, *or* on the day he succeeds to the business of a liable employer. To terminate liability (other than by going out of business), an employer must show that he has not paid remuneration totalling $300 or more in any of the four consecutive calendar quarters prior to the date on which he wishes to terminate. Liability ends as of the start of the next calendar quarter, provided application to terminate is filed before that date.

Each "subject employer" is liable for contributions for each employee in covered employment. Contributions are based on the first $6,000 paid to each employee during any calendar year. The beginning contribution rate is usually set at 3.7%, which includes a 1.0% subsidiary tax.

Employers are also subject to the Federal Unemployment Tax if during the current year or the prior year they (1) paid wages of $1,500 or more in any calendar quarter or (2) had one or more employees at any time in each of 20 calendar weeks during such year.

The State Unemployment Insurance Law provides for a merit rating system for contributing employers. The law prescribes the setting up of an individual account for each employer, to which his contributions are credited and to which benefits paid to former employees are debited. As of each December 31, the employer, if he has been liable for five quarters, is rated according to the balance in his account as a percentage of his payrolls. This individual rating determines the tax rate at which the employer will pay contributions to the State during the succeeding calendar year. Favorable employment experience generally tends to assist in receiving a contribution rate in the lower portion of the rating scale. Safeguards have been provided to keep the Unemployment Insurance Fund in a sound and solvent condition.

The unemployment insurance tax system is on a cooperative State-Federal basis, with contributions collected from employers only and paid to employees when they become unemployed.

Further information on this and other matters pertaining to application of the law to your particular business is obtainable from the Unemployment Insurance Division, State Office Building Campus, Albany, N.Y. 12201. Attention: Liability and Determination Section.

Social Security. The Federal Social Security Act is designed to provide for the worker's old age and to assure some income to his dependents after his death. This is the old age and survivors insurance system, the cost of which is borne by both employees and employers in covered employments.

Every such "subject" employer who employs one or more persons is liable for this old age tax and on entering business must file application for an employer's identification number on form SS-4, obtainable from the nearest office of the District Director of Internal Revenue where you send your Federal personal income tax returns.

The employer currently pays a 6.05% tax on wages up to $17,700 a year ($1,070.85) for each employee and the employee pays a like tax on all his wages up to the same amount. The employee's share is deducted by the employer at the close of each pay period. Self-employed persons pay a 8.10% tax on wages up to $17,700 a year ($1,433.70).

Details on this tax, reports and payments should be obtained from your District Director of Internal Revenue. Circular E, "Employer's Tax Guide," is particularly useful on both the social security and unemployment insurance taxes, since the percentage of tax and taxable wage amounts may change from year to year.

Coverage of the old age tax has been extended to include individuals and partners who are self-employed. Such individuals must obtain a social security card from the nearest Social Security Administration Office. Report of the amount of such self-employed net earnings to be credited to the individual's social security account, and the tax to pay for this insurance, have been made a part of the Federal individual income tax return. With few exceptions, anyone having his own trade or business and earning $400 or more net in a year as sole owner or as a partner is subject to the old-age tax. The Federal security agency also publishes a helpful pamphlet entitled, "Special Information for Self-Employed People."

Disability Benefits Insurance. Article 9 of the Workmen's Compensation Law provides for protection for a worker's disability from non-occupational injury or sickness. Known as the Disability Benefits Law, this measure supplements the State Workmen's Compensation and Unemployment Insurance Laws, but there are certain inherent differences which should be noted by the employer as explained below.

The Disability Benefits Law is administered by the Chairman of the Workmen's Compensation Board, 2 World Trade Center, New York, N.Y. 10047, to whom inquiries should be addressed for answers to specific problems.

An employer becomes subject to this law if he employs one or more employees (in covered employment) for thirty days in any calendar year. Upon becoming subject, the employer is required to procure protection, generally in the form of insurance, from the State Insurance Fund or a company authorized to write accident and health insurance in New York State. An employer may operate as a self-insurer by furnishing satisfactory proof of his ability to pay benefits, and depositing securities or furnishing a bond as required by the Chairman of the Board.

The law also permits alternative forms of protection, either by a plan which was in existence on April 13, 1949, and remained effective after July 1, 1950, or by a new plan or agreement with a carrier, with disability benefits at least as favorable as provided for under the law.

Disability benefits are payable to employees at the rate of one-half of average weekly wages with a maximum of $105 per week and a minimum of $20 per week for a period of not more than 26 weeks. If the employee's average weekly wage is less than $20, his benefit is such average weekly wage. A waiting period of seven days is prescribed by the law and payments are made by the employer of his insurance carrier upon satisfactory medical evidence of disability. Employees who become ill or injured while they are unemployed receive similar benefits from a special fund administered by the Board.

Contributions may be collected by the employer from his employees at the rate of one-half of one percent of wages with a maximum of 30 cents per week per employee, and the employer contributes the excess cost of the insurance plan as determined by the Board.

Labor Management Relations Act. The Act is administered by the National Labor Relations Board whose activities, as under the original Act, fall into two main categories: prevention of unfair labor practices; and the determination of collective bargaining representatives.

Further information regarding the Labor Management Relations Act or any problems arising thereunder may be obtained from the regional office of the National Labor Relations Board. There are two regional offices in

New York State — one is located at 26 Federal Plaza, New York, N.Y. 10007;

the other at U.S. Court House, Buffalo, N.Y. 14202.

Labor Disputes. Where differences arise over the interpretation of an existing contract, the law — Labor Management Relations Act — strongly encourages final adjustment by a method agreed upon by the parties, with the use of the Federal Mediation and Conciliation Service considered to be a last resort and in exceptional cases.

Where disputes are of such importance as to endanger the health or safety of the Nation, the law is designed to settle the differences of the parties through a special proceeding, without resort to strike or lockout until after investigation, publicity, mediation and a vote by the employees concerned.

All counties of New York State are served by the regional office of the Federal Mediation and Conciliation Service located at 26 Federal Plaza, New York, N.Y. 10007.

Collective Bargaining Representatives. The State Labor Relations Act confers full authority upon the State Labor Relations Board to certify, after investigation, and hearing the collective bargaining representative chosen by a majority of a given group of employees. Ordinarily this choice is determined by means of an election. Under the New York law, employers as well as employees have the right to file a petition for certification of collective bargaining representatives.

Further information regarding the Labor Relations Act of New York State may be obtained from the State Labor Relations Board at its main office, 2 World Trade Center, 33rd Floor, New York City 10047, or at its offices in the State Campus, Albany, N.Y. 12226, and State Office Building, Buffalo, N.Y. 14202.

Law Against Discrimination. During the 1945 session of the State Legislature, a new statute, the Law against Discrimination, was enacted. This, together with subsequent amendments, added to the State labor regulations described in this section a series of "unlawful discriminatory practices," which are enforced by the State Division of Human Rights, in the Executive Department. A purpose of the law is to establish the principle that in employment there shall be no discrimination by reason of age, race, creed, color, national origin, or sex.

For detailed information, inquiries should be addressed to any of the division's offices located at 270 Broadway, N.Y., N.Y. 10007; 217 Lark Street, Albany, N.Y. 12210; Binghamton State Office Building, 44 Hawley Street, Binghamton, N.Y. 13901; 295 Main Street, Buffalo, N.Y. 14203; 183 Fulton Ave., Hempstead, L.I., N.Y. 11550; 65 Broad Street, Room 606, Rochester, N.Y. 14616; 100 New Street, Syracuse, N.Y. 13202; and 222 Mamaroneck Avenue, White Plains, N.Y. 10605.

Industrial Relations — State Law Labor Relations Act of New York State. The Labor Relations Act of New York State was designed to guarantee employees of industries engaged in intrastate commerce the same rights, and protection in the exercise thereof, that employees of industries engaged in interstate commerce are guaranteed under Federal law and is administered by the State Labor Relations Board.

Unfair Labor Practices. The Labor Relations Act of New York State lists ten types of "unfair labor practices":

1. Spying upon activities of employees in the exercise of their right to organize and bargain collectively.

2. Blacklisting employees because of their participation in union activities.

3. Domination of, or interference in, the formation or administration of any employee organization.

4. Requiring, as a condition of employment, that workers join a company union or refrain from organizing or joining a union of their own choosing.

5. Encouraging membership in a company union or discouraging membership in any other labor organization, by discrimination in regard to hire, tenure or other working conditions.

6. Refusal to bargain collectively with employee representatives.

7. Refusal to discuss grievances with employee representatives.

8. Discharging or otherwise discriminating against an employee for filing a complaint with, or giving testimony before, the State Labor Relations Board.

9. Blacklisting or discriminating against any employee exercising any right created by the law.

10. Any other acts which interfere with, restrain or coerce employees in the exercise of their right to organize and bargain collectively.

Competition and Trade Practices

Up to this point we have reviewed in broad outline those regulations pertaining to the form of business organization, licensing and labor or employee relations. We come now to those forms of regulations designed to promote socially desirable trade practices and to check undesirable ones. In the case of small business enterprises, these regulations center around maintaining competition and keeping such competition on an ethical basis. For competition is still the rule, "the life of trade." The exceptions are such types of enterprise as public utilities, in which public policy has decided upon regulated monopoly as the form best suited to serve the public interest without undue waste of capital.

This public insistence upon competition, while keeping it on a high level and avoiding unfair competitive practices, is important to understand. It means that the government will not guarantee your profits, or hold down your more able competitors so that you can succeed with less business ability. But it also means that you are relatively free to run your business in your own way—that, under our system of free enterprise, your success or failure is largely left up to you.

Competition and Monopoly — The Sherman Act. The broad basis for popular insistence upon competition stems from the theory that rivalry among sellers of goods and services will, on the whole, yield better goods and services at lower prices than relying on the unregulated judgment of a monopolist. But the game has to have rules to bring such beneficial results, and indeed to preserve the game itself, for buyers can be deceived about quality and quantity, and sellers can "gang up" on the customers instead of competing for their business, and thus create monopolies. Bargaining power can be substituted for bargaining skill; and instead of resulting in better goods at lower prices, it can result in the crushing of the small by the strong through the sheer weight of superior capital resources and the consequent ability to stand temporary losses.

The first important Federal legislation in this field was the Sherman Anti-Trust Act of 1890. This Act made unlawful any contracts, combinations and conspiracies in restraint of interstate trade and commerce. In 1899 New York State passed similar legislation declaring contracts or combinations void which created monopolies or restrained or prevented competition. Both are still law.

Between the generality of their language, however, and the attempts of the courts to distinguish between "good" and "bad" trusts, it was difficult for businessmen to determine which competitive practices were valid and which would subject them to prosecution. Accordingly Congress passed two further anti-trust laws in 1914: the Clayton Act and the Federal Trade Commission Act. It is with the provisions of these two acts that small businesses are primarily concerned, for they deal with specific competitive practices and attempt to define those either by enumeration of unlawful practices (Clayton Act) or by setting up a Commission to so enumerate and to prosecute (F.T.C. Act).

The Clayton Act. Under Section 2 of the original Clayton Act sellers in interstate commerce were forbiden to discriminate in price between different buyers where such differences were not based upon variations in grade, quantity, quality, selling or transportation costs or the necessity for meeting bona fide competition, and where such price discrimination tended to create a monopoly or substantially lessen competition. The major purpose of these provisions was to prevent one seller from injuring another, rather than to protect buyers, notably retailers.

During the twenties and early thirties some independent retailers became alarmed over the growth of chain stores, and pushed for the passage of legislation to prevent price concessions by sellers to chain stores which were not also extended to volume purchases of the independents. The Robinson-Patman Act of 1936 amended Section 2 of the Clayton Act to define illegal price discriminations more sharply. In effect it put the burden upon the seller to prove that a special price to a particular buyer was based upon actual economies due to a difference in the cost of selling to him, and no more than that difference. The seller can still make the defense, however, that the lower price was made to meet an equally low price of a competitor.

The monopolistic practices condemned by the Clayton Act are prosecuted by either the Department of Justice (as in the case of the Sherman Act) or by the Federal Trade Commission.

The Federal Trade Commission Act. This Act created the Federal Trade Commission and forbade "unfair methods of competition in commerce." This was later amended to include "unfair or deceptive acts or practices in commerce." While the Sherman Act deals with combinations in restraint of trade, and the Clayton Act made illegal certain specific practices (such as price discrimination) which were viewed as leading to monopoly, the Federal Trade Commission Act attempts to stop practices which are "unfair," of whatever character. The coverage of the Federal Trade Commission is much broader than that under the Sherman or Clayton Acts, as the definition of what practices are "unfair" is left up to the Commission and (finally) the Supreme Court. Actually the Commission has been influenced in its decisions by the kinds of practices condemned under both the common law of restraint of trade and under Federal and State anti-trust laws. These include deceptive acts or practices, misrepresentation, commercial bribery, boycotts, lotteries and — before the passage of the Miller-Tydings Act discussed below — resale price maintenance.

In 1938 the Federal Trade Commission Act was amended to outlaw any "false advertisement" by mail or other means in interstate commerce, to induce the purchase of foods, drugs, devices or cosmetics. Liability was limited to the manufacturer, packer, distributor or seller of the commodity, exempting the publisher or radio broadcaster of the advertisement.

Resale Price Maintenance – The Miller-Tydings and State Fair Trade Laws. To the small businessman, the anti-trust regulations involving his competitive practices most intimately are those relating to the pricing of his goods. It was noted above that under the Clayton Act, and the Robinson-Patman amendment thereto, discrimination in price is forbidden which harms competition among sellers, buyers and sellers, or buyers in interstate commerce, unless based on actual economies in selling a particular customer or to meet actual competition. Under the Sherman and Federal Trade Commission Acts, however, agreements between a seller and his supplier to maintain a price fixed by the supplier were treated as unlawful: either as agreements in restraint of trade (Sherman Act) or as unfair methods of competition (F.T.C. Act).

The feeling persisted among large elements of the business community, however, that the insistence on the part of the manufacturer of a trade-marked product that its resale price be maintained in the retail market was a fair policy and not contrary to the public interest. Starting with California in 1931, by 1950, 45 states had passed laws to permit manufacturers to fix resale prices by contract. The Miller-Tydings Act of 1937, followed by the McGuire Act of 1951, reflected this shift in point of view and amended the Sherman Act to make lawful all resale price maintenance contracts in interstate commerce where permitted by state law and where the product is trademarked. Thus, where a state permits resale price agreement, the parties to such a contract cannot be prosecuted under the Sherman Act as parties to a contract in restraint of interstate trade.

New York Fair Trade Law. In 1935 the Legislature of New York passed a law "to protect trademark owners, distributors and the public against injurious and uneconomic practices in the distribution of articles of standard quality under a distinguished trademark, brand or name." After amendment in 1938, this legislation became Article 24-A of the General Business Law in 1940, under the title "Fair Trade Law."

The New York Fair Trade Law was repealed in May, 1975.

It should be emphasized that all of the laws relating to competition and trade practices cannot be obtained in detail from the Federal and State statutes themselves. Whether particular practices fall within the sphere of prohibited action is a question you should take up with a lawyer, since most of the law relating to the Sherman, Clayton and Federal Trade Commission acts and the State Anti-Monopoly and Fair Trade acts is in the form of administrative decisions or the decisions of the Federal and State courts.

Registrable Marks. Trademarks, service marks, collective marks and certification marks used in interstate commerce may be registered in the United States Patent Office, Washington, D.C., upon compliance with the Lanham Trade Mark Act.

A trade mark is a word, name, symbol, or device, or any combination thereof which identifies and distinguishes goods. A service mark is a mark which identifies and distinguishes services and includes various distinctive features of advertising which identify a service. A collective mark is a mark used by the members of a cooperative, association or other group or organization to identify and distinguish the goods or services of such members and includes marks used to indicate membership in a union or other organization. A certification mark is a mark used in connection with the goods or services of any person other than the owner of the mark to certify regional origin, quality, accuracy, material, mode of manufacture, production by labor union, or other characteristics of the goods or services.

The greatest single advantage of registering a mark is that registration gives constructive notice of the registrant's claim of ownership of the mark. This means that so long as the mark is registered, everyone is charged with notice of the claim of ownership, and no rights may be claimed in the mark by another who commenced to use it after the registration was issued.

In New York State, trademark and service mark registration is available to local concerns that cannot register their marks under the Lanham Act because their marks are not used in interstate commerce.

Under Article 24 of the General Business Law, a person who adopts and uses a trademark or service mark in New York State may file in the office of the Secretary of State, Miscellaneous Records Section, 162 Washington Avenue, Albany, N.Y. 12210 on a form furnished by the Secretary of State, an application for the registration of his mark. Upon compliance with the requirements of Article 24, the Secretary of State will issue a certificate of registration to the applicant. The application for registration must be accompanied by a filing fee of ten dollars payable to the Secretary of State.

New York Upholstery and Bedding Law. Related in purpose to the Food and Drug laws are regulations of manufacturers, preparers-renovators, and dealers in bedding, upholstered furniture and filling materials. They deal with the prevention of contagious diseases through use of old or second-hand material which has not been sterilized and tagged as used. Anyone proposing to manufacture, repair-renovate or sell bedding, upholstered furniture or filling materials should first obtain the details concerning these regulations from the Division of Licensing Services, New York State Department of State, 270 Broadway, New York, N.Y. 10007.

Textile Fiber Products Identification Act. This Act became effective on March 3, 1960, and regulates the marketing, handling, labeling, advertising and selling of all household products made of textile fibers with few exceptions. Among items specifically included are wearing apparel, costumes and accessories, draperies, floor coverings, furnishings, and bedding.

A copy of the Rules and Regulations under the Textile Fiber Products Identification Act may be obtained from the Federal Trade Commission, Bureau of Textiles and Furs, Washington, D.C. 20580.

New York Uniform Commercial Code. The Uniform Commercial Code was adopted in New York State in 1962 and became effective September 27, 1964.

The Code is designed to meet conditions of modern business and it presents a general and comprehensive law relative to commercial transaction. It controls the fields of negotiable instruments, sales, warehouse receipts, bills of lading, stock transfers, conditional sales and trust receipts. It regulates bank collections, bulk sales, chattel mortgages and factor liens and provides statutory authority for the financing of accounts receivable. The mailing address of the Uniform Commercial Code Section of the N.Y.S. Department of State is P.O. Box 7021, Albany, New York 12231.

To meet the need for increased revenues to support an expanded program of State aid to the localities, legislation was adopted in 1965 (Chapter 93, Laws of 1965) imposing a statewide retail sales and use tax, effective August 1 of that year.

The New York State sales tax, currently at 4 percent, is levied on the retail sale of tangible personal property, utility services, restaurant meals, take-out foods, hotel rooms, admission charges and dues, and other specified services. A compensating use tax is levied at the same rate. Exemptions include ingredients and components, machinery, equipment, fuel and utility services used directly and predominantly in manufacturing, mining, agriculture, research and development in the experimental or laboratory sense, except in New York City where only materials or components are exempt. Some localities impose additional sales and use taxes from 1 percent to 4 percent, making a total sales tax range of from 4 to 8 percent. Vendors of property and services subject to the tax are responsible for both the collection and the remittance of the tax. Full information, forms for making returns and a Certificate of Authority to collect this tax may be obtained from the Sales Tax Bureau of the Department of Taxation and Finance, State Campus, Albany, N.Y. 12227.

The Fair Credit Reporting Act

The Fair Credit Reporting Act has been enacted to insure that credit bureaus provide accurate consumer credit information that is fair and equitable to the consumer. While the central focus of the Act is to regulate the methods and practices of consumer reporting agencies (defined as any person which, for monetary fees, dues, or on a cooperative nonprofit-basis, regularly engages in whole or in part in the practice of assembling or evaluating consumer credit information for the purpose of furnishing consumer reports to third parties), the new law not only imposes certain requirements on the use of the consumer reports by businessmen that offer credit to their customers, but also regulates the use of consumer reports when the information obtained is used in connection with the review or collection of an account, for employment purposes, or for the underwriting of insurance.

The law provides that whenever credit involving a consumer is denied or the charge for such credit is increased either wholly or partly because of information contained in a consumer report from a consumer reporting agency, the user of the consumer report shall so advise the consumer and supply the name and address of the consumer reporting agency making the report.

In cases where credit is denied or the charge increased because of information obtained from a person other than a consumer reporting agency bearing on the consumer's credit worthiness, credit standing, credit capacity, character, general reputation, personal characteristics or mode of living, the user of such information shall, within a reasonable period of time, (received within sixty days) upon the consumer's written request for the reasons for any denial of credit, disclose the nature of the information to the consumer. The user of the information shall clearly and accurately disclose to the consumer his right to make such written request at the time denial of credit is communicated to the consumer.

Article 10-A of the Personal Property Law, effective September 1, 1970:

The purpose of the act is to afford consumers, subjected to high pressure door-to-door sales tactics, a "cooling-off" period.

Home solicitation sale is defined as a consumer transaction in which the purchase price is payable in four or more installments, and the seller is a person doing business who engages in a personal solicitation of a sale at the residence of the buyer and the buyer's agreement or offer to purchase is there given to the seller. A cash sale that meets all the other requirements is still deemed a home solicitation sale if the seller makes or assists in obtaining a loan for the buyer to pay any part of the purchase.

In most cases, the buyer may cancel a home solicitation sale until midnight of the third business day after the day on which the buyer agreed or offered to purchase the merchandise.

The seller must notify the buyer of his right to cancel within three days by means of a perforated card as set forth below:

YOU MAY CANCEL THIS SALE WITHIN THREE DAYS

If you decide within three days that you want to cancel the sale, tear off and mail the bottom of this card. To cancel, the card must be mailed within three days after you sign the contract. If you cancel, you may lose your down payment.

. . . .

Contract Signed   (Date)
I hereby cancel this sale   (buyers signature)

The card must be printed in capital and lower case letters of not less than twelve point bold faced type, and the lower half should have the seller's business address on the other side.

The three day period does not begin to run until the seller has given proper notice as set forth above.

If the seller does not comply with this provision of this act, the buyer may cancel by any means whatsoever.

The seller may retain as a cancellation fee 5% of the cash price but not exceeding the amount of the cash down payment.

If you intend to engage in any business that will involve door-to-door sales, it is suggested that you consult your attorney as to your rights and responsibilities under the act.

Summary

Should you wish any further information which is not available from the sources listed in this publication, the New York State Department of Commerce is ever ready to provide additional business counseling or source information. All Department services are free and available at any of its offices listed on the back cover.

The Department has inaugurated a toll-free telephone service for the convenience of New York State callers. The number for New York callers is 800-342-3683.

Insurance Requirements CHAPTER B

One of the costs of doing business is insurance coverage against specified contingent losses, such as fire, accident, and death. In the event of a serious loss that is not covered by insurance, a small store owner may be forced into a business extreme—bankruptcy. So part of the advice you should seek from an attorney is a listing and explanation of insurance needs.

After obtaining this information, obtain further information from an insurance broker who is well informed about small store insurance coverage. Many insurance companies distribute pamphlets that detail comprehensive insurance information, typically their eligibility rules, summary coverages, premiums, and general rules.

The following are some of the important contingencies against which merchants should carry insurance:

* the building (if owner-occupied),
* business personal property,
* premises liability,
* product liability,
* personal injury liability,
* employer's nonownership automobile liability,
* employee dishonesty,
* burglary and robbery,
* fire,
* earthquakes,
* accounts receivable,

* exterior signs, and
* air conditioning equipment.

You should not, in any case, start to do business without adequate insurance coverage. The possibility of becoming a victim of circumstances beyond your control deserves a high priority in your initial store planning.

Small Business Administration Checklists

I. Stock assortment

  A. Unit control systems

    1. Do you have an adequate system for checking on staple items?
    2. For other than staple items, do you have an adequate unit control system in operation?
    3. Do you have an effective system for checking on slow-selling stock?
    4. Do you have an effective system for spotting potential fast-selling stock?
    5. Do you keep a close check on customer demand by a want slip system?

  B. Balance of stock

    1. Is the stock in each of your merchandise classifications balanced to the rate of sale in each?
    2. Is your stock balanced by price line, color, size, and type?
    3. Do you have too many price lines?
    4. Are your prices and price lines the right choice to meet your competition?
    5. Do you carry deep stocks in each of the running styles?
    6. Do you carry deep stocks in heart sizes, colors, and materials?
    7. In fringe sizes, colors, etc., do you deliberately keep low stocks and depend on substitution to avoid lost sales at these points.

8. Do you keep a proper balance among the following classes of stock: Staple, assortment, prestige, and clearance?
9. Do you maintain a basic stock assortment even in dull months?

C. Selection

1. Do you avoid stocking items from different suppliers and in different brands that virtually duplicate one another?
2. Do you select each item in stock with a distinct customer group or target in mind?
3. Do you choose items for promotion that have outstanding merit in price, fashion, or utility?
4. Do you place adequate emphasis on special value promotions, neither too much nor too little?
5. Do the characteristics of the stock give your store a clearly defined personality or image that attracts people in the trading area?
6. Do you keep in close touch with all new market developments by cooperating with a buying office or voluntary group and by seeing all salesmen who call?

. . .

D. Salesmanship

1. Is your salesforce well chosen?
2. Is your salesforce adequately trained in merchandise information and in customer handling?
3. Do your salespeople get adequate merchandise information?
4. Do you provide your salespeople with sufficient premiums, rewards, and contests to maintain their interest?
5. Do you give considerate attention to their suggestions and grievances?
6. Is each of your buyers a good leader?

I. Increasing your markon

A. Buying for less

1. Do you take advantage of all discount opportunities?
2. Do you watch purchases under seasonal rebate agreements so that they will not fall below limits?
3. Do you keep your transportation costs to a minimum by using the most economical common carrier, packing methods, and consolidations?
4. Do you concentrate your purchases with key suppliers?
5. Do you actually use the facilities of a resident buying office to obtain better values?
6. Could you realize savings by placing orders further ahead?

7. Could you realize savings by placing blanket orders?
8. Have you an undeveloped opportunity to use private brands to compete with national brands?

B. Selling for more

1. Do you take every opportunity to buy exclusive merchandise?
2. Do you price every item on its merits (rather than applying at an average markup on most goods)?
3. Are goods costing the same put into stock at different prices when there is a difference in value in the customers' eyes?
4. Could you raise price line endings slightly without detracting from your sales volume?

C. Promoting higher-markup goods.

1. Do you know the markup of each price line and in each classification?
2. Do you make an adequate effort to feature in your advertising those price lines and items that bear a long markup?
3. Is your long-markup merchandise adequately displayed in the store?
4. Are your salespeople trained to give special attention to the higher markup goods in stock?
5. Do you give rewards for selling high markup goods?

II. Curtailing your reductions

A. Buying

1. Will your markdowns by reduced by rising wholesale prices?
2. Do your buyers make careful buying plans before they go to market?
3. Do your buyers frequently overbuy promotional merchandise, later forcing you to take heavy markdowns on remainders?
4. Are your stocks peaked well in advance of the sales peak?
5. Do you curtail reorders at the peak of the selling season?
6. Are you developing classic lines with a long life?
7. Are merchandise shortcomings leading to customer returns and markdowns? (If so, demand higher quality standards.)

B. Selling

1. Are your salespeople adequately presenting the older goods in your stock?
2. Do you have a good followup system to insure that goods don't become slow sellers?
3. Do you carefully instruct your salespeople in the selling points of merchandise that is slow moving?
4. Are your salespeople using forced selling methods that lead to returns and eventual markdowns?

C. Control

    1. Do you have any opportunities to increase your stock turn and reduce the length of time goods are on hand before being sold?

    2. Do you take your markdowns early enough?

    3. Do you take them too soon?

    4. Do you set the first markdown low enough to move most of the goods marked down?

    5. Have you established special markdown prices?

    6. Do you have a system of good physical control of stock that avoids shortages?

III. Increasing your cash discounts

A. Are you getting the largest possible cash discounts from your suppliers?

B. Do you pay all your bills on time so as to obtain the discounts offered?

C. Are you taking advantage of anticipation opportunities?

IV. Lowering your workroom and alteration costs

A. Are charges to your customers desirable, and are they adequate?

B. Is your workroom being run as economically as possible?

C. Would it be feasible to eliminate your workroom operation?

I. Layout

    1. Are your fixtures low enough and signs so placed that the customer can get a bird's-eye view of the store and tell in what direction to go for wanted goods?

    2. Do your aisle and counter arrangements tend to stimulate a circular traffic flow through the store?

    3. Do your fixtures (and their arrangement), signs, lettering, and colors all create a coordinated and unified effect?

    4. Before any supplier's fixtures are accepted, do you make sure they conform in color and design to what you already have?

    5. Do you limit the use of hanging signs to special sale events?

    6. Are your counters and aisle tables *not* overcrowded with merchandise?

    7. Are your ledges and cashier/wrapping stations kept free of boxes, unneeded wrapping materials, personal effects, and odds and ends?

    8. Do you keep trash bins out of sight?

1. Do your signs referring to specific goods tell the customer something significant about them, rather than simply naming the products and their prices?

2. For your advertised goods, do you have prominent signs, including tear sheets at the entrances, to inform and guide customers to their exact location in the store?

3. Do you prominently display both advertised and nonadvertised specials at the ends of counters as well as at the point of sale?

4. Are both your national and private brands highlighted in your arrangement and window display?

5. Wherever feasible, do you give the more colorful merchandise in your stock preference in display?

6. In the case of apparel and home furnishings, do the items that reflect your store's fashion sense or fashion leadership get special display attention at all times?

7. In locating merchandise in your store, do you always consider the productivity of space — vertical as well as horizontal?

8. Is your self-service merchandise arranged so as to attract the customer and assist her in selection by the means indicated below:
   a. Is each category grouped under a separate sign?
   b. Is the merchandise in each category arranged according to its most significant characteristic — whether color, style, size, or price?
   c. In apparel categories, is the merchandise arranged by price lines or zones to assist the customer to make a selection quickly?
   d. Is horizontal space usually devoted to different items and styles within a category (vertical space being used for different sizes — smallest at the top largest at the bottom)?
   e. Are impulse items interspersed with demand items and *not* placed across the aisle from them, where many customers will not see them?

Small Business Administration Loan Information

D

Small Business Administration's primary method of assisting a business financially is by guaranteeing business loans made by banks. SBA may guarantee up to 90% or $350,000, of a loan made by a commercial bank, to start a
new business or expand an existing business. In an exceptional situation, the
guaranty may be as high as $500,000.

The initial step involves the submittal of a loan proposal to a commercial bank, preferably one where you maintain an account, indicating how
much money will be needed, how the money will be used, and how the
business will generate enough income to repay the loan.

Generally, a banker is impressed with the applicant's ability as a manager if a well documented plan is submitted. In the discussion with the
banker, if the bank is unwilling to make a regular bank loan, you should
ask if the bank will consider making the loan with a guarantee from SBA.

The following items should be submitted for consideration:

1. A business plan consisting of a brief history of the business and its
   problems, including an explanation of why the loan is needed and
   how the money will be used to help the business.

2. A written estimate for all equipment and leasehold improvements
   to be purchased with the loan money.

3. Personal resumes of the owners of the business.

4. Signed Balance Sheets and Profit and Loss Statements current
   within 90 days and for the last three fiscal years of the business
   has been operating.

5. Federal Income Tax Returns of the business for the last three
   years and Federal Income Tax Returns for the business owners
   for the last two years.

**LOAN APPLICANT
INSTRUCTION SHEET**

6. A copy of the business lease or a letter from the landlord with the terms of the proposed lease.

7. A copy of the Certificate of Doing Business (registration of the business with the County Clerk). If the business is incorporated, stamp the corporate seal on the application form.

8. A detailed projection of earnings for the first year of business operation must be submitted. Be certain to explain how the expected sales volume will be achieved.

9. List collateral to be offered as security for the loan.

10. Personal Financial Statement.

Before You See the SBA Loan Officer

Most of our regular business loans are made by banks and partially guaranteed by the SBA. While direct loan funds may be available from time to time, *you must first attempt to secure your loan on the basis of an SBA guaranty before you can be considered for a direct loan.*

If you have not yet seen your banker regarding your loan needs, we suggest that you do so before you speak with the SBA Loan Officer. If your bank is willing to make your loan with our guaranty, there will probably be no need for you to return to our office.

If your bank will not make you a loan directly, or in cooperation with the SBA, you may be considered for a direct loan, *if we have the funds. The fact that you may be considered for a direct loan, does not automatically qualify you for the loan. You must show ability to repay.*

If you are seeking a loan to establish a business, we require that you have a reasonable amount of your own money to invest. We cannot provide you with 100% financing to start a business.

If you own an established business and do not have any financial statements with you, we recommend you obtain them before you speak with the SBA Loan Officer. Bring with you copies of your financial statements for the period most recently ended and for the last one or two fiscal years.

The attached pamphlet explains our policy in greater detail and gives you a step-by-step procedure in applying for the loan.

If you need SBA Management Assistance, advise the receptionist. She will be happy to refer you to either a SCORE counsellor or a Management Assistance Officer.

If the bank prefers or agrees to consider the loan with SBA participation, three SBA forms are required:

1. The application for the loan (SBA Form 4).

2. A statement of personal history (SBA Form 912) on each principal.

3. A personal financial statement (SBA Form 413) on each principal (or personal financial statement on bank's form).

If the bank approves the loan, the application and supporting documentation will be forwarded to the SBA for consideration.

An SBA officer will evaluate the loan application based on the following criteria:

1. Eligibility as a small business and eligibility for the particular lending program.

2. Availability of funds—does the applicant have funds available from another personal source or from an outside source?

3. Evaluation of balance sheet.

4. Working capital — is it adequate?

5. Collateral — what is being offered as collateral? Is it adequate to secure the loan?

6. Earnings — past and/or projected earnings must be analyzed, fixed debt must be explained. Projected figures will be compared with industry averages. Applicant must show ability to repay loan from cash flow of business.

7. Equity — is invested capital or equity adequate?

8. Management — does the applicant have experience in the line of business? Are you capable of managing the business successfully?

9. Adequacy of lease.

10. Adequacy of hazard insurance.

If the bank is unwilling to make a loan directly, or in participation with SBA, you should ask the banker for a letter of decline, contact a second bank and follow the same procedure.

Direct Loans

If a second bank also declines your application, you may then apply directly to the SBA for a loan. The maximum amount that you may borrow on a direct loan basis is now $150,000. You should bear in mind that *funds available for direct loans are very limited and the Agency is highly selective in making loans of this type.*

The documentation required for submittal of a Direct Loan Application is the same as needed for a Guaranteed Loan from a bank.

SBA BUSINESS LOANS

Small Business Administration business loans have helped thousands of small firms get started, expand, grow and prosper.

Small manufacturers, wholesalers, retailers, service concerns, farmers, and other businesses may borrow from the Agency to construct, expand, or convert facilities, purchase buildings, equipment, materials or obtain working capital.

By law, the Agency may not make a loan if a business can obtain funds from a bank or other private source. You, therefore, must first seek private financing before applying to SBA. This means that you must apply to your local bank or other lending institution for a loan. If you live in a large city — one with more than 200,000 people — you must apply to two banks before applying for a direct SBA loan.

Applicants for loans must agree to comply with SBA regulations that there will be no discrimination in employment or service to the public, based on race, color, religion, national origin, sex or marital status.

LENDING OBJECTIVES

SBA, by the direction of Congress, has as its primary goal the preservation of free, competitive enterprise in order to strengthen the Nation's economy.

SBA's specific lending objectives are to (1) stimulate small business in deprived areas (2) promote minority enterprise opportunity and (3) promote small business contribution to economic growth.

For business loan purposes, SBA defines a small business as one that is independently owned and operated, not dominant in its field and meets employment or sales standards developed by the Agency. For most industries, these standards are as follows:

Manufacturing—Number of employees may range up to 1,500, depending on the industry in which the applicant is primarily engaged.

Wholesaling—small if yearly sales are not over $9.5 to $22 million, depending on the industry.

Services—Annual receipts not exceeding $2 million to $8 million depending on the industry in which the applicant is primarily engaged.

Retailing—small if annual sales or receipts are not over $2 to $7.5 million, depending on the industry.

Construction—General construction: average annual receipts not exceeding $9.5 million for three most recently completed fiscal years. Special trade construction: average annual receipts not exceeding $1 or $2 million for three most recently completed fiscal years, depending on the industry.

Agriculture—Annual receipts not exceeding $1,000,000.

Ask the nearest SBA field office which standard applies to your type of business.

A loan applicant must:

1. Be of good character.
2. Show ability to operate his business successfully.
3. Have enough capital in an existing firm so that, with an SBA loan, he can operate on a sound financial basis.
4. Show the proposed loan is of such sound value or so secured as reasonably to assure repayment.
5. Show that the past earnings record and future prospects of the firm indicate ability to repay the loan and other fixed debt, if any, out of profits.
6. Be able to provide from his own resources sufficient funds to have a reasonable amount at stake to withstand possible losses, particularly during the early stages, if the venture is a new business.

SBA emphasizes maximum private lender participation in each loan. This policy has made it possible for SBA to respond to a far greater number of requests for financial assistance than is possible under the direct lending program.

When the financing is not otherwise available on reasonable terms, SBA may guarantee up to 90 percent or $350,000 (or $500,000 in special situations), whichever is less, of a bank loan to a small firm.

If the loan is not obtainable from a private lender and if an SBA guaranteed loan is not available, SBA will then consider advancing funds on an immediate participation basis with a bank. SBA will consider making a direct loan only when these other forms of financing are not obtainable and funds are available for direct lending.

The Agency's share of an immediate participation loan may not, at the present time, exceed $150,000. Direct loans may not exceed $150,000 and at times may not be available due to Federal fiscal restraints. In exceptional circumstances, if certain standards are met, these ceilings may be waived by Regional Directors.

SBA business may be for as long as ten years, except those portions of loans for the purpose of acquiring real property or constructing facilities may have a maturity of 20 years. However, working capital loans usually are limited to six years.

MATURITY

Interest rates on SBA's portion of immediate participations, as well as direct loans, may not exceed a rate set by a statutory formula relating to the cost of money to the Government. Within certain limitations bank sets the interest rate on guaranteed loans and its portion of immediate participation loans.

INTEREST

Security for a loan may consist of one or more of these:

COLLATERAL

1. A mortgage on land, a building and/or equipment.
2. Assignment of warehouse receipts for marketable merchandise.
3. A mortgage on chattels.
4. Guarantees or personal endorsements, and some instances, assignment of current receivables. A pledge or mortgage on inventories usually is not satisfactorily collateral, unless the inventories are stored in a bonded or otherwise acceptable warehouse.

Because it is a public agency using taxpayers' funds, SBA has an unusual responsibility as a lender. It therefore will not make loans:

INELIGIBLE APPLICATIONS

1. If the funds are otherwise available on reasonable terms.
2. If the loan is to (a) pay off a loan to a creditor or creditors of the applicant who are inadequately secured and in a position to sustain loss, (b) provide funds for distribution or payment to the principals of the applicant, or (c) replenish funds previously used for such purposes.
3. If the loan allows speculation in any kind of property.
4. If the applicant is a nonprofit enterprise.
5. If the applicant is a newspaper, magazine, book publishing company, or similar enterprise, except radio, cable, or TV broadcasting companies.
6. If any of the gross income of the applicant (or of any of its principal owners) is derived from gambling activities, except for those small firms which obtain less than one-third of their income from the sale of state lottery tickets under a state license, or from gambling activities in those states where such activities are legal within the State.
7. If the loan provides funds to an enterprise primarily engaged in lending or investing.

8. If the loan finances real property that is, or is to be, held for investment.

9. If the loan encourages monopoly or is inconsistent with accepted standards of the American system of free competitive enterprise.

10. If the loan is used to relocate a business for other than sound business purposes.

Amusement and recreational enterprises are eligible for SBA assistance. However, they must be open to the public, and properly licensed by appropriate State or local authority.

Loans may be approved to effect a change in the ownership of a business if they would aid in the development of a small business, keep it in operation, and/or contribute to a well-balanced national economy by facilitating ownership of small business concerns by persons whose participation in the free enterprise system has been hampered or prevented because of economic, physical or social disadvantages, or disadvantages in business or resident locations.

RECREATIONAL ENTERPRISES AND CHANGE OF OWNERSHIP

Small Business Administration Field Office Addresses

Boston	Massachusetts 02114, 150 Causeway Street
Holyoke	Massachusetts 01040, 326 Appleton Street
Augusta	Maine 04330, Federal Building, U.S. Post Office, 40 Western Avenue
Concord	New Hampshire 03301, 55 Pleasant Street
Hartford	Connecticut 06103, Federal Office Building, 450 Maine Street
Montpelier	Vermont 05602, Federal Building, Second Floor, 87 State Street
Providence	Rhode Island 02903, 702 Smith Building, 57 Eddy Street
New York	New York 10007, 26 Federal Plaza, Room 3100
Hato Rey	Puerto Rico 00919, 255 Ponce De Leon Avenue
Newark	New Jersey 07102, 970 Broad Street, Room 1635
Syracuse	New York 13202, Hunter Plaza, Fayette and Salina Streets
Buffalo	New York 14202, 111 West Huron Street
Albany	New York 12207, 99 Washington Avenue
Rochester	New York 14604, 55 St. Paul Street
Philadelphia	Bala Cynwyd, Pennsylvania 19004, 1 Decker Square
Harrisburg	Pennsylvania 17108, 7-11 Market Square
Wilkes-Barre	Pennsylvania 18703, 34 South Main Street
Baltimore	Towson, Maryland 21204, 7800 York Road
Wilmington	Delaware 19801, 901 Market Street
Clarksburg	West Virginia 26301, Lowndes Bank Building, 109 North Third Street
Charleston	West Virginia 25301, Charleston National Plaza, Suite 628
Pittsburgh	Pennsylvania 15222, Federal Building, 1000 Liberty Avenue

Richmond	Virginia 23240, Federal Building, 400 North Eighth Street	**235**
Washington	D.C. 20416, 1030 15th Street, N.W.	

Atlanta	Georgia 30309, 1401 Peachtree Street, N.E.
Birmingham	Alabama 35205, 908 South 20th Street
Charlotte	North Carolina 28202, Addison Building, 222 South Church Street
Columbia	South Carolina 29201, 1801 Assembly Street
Jackson	Mississippi 39205, Petroleum Building, Pascagoula and Amite Streets
Gulfport	Mississippi 39501, Security Savings and Loan Building
Jacksonville	Florida, 32202, Federal Office Building, 400 West Bay Street
Louisville	Kentucky 40202, Federal Office Building, 600 Federal Place
Miami	Florida 33130, Federal Building, 51 Southwest First Avenue
Tampa	Florida 33607, Federal Building, 500 Zack Street
Nashville	Tennessee 37219, 500 Union Street
Knoxville	Tennessee 37902, 502 South Gay Street
Memphis	Tennessee 38103, Federal Building, 167 North Main Street
Chicago	Illinois 60604, Federal Office Building, 219 South Dearborn Street
Springfield	Illinois 62701, 502 East Monroe Street
Cleveland	Ohio 44199, 1240 East Ninth Street
Columbus	Ohio 43215, 34 North High Street
Cincinnati	Ohio 45202, Federal Building, 550 Main Street
Detroit	Michigan 48226, 1249 Washington Boulevard
Marquette	Michigan 49855, 201 McClellan Street
Indianapolis	Indiana 46204, 575 North Pennsylvania Street
Madison	Wisconsin 53703, 122 West Washington Avenue
Milwaukee	Wisconsin 53203, 735 West Wisconsin Avenue
Eau Claire	Wisconsin 54701, 500 South Barstow Street
Minneapolis	Minnesota 55402, 12 South Sixth Street
Dallas	Texas 75202, 1100 Commerce Street
Albuquerque	New Mexico 87110, 5000 Marble Avenue, N.E.
Houston	Texas 77002, 808 Travis Street
Little Rock	Arkansas 72201, 611 Gaines Street
Lubbock	Texas 79408, 1205 Texas Avenue
El Paso	Texas 79901, 109 North Oregon Street
Lower Rio Grande Valley	Harlingen, Texas 78550, 219 East Jackson Street
Corpus Christi	Texas 78408, 3105 Leopard Street
Marshall	Texas 75670, 505 East Travis Street
New Orleans	Louisiana 70113, 1001 Howard Avenue
Oklahoma City	Oklahoma 73118, 50 Penn Place
San Antonio	Texas 78205, 301 Broadway
Kansas City	Missouri 64106, 911 Walnut Street
Des Moines	Iowa 50309, New Federal Building, 210 Walnut Street
Omaha	Nebraska 68102, Federal Building, 215 North 17th Street
St. Louis	Missouri 63101, Federal Building, 210 North 12th Street
Wichita	Kansas 67202, 120 South Market Street
Denver	Colorado 80202, 721 19th Street, Room 426
Casper	Wyoming 82601, 100 East B Street
Fargo	North Dakota 58102, 653 Second Avenue, N.

Helena	Montana 59601, 613 Helena Avenue	**236** Small Business Administration Field Office Addresses
Salt Lake City	Utah 84138, Federal Building, 125 South State Street	
Sioux Falls	South Dakota 57102, National Bank Building, Eighth and Main Avenue	

San Francisco	California 94102, Federal Building, 450 Golden Gate Avenue
Fresno	California 93721, Federal Building, 1130 O Street
Honolulu	Hawaii 96813, 1149 Bethel Street
Agana	Guam 96910, Ada Plaza Center Building
Los Angeles	California 90014, 849 South Broadway
Las Vegas	Nevada 89121, 301 East Stewart
Phoenix	Arizona 85004, 112 North Central Avenue
San Diego	California 92101, 110 West C Street

Seattle	Washington 98104, 710 Second Avenue
Anchorage	Alaska 99501, 1016 West Sixth Avenue
Fairbanks	Alaska 99701, 501½ Second Avenue
Boise	Idaho 83701, 216 North Eighth Street
Portland	Oregon 97205, 921 Southwest Washington Street
Spokane	Washington 99210, Courthouse Building, Room 651

Note: Telephone numbers of these offices may be obtained by finding the Small Business Administration office under "United States Government" in the appropriate city telephone directory.

Index

237